Praise for
Queering Anti-Zionism

"Corinne Blackmer exposes the ways in which prominent academics have once again placed their ideological ambitions (i.e., anti-Zionism) above empirical evidence. Her book recalls the groundbreaking work of physicists Alan Sokal and Jean Bricmont, who exposed the misrepresentation of scientific concepts by prominent postmodern thinkers in their aptly titled *Fashionable Nonsense*. *Queering Anti-Zionism* similarly reveals the misappropriation of human rights discourse by celebrated academics who often willfully display a profound indifference to facts and logic. Scholars and students who have been steeped in or exposed to queer theory will find refuge in and/or lively engagement with this eloquent work."

—R. Amy Elman, professor of political science, Kalamazoo College, and author of *The European Union, Antisemitism, and the Politics of Denial* and *Sexual Equality in an Integrated Europe*

"*Queering Anti-Zionism* embodies engaged scholarship at its best. Blackmer displays her unique talents and commitments as a pro-Zionist Queer scholar-activist to provide an informed analysis and critique of how key queer anti-Zionist commentators have engaged in anti-Israel propaganda and rhetoric. This is a book of exceptional integrity and accomplishment."

—David Ellenson, chancellor emeritus, Hebrew Union College–Jewish Institute of Religion, former director, Schusterman Center for Israel Studies, Brandeis University

"Corinne Blackmer offers a powerful narrative about the destructive force of identity politics. It draws too tight a circle around the words and people allowed to enter its sacred struggle for social justice. And no entry to Zionists fuels a concoction of distortions about Israeli history and society."

—Donna Robinson Divine, Morningstar Family Professor Emerita of Jewish Studies and professor emerita of government, Smith College

"*Queering Anti-Zionism* is an important corrective to the Manichaean view of the Israeli-Palestinian conflict that has overtaken queer academia. Corinne Blackmer challenges point-by-point the oversimplifications, false equivalencies, and misrepresentations presented by leading queer critics of Zionism; she offers in their place a balanced and informed understanding of the complexities of the conflict. This is a brave and very necessary book."

—Lillian Faderman, author of *Naked in the Promised Land*, *My Mother's Wars*, and *Woman: The American History of an Idea*

"After being maliciously attacked as a lesbian and a Jewish-Zionist, Corrine Blackmer set out to write about how the BDS—Boycott, Divestment, and Sanctions—movement is damaging the field of queer studies. The result is an engaging book that offers valuable insight into how this discipline has become a breeding ground for repellent ideologies and propaganda that contradict postmodernist positions, fail to do justice by Palestinian LGBTQ individuals, stymie efforts to foster Israeli-Palestinian mutual understanding and coexistence, and ostracize and marginalize Jews."

—Miriam F. Elman, associate professor of political science, Syracuse University, and executive director, Academic Engagement Network

QUEERING ANTI-ZIONISM

QUEERING ANTI-ZIONISM

ACADEMIC FREEDOM, LGBTQ INTELLECTUALS, AND ISRAEL/PALESTINE CAMPUS ACTIVISM

CORINNE E. BLACKMER

WAYNE STATE UNIVERSITY PRESS
DETROIT

Copyright © 2022 by Wayne State University Press, Detroit, Michigan, 48201. All rights reserved. No part of this book may be reproduced without formal permission. Manufactured in the United States of America.

Library of Congress Cataloging Number: 2022933656

ISBN 978-0-8143-4998-4 (paperback)
ISBN 978-0-8143-4999-1 (hardback)
ISBN 978-0-8143-5000-3 (e-book)

Cover design by Michel Vrana

Wayne State University Press rests on Waawiyaataanong, also referred to as Detroit, the ancestral and contemporary homeland of the Three Fires Confederacy. These sovereign lands were granted by the Ojibwe, Odawa, Potawatomi, and Wyandot Nations, in 1807, through the Treaty of Detroit. Wayne State University Press affirms Indigenous sovereignty and honors all tribes with a connection to Detroit. With our Native neighbors, the press works to advance educational equity and promote a better future for the earth and all people.

Wayne State University Press
Leonard N. Simons Building
4809 Woodward Avenue
Detroit, Michigan 48201-1309

Visit us online at wsupress.wayne.edu.

CONTENTS

Prologue: *My Education in Homophobia,*
Anti-Zionism, and Extremism   VII

Introduction: Pinkwashing, Israel/Palestine Campus
Activism, and Academic Freedom   1

1. Sarah Schulman's Queer Adventures in Israel/Palestine   31

2. Jasbir Puar, or, Zionophobia in Homonationalist Times   53

3. Angela Davis: Israel as the Queer Intersectional Outsider   77

4. Dean Spade's BDS Activist Malpractice   95

5. Judith Butler's One-State Solution Trouble   111

Conclusion: Queering the Future of the
Israel/Palestine Conflict   133

Notes   143
Index   187

PROLOGUE

MY EDUCATION IN HOMOPHOBIA, ANTI-ZIONISM, AND EXTREMISM

Anti-Zionist and Homophobic Hate Crimes

In March 2008, as the Israeli Defense Forces' (IDF's) Operation Hot Winter responded to Hamas and other terrorist groups firing Grad and Qassam rockets onto Israeli citizens all over the southern part of the country, I became the target of a series of hate crimes on my campus. Though in some ways they are far apart, I found it next to impossible not to draw a link between these events.

I am an out lesbian and Jewish woman. Proud of my identities and having experienced little cause for apprehension or self-consciousness about them on my campus, I covered my office door with materials proclaiming my affiliations. I also teach courses in sexuality, gender, and Judaic studies. As a professor dedicated to teaching students to practice critical reason, value uncertainty, respect open inquiry, and question "black versus white" and "us versus them" thinking, I regularly approach subjects through the controversies surrounding them. Seeking to foster a yearning for complexity and new knowledge, I regarded it as desirable that my freshmen, sophomore, and upper-division courses often roiled in lively debate, and I worked hard so that my students left my

---

The views expressed here are my own and do not necessarily reflect those of the United States Holocaust Memorial Museum.

classes more committed to diversity of opinion and social justice than they had been when they had entered. My courses did not touch on Israel and Palestine but, rather, on issues surrounding various Jewish and Christian interpretations of the Hebrew Bible, and contested meanings of gender identities and sexuality differences. Finally, my colleagues and my administration had always been enthusiastically supportive of my endeavors in cross-cultural critical thinking.

Therefore I had little to prepare me when, one morning, an anxious-looking colleague approached me and showed me that materials on the door of my office had been defaced—torn, and scrawled over with profane, hateful language that was anti-LGBTQ, antisemitic, and anti-Zionist. The damaged items included the front page of the *New Haven Register*, dated November 12, 2007, featuring a jubilant Jewish lesbian couple on the day that marriage equality became legal in Connecticut, a map of Israel, a photograph of myself holding flowers and wearing a *kippah*, a picture of the Western Wall in Jerusalem, a newspaper reprint of Iranian men being hung and Saudi Arabian men being flogged for being gay; the Israeli and LGBTQ rainbow flags, respectively, and a photograph of a gay man on the beach in Tel Aviv wearing a T-shirt proclaiming "Proud to Be a Jewish Queer." The defacements were, in their fashion, meticulous, as each item had received its particular message, while the map of Israel was shredded into pieces without further comment. I also saw that I had received several telephone calls on the office line—among them three that contained implicit and explicit threats against both me and my family. One consisted of a loud hammer banging down methodically, punctuated by a muffled voice intoning, "Die Pervert Zionist! Die Pervert Zionist!"

I saved the messages and called the campus police. I thought about how Israeli military operations, no matter how unavoidable because of Hamas's unremitting acts of military aggression, made me anxiously anticipate the inevitable stream of anti-Zionist protests, Boycott, Divestment, and Sanctions (BDS) advocacy aimed at Israel, biased pronouncements from the United Nations, anti-Israel social media campaigns, and wall-to-wall coverage out of proportion to that afforded analogous conflicts across the world. When the officer finally arrived, she took my statement and one scrawled-over photograph as evidence, and asked me if I knew anyone who might have done this to me. I said I could readily imagine the *kind* of person who could do this to me, and explained my identities and affiliations, but not a specific person. I did not have any concrete enemies as far as I knew.

The officer's implicit, reflexive perspective on the crime also dismayed me. Throughout the interview, she seemed clearly to assume that I had only been the victim of homophobic animus. All other threats and the defacing were ignored, as if incidental, accidental, and, indeed, nonsignifying. I realized she could understand homophobia but not anti-Zionism—which was not a recognized form of hate speech, as too many pro-Israel students, faculty, and staff at American college campuses have learned to their politically naïve dismay. The personnel at my school were certainly not particularly to blame for this reaction, as I would encounter this mode of response throughout this experience among almost everyone. Only two parties, my family and the congregants at my synagogue, understood easily that someone could be targeted for being a Jewish lesbian and Zionist simultaneously. Finally, and perhaps ironically, I realized that I, as a member of the faculty senate, had contributed to the campus climate that could lead to such erasure by (a) failing to suggest including Zionism as a form of diverse political opinion and identity in our university's initiatives, and (b) not bringing anti-Zionism up for discussion and critique, as I was fearful of the ways it could be used as a weapon against Jewish students, Zionists, and other allies of Israel.

I stumbled my way through the teaching day. I happened to run into a journalism professor I knew and told him about the episode. He promised he would do what he could to help. When I came back to my office later that afternoon, I had telephone calls from two Connecticut television networks wanting to interview me for the evening news, along with a reporter from the *New Haven Register*. Again I found myself perplexed by how they responded to the hate crime that had occurred. They, too, reacted as if I had been victimized only as a lesbian. No one could or would hear me, despite my confused protestations, and I realized that, placed in conjunction, the categories of "lesbian" and "Jew" (never mind Zionist—a concept that was simply off the map) did not make sense to them. There were many ways of understanding this, some more plausible than others. Perhaps they thought that a lesbian presenting herself as Jewish would offend Orthodox Jews watching the news; perhaps they subtly employed homophobic perceptions of Judaism that could not apprehend a lesbian as "really" Jewish; perhaps they understood anti-Zionism as a form of protected speech rather than hate speech; perhaps "invariably" homophobic religion and sexual minority identity did not mix for them; perhaps they preferred to evade the "too hot" topic of Zionism; or perhaps the reporters, like the police officer, wished only to maintain a singular focus on the homophobia, to simplify their task.[1]

I was left with only speculation. With these limiting assumptions, they were unlikely, I feared, to catch the perpetrator(s). It also occurred to me that my situation was not entirely unlike that of students who had once come to me for assistance, only to receive ambivalent, equivocating messages about whether they were, as Jews and Zionists, actual victims of unjust religious and cultural prejudice or merely reluctant players in an international game of politics. Finally, I felt uncomfortably like someone who had been cut into jigsaw pieces that did not fit together.

Walking down the hall shortly after class, I absent-mindedly noticed the office door of a colleague. On it was the famous prohibition against men "lying with another male" in Leviticus 18:22, accompanied by passages about mixing fibers and stoning adulterers, meant to illustrate the sexist and homophobic primitivism of Jewish biblical law. My colleague only intended to show the humorous illogic of anti-gay animus, but in context it struck me as unconsciously antisemitic and engaged in ideological Christian supercessionism. I felt angry, targeted, as Judaism was scarcely the sole or even major purveyor of homo-hatred in the Western world.

In the several days that followed, I became sunk in contemplation of the *strange, unaccountable,* and, indeed, *uncanny* nature of my experience of contemporary anti-Zionism. While being a lesbian was more or less a continual if nominally tolerable prejudicial disadvantage, one could, within the space of a single day, be reminded of the sterling successes of the State of Israel and the respect accorded Jews, on the one hand, and the threats of extirpation and hatred both still faced, on the other. In contrast to the steady drone of homophobia, anti-Israel animus was like an episodic series of traumatic shocks. There were worlds between me and the historical catastrophes of pogroms, the Holocaust, and the dispossession of Middle Eastern Mizrachi Jews, but at the same time I could not but be aware of the unremitting efforts of those who opposed the existence of Israel to perpetuate their hatred and refusal to compromise.

For instance, three days after the initial incident, I enjoyed a splendid time at Shabbat services at my synagogue, where the congregants offered their support, and my rabbi, seeking to comfort me while speaking truth, reminded me that "the loathing for our people has never been personal." I spent part of the next day reading about remarkable Israeli technologies of de-desertification and innovative treatments for cancer. Then I arrived at school on Monday to see that new materials I had placed on my door had, again, been defaced, and more hate-filled messages had been left on my office telephone.

I went through the same drill with another investigating officer, who now said he would set up a video camera to see if the perpetrator could be apprehended. That same afternoon, as I was walking toward my car to go home, I ran into faculty members who, along with some students, were protesting the policies of the Israeli government in Gaza. The reporters and police had erased my identities as a Jew and Zionist, while these folks now held signs accusing Israelis—by whom they meant Jews and Zionists—of being racist Western colonialists, ethnic cleansers, and Nazi Zionists. One faculty member at the protest, who had heard about my being targeted, commiserated by telling me I had been the unfortunate victim of the "homo-hating patriarchy." While I reflected on the uncomfortable irony of this person targeting me in one way while expressing compassion for my being targeted in another way, I arrived at my car to see that it had been daubed with mud in the shape of a swastika.

Yet another visit to the police, feeling invisible, disconsolate, and terrified that the perpetrator(s) had followed me to my car and, in all likelihood, knew where I lived.

The thrice-repeated hate crimes against me ended as suddenly as the protests against the Israeli campaign in Gaza, and, other than this connection, I will never know why. The perpetrator(s) of these hate crimes against me were never apprehended—a result of many factors, including the absence of an accurate profile. I live with the realization that one or more people out there wish me harm and long for me to disappear, simply because I am a lesbian, Jewish, and Zionist, and not necessarily in that order.

Subsequent Ordeals in the Classroom

A few years later, after the initial shock and trauma had subsided, I begin to think, in a more serious and sustained fashion, about the nature of hate crimes per se. I wondered what, if anything, I and my colleagues could do to create an environment that might discourage future hate-driven threats, assaults, and vandalism, and, more important, provide greater support and educational resources for victims of discrimination, bullying, or ignorance. I knew that hate crimes were not directed against an individual but rather against perceived group membership; that they were motivated often by a *cluster* of prejudices rather than just one; that social environments structured to advantage certain identity characteristics over others could encourage hate crimes; that offenders may believe that society supports their violent prejudices; and that of the four schematic types of perpetrators (i.e., thrill-seeking individuals, defensive offenders, retaliators, and those on a mission), I had most likely been targeted by the perpetrator(s) in an act of retaliation for a perceived attack against their own group, coupled with a mission to eradicate difference.

Further, I had long taken interest in the history and dynamics of the Israel/Palestine conflict, and began to think about doing something tangible to improve the campus climate, lessen my own and others' loneliness, and ease subterranean tensions and hostilities. Since the women's and gender studies program at my university had espoused anti-Zionism far before the National Women's Studies Association (NWSA) curtailed academic freedom by passing a sweeping BDS resolution in 2015,[2] I was robbed of the kind of feminist solidarity that could discourage hate crimes or help victims in healing. In addition, aware that a cluster of prejudices generally motivated those who committed hate crimes, I understood that the anti-Israel biases of women's studies programs put me at greater risk of repeated crimes. Their prejudices severed the feminist from the Jewish parts of my identities and left me dangerously isolated and therefore prey to future attacks. Thus, feeling the need for positive and protective community, I joined the Judaic studies steering committee, where I found colleagues who supported all aspects of who I was.

As earlier mentioned, I had always been a principled proponent of academic freedom and free speech, and saw the university's mission of producing new knowledge as inextricably bound up in its acting as a forum for the free and open exchange of ideas. I held it as an article of faith that, as Robert M. Hutchins famously notes, "without a vibrant commitment to free and open inquiry, a university ceases to be a university."[3] I therefore opposed the BDS movement as an infringement of academic freedom (while supporting the rights of BDS proponents to voice their beliefs), and I also opposed policies promoting safe places, speech codes, disinvitation of controversial speakers, cancel culture, and trigger warnings. Such practices, I believed, abridged freedom of speech and association, as well as academic freedom, and did not prepare students for the unsafe and often traumatically triggering world beyond the university. More important, they did not teach them to hone the kind of questions they asked and arguments they formulated in response to those who disagreed with them. I thought such practices did not teach critical reasoning, and how to yearn for complexity as opposed to partisan black-and-white thinking that replicated insider-outsider schemas. As a political activist and a feminist Jewish lesbian, I had long been exposed to unsafe spaces, including, for instance, in the work I had done outside the university in ACT UP as an AIDS activist, and in bringing what had been the hotly controversial issue of marriage equality before the public.

In this context, I considered the Israel/Palestine conflict, which posed such a threat to free speech and academic freedom, as an ideal venue for teaching critical thinking, and for exploring how people dealt with ideologically charged issues. I finally decided to teach a new course on the subject, called Narrating the Israel/Palestine Conflict. The class would focus on the various partisan and conciliatory narratives surrounding this issue without privileging any of them. I understood that college students, faculty members, and professionals exemplified, in the words of Kenneth Stern, "how we as human beings process information and come to conclusions, based on who we are, especially when our identity is tethered to an issue of perceived social justice or injustice."[4] I envisioned creating an empathetic pedagogical environment for Jewish students, Zionists, anti-Zionists (and both camps' allies) but also for the majority of undecided parties interested in learning, in an environment dedicated to reasoned argument and evidence, about the Israel/Palestine conflict.

The requisite committees enthusiastically approved the course (with one of my colleagues, who appeared somewhat awestruck, saying that I was "uncommonly brave" to be willing to teach this subject matter), and the semester arrived. The course fulfilled a freshman requirement in critical thinking, and I found my first group of university students to be an overall uninformed but eager and curious group who wanted to know more about the conflict and why it had persisted for so long.

Drawing on the work of James Waller, a noted expert in genocide and Holocaust studies, I opened the semester by telling the class that our task—learning critical thinking in the context of the Israel/Palestine conflict—was a doubly challenging one. We had to consider the highly contested nature of this subject matter in the light of our evolutionarily based tendencies to engage in group thinking.[5] I said that we might, as contemporary individuals, use our minds to conduct Google searches, read news reports, or play video games, but that our brains had formed when humans had lived in small, often frightened and threatened, groups. We were geared to see strangers as intruders who too often deserved our hate. Under the influence of charismatic leaders who played on our fears, and untrained in critical reasoning, we were susceptible to racism and xenophobia—and even hate-driven impulses to eradicate our perceived enemies.

Further, citing the seminal work of Stanley Milgram and later studies, I said that we could find pleasure in conformity, since obeying authority relieved painful personal and social dilemmas around social status, decision-making, and belonging. We needed to seek for fellow feeling and recognize that our penchant to follow leaders and exclude dissent made it difficult to think coherently when we perceived the conflict in the kind of stark binary terms with which we would become familiar over the course of the semester: democratic versus authoritarian, good versus evil, settler-colonialist versus indigenous, terrorist versus state terrorist, genocidal versus limited use of deadly force, among others. Referring to Michael Hogg, and his work on "uncertainty-identity theory,"[6] I noted that the feelings of anxious ambivalence we all had about our perceptions, values, identities, and allegiances—which we should prize as the fruits of a mind attuned to thinking critically about complex issues with few clear right and wrong answers—made us uncomfortable, and that to reduce such incertitude, we could become zealots who punished dissent and criticism, insisted on consensus and solidarity, and dehumanized outsiders and rebels. As Hogg put it, "Ideological orthodoxy prevails . . . and is protected by suppression of criticism . . . and marginalization of deviance."[7] If strong partisanship on each side of the Israel/Palestine conflict could diminish academic freedom on campuses, as each side sought to chill the speech and deny the humanity of the other party, either through boycott campaigns, blacklists, hecklers' vetoes, or legal actions, then learning about the conflict in an open environment that respected those values of free and open inquiry strengthened the mission of the university.[8]

I noted that while students could, upon reviewing the issues dispassionately, decide that they were either pro-Palestinian or pro-Israeli, the course would reject the notion that they had to be partisan or, for that matter, artificially "balanced." We would come to appreciate the challenges involved in resolving the conflict, and the inadvisability of arriving at facile solutions that elided profound historical differences. The beliefs and articles of faith of each side could not be wished or washed away. I reminded them that they would be disturbed by uncomfortable and unfamiliar ideas about the world, and I told them that we would in part learn about our subject matter through modeling differences of opinion and perspective. We would foster an environment of learning to think effectively about difficult issues rather than further weaponizing the conflict. I said, as Kenneth Stern remarks, that "strong passion, informed by one's core beliefs but lacking insight into the other side's sacred values, may lead to intuitive reactions that are counterproductive to one's goals."[9] I ended by remarking that, to help maintain our focus on facts and history, we would focus on primary documents, and that I believed that instructors indoctrinated—as opposed to taught—when they presented particular propositions and opinions that remained open to debate as dogmatically true, and refused students opportunities to contest them.[10]

The students responded enthusiastically to my words, and they were pleased, if somewhat anxiously so, to have encouragement to formulate their own views and opinions. But there was one among the group who appeared to deliberately ignore my words and who gave me pause: an extreme anti-Zionist who explicitly supported BDS and Palestinian terrorism as legitimate responses to Israeli aggression, and whose writing and oral comments expressed an assured zealotry and dead-serious conviction of rightness the likes of which I had never witnessed before in any classroom, even after many years of teaching highly controversial subjects.

The class progressed largely without incident, fortunately, except that the anti-Zionist student objected nearly continuously to even the blandest factual statements about the conflict. Some students voiced their irritation and impatience with the way this student commandeered the classroom. One could also see that they felt bullied, marginalized, and shut down, particularly since this student never engaged in give-or-take discussion or considered other students' points of view. Indeed, the anti-Zionist showed vivid contempt and pained outrage toward anyone who expressed even qualified support for Israel, the two-state solution, or, for that matter, any form of conciliation or consideration of diverse viewpoints and investments.

Further, to accustom students to appreciating and learning about multiple points of view on the conflict, I had them randomly pick from a box the names of different figures whose beliefs and perspectives they would be required to research and represent. With considerable sardonic irony, the anti-Zionist chanced to select Golda Meir. I was not surprised when this student angrily refused to represent any but a Palestinian figure, claiming that the assignment was unfair, coercive, and demanded that students abandon their convictions to receive a good grade.

Having the students work in pairs or *havruta* (a traditional Jewish pedagogical practice) so that they could discuss, exchange, and debate their ideas collaboratively, I had near the beginning of the semester also given the students a more familiar short assignment to evaluate arguments—based on facts and evidence—that Israel had or had not engaged in attempted genocide against the Palestinians. This assignment was not simply a slam dunk with a predetermined right answer. Rather, the idea was to gain practice not only with marshalling facts and evidence but also with evaluating the potentially thorny issues of intentionality. In brief, were the Israeli Defense Forces taking military actions whose intent was ethnic cleansing/genocide against the Palestinians, or, rather, taking control of violent actors in forays that could also result in accidental death through the use of lethal force? My anti-Zionist refused to work in partnership with another student partner and instead wrote a blistering two-page essay, asserting vociferously that the Israelis had not merely intended but also had committed genocide against the Palestinians to eliminate their enemies, who were the legitimate indigenous heirs to the lands the Israelis illegally occupied as settler colonialists. It was an enraged screed that provided no facts or evidence whatsoever for its positions, and that completely bypassed giving an evaluation of probable intention. Instead of simply giving a failing grade, I asked to see this student in my office. There, I attempted to reason and encourage the student to adduce evidence, but the anti-Zionist soon marched out, accusing me of being an anti-Palestinian and

Islamophobic racist who wanted to ruin an academic career because I was a Zionist.

Flummoxed and somewhat worried by this student, I was pulled aside a few days later by my dean, who informed me that a student had come to her office and made what she called strident comments against me. Although she recognized that these were out of character with respect to what she knew of me, she had referred the student (as she was obliged to do) to the director of the office of diversity and equity.

The call came soon after. Here was someone I did not know, who took a very different attitude toward me than my dean had with respect to my anti-Zionist student. The director was reflexively, obviously anti-Israel and, noting that this student had an excellent academic record, was inclined to give credence to accusations that I was Islamophobic and racist. The director asked me to complete a lengthy statement explaining my side of the story, and then told me that I should reflect on whether I acted questionably in threatening to give a failing grade simply because a student disagreed with my subjective interpretations. I differed strongly with this view of the matter and gave my reasons. Accusations of genocide implicate human beings in the most profound ethical violations against humanity, I argued, and the standard of evidence for them must be extremely high; casual or baseless accusations were both epistemically and morally unacceptable. The director retreated somewhat, and subsequently arrived at the remedy to have this student graded by a different professor with whom the student might, she concluded, see more eye to eye.

I was at once relieved and deeply vexed by this solution, as it deprived me of legitimate pedagogical authority without cause at the same time that it restored peace and good order to my classroom. I subsequently learned that this student did not receive a passing grade from the other professor, who also critiqued the work for lack of reasoned argument and evidence, and, although feeling somewhat vindicated, I was also saddened that the conflict had claimed yet another potentially fine intellect in this instance. Nevertheless, the strain of dealing with this student in the classroom; the need to take time to write a lengthy statement defending my pedagogical practices against accusations of racism and bias; and the anti-Zionist's seemingly seemingly boundless hatred of Israeli Jews and the mere existence of Israel exhausted me and provided me with fresh reminders of the intransigence of the conflict, and its power to transform otherwise thoughtful, capable people into zealots and quasireligious true believers who identified themselves as ideological warriors engaged in a life-and-death battle to defend the Truth.

My Second Coming Out

During those traumatic but transformative years following the hate crime, I also decided to help heal and solve the puzzles of myself by, finally, integrating my multiple but sometimes disjointed identities. Since 2010, I have become the Jewish lesbian who, rather than standing by chagrined and upset, cheers for the Israeli and Palestinian LGBTQ delegations at Gay Pride parades. Some other queer parade-goers, showing their instinctive anti-Israel animus, boo and heckle while moving away from me and my friends, pariahs within our supposedly collectively marginalized community.

I am the Jewish lesbian who, as a professor, shows Israeli LGBTQ films in my classes, such as *Keep Not Silent* (2004, dir. Llil Alexander), about Orthodox lesbians, or *Gay Days* (2009 dir. Yair Qedar), about the early days of the queer rights movement in Israel, or *Flawless* (2018, dir. Tal Granit and Sharon Maymon), about the adventures of a young Israeli transgender woman.

I am the Jewish lesbian professor who, when teaching courses in sexuality and ethics, discusses the formal legal landscape for LGBTQ persons in the Western and non-Western worlds—in the Middle East and throughout Africa, Asia, Eurasia, and Central and South America. While punishments in many nations are enforced unevenly and, at best, capriciously, the landscape reveals deeply ideological and religious animus against LGBTQ persons. In addition, advances in LGBTQ rights in many nations has caused a backlash in others, which use homophobia and nationalism to define themselves against the West.

But I am also the Jewish lesbian professor who had to learn to confront head on loathing from two external sources: a perpetrator of serial hate crimes who detested Jewish Zionists and lesbians sufficiently to vandalize and issue death threats, and a student who loathed the mere existence of Israel.

Although those experiences were extremely painful, they paled when compared to the anguish caused by the anti-Zionist accusers from within my LGBTQ communities. They constituted a different kind of enemy, now from the marginalized group who suffered discrimination, with whom I had always felt great solidarity and for whose sake I had devoted much time and effort as an activist and advocate. They took all the liberal ideals of inclusion and respect for plurality in which I believe so deeply and used them against my Jewish and academic freedom-loving selves. I already had been (obviously) excluded from the communities of my enemies, the religious bigots and the criminal haters, and now these haters threatened to exclude me from the communities in which I had previously found refuge, mutual identification, and support.

Coming out of that capacious Zionist closet was the necessary first step for me. Since doing so I have found disparate communities of individuals who understand and support me, and whose affectionate care has encouraged me to reach out to others.

Since then, I have taught the Israel/Palestine conflict many times. In the process I have been inspired by and learned much from contemporary Zionist activists such as R. Amy Elman, Lillian Faderman, Rachel Fish, David Ellenson, Miriam Elman, Cary Nelson, and Rachel S. Harris. They all fervently support Palestinian rights alongside Zionism—Jewish national self-determination in Israel—which they do not regard as mutually exclusive positions. I've also learned from LGBTQ activists in Israel/Palestine who are forging paths that do not subscribe to antisemitism. Some Palestinian gays and lesbians have nuanced perspectives on the relationships between occupation and homophobia, and they refuse to privilege their LGBTQ identities over their Palestinian identities or vice versa. They understand how negative social, political, and religious views of gayness in Palestine are worsened by the occupation.

They have intersectional identities, and they place their politics in a complex context of Israeli occupation, nationalist resistance, the hypocritical corruption of the Palestinian Authority, the tragic ascendance of Islamist politics, which threatens women and religious minorities as much as LGBTQ people, and, at last, a Palestinian wartime ethos that positions heterosexual reproduction and the heteronormative family as crucial to national survival. The culprit is not Islam—which is not any more inherently homophobic than Judaism or Christianity. Rather, Islamism (or Islamic fundamentalism) has ascribed dire new meanings to homosexuality—again, as well as to the rights of women and religious minorities.

So too, in Israel, do many LGBTQ voices resist the allure of cooption by the state and the prejudice of ultra-Orthodox Judaism. As liberal Zionists they draw connections between the homophobic and traditional gender ideologies of the settlers and the occupation. Like me, they understand and even respect the engrained passions that animate partisans on both sides, but continue to work for compromise, conciliation, and the peaceful resolution of the Israel/Palestine conflict.

INTRODUCTION

PINKWASHING, ISRAEL/PALESTINE CAMPUS ACTIVISM, AND ACADEMIC FREEDOM

How BDS Annexed the LGBTQ Movement

In her influential article for the *New York Times*, "Pinkwashing and Israel's Use of Gays as a Messaging Tool" (2011),[1] Sarah Schulman, a Jewish lesbian writer, academic, and supporter of the Boycott, Divestment, and Sanctions (BDS) movement, brought the concept of pinkwashing to the general public.[2] She contended that protections for lesbians and gays in the Western world had led to a "nefarious phenomenon": namely, the "co-opting of white gay people by anti-immigrant and anti-Muslim forces in Western Europe and Israel." Gays and lesbians had been hijacked into adopting these prejudices since their fragile acquisition of new rights, and thus regarded Muslim immigrants as "homophobic fanatics." In their unwarranted Islamophobia, they not only disregarded other homophobic religious groups, such as fundamentalist Christians, the Roman Catholic Church, and Orthodox Jews, but also ignored the existence of Islamic LGBTQ organizations and progressive pro-gay Muslims. In brief, Western gays had reflexively dehumanized Muslims. The former failed to imagine how Muslims could resist homophobic and sexist practices; allegiances which Westerners had, in any event, exaggerated or decontextualized.

If Schulman makes these grandiose generalizations about the cultural politics and prejudices of Western gays and lesbians, for which she offers no proof, she also, ironically, erases LGBTQ and feminist Muslim immigrants, many of whom likely left for the West[3] to escape engrained homohatred or misogynistic persecution, and continued to fear persecution from Muslim immigrant communities in their adopted Western countries.[4] She continues in this flawed line of argumentation, stating that, starting in 2005, an American public relations firm, working in conjunction first with the Israeli Ministry of Tourism and overseas consulates and, later, with the Israeli Ministry of Foreign Affairs, launched a campaign called "Brand Israel," directed at "hunky" and "beef-cakey" gay men aged 18–34. This public relations campaign portrayed Israel as a "relevant and modern" country that was gay-friendly, and marketed Tel Aviv as an "international gay vacation destination." In a stunning non sequitur that forced an association between the BDS movement and the Israeli Ministry of Tourism's ordinary if, for gays, laudable promotion of Israel as an LGBTQ-friendly destination, Schulman claimed that the Israeli government was using queers as the means to distract attention from the ongoing Israel/Palestine conflict. Schulman, borrowing from others, defined these twin dynamics as "pinkwashing," which she characterized as "a deliberate strategy to conceal the continuing violations of Palestinians' human rights behind an image of modernity signified by Israeli gay life." According to Schulman, pinkwashing played on the sensibilities of naïve gay and lesbian people who had only begun to acquire equal legal recognition and thus "mistakenly judge how advanced a country is by how it responds to homosexuality."[5]

For Schulman and the other seminal LGBTQ supporters of BDS this book explores—Jasbir Puar, Angela Davis, Dean Spade, and Judith Butler—sexuality rights have become central in struggles for and against the putatively civilizing missions of globalization and modernization. As these influential intellectuals assert, this might in part explain why gay rights have achieved such success in recent times in Western nations.[6] Indeed, as Katherine Franke notes, "*Modern* states are expected to recognize a sexual minority within the national body and grant that minority rights-based protections. *Premodern* states do not. Once recognized as modern, the state's treatment of homosexuals offers cover for other sorts of human rights shortcomings. So long as a state treats its homosexuals well, the international community will look the other way when it comes to a range of other human rights abuses."[7]

This pinkwashing non sequitur lies at the heart of the relations among the LGBTQ politics, Israel/Palestine campus activism, and academic freedom that *Queering Anti-Zionism* explores in the work of these activist intellectuals. Their work draws on postmodern queer, intersectional, or discursive theories to frame the activists' pro-BDS visions of the Israel/Palestine conflict, and to affix an ever-broadening series of academic fields to BDS, thus making them mouthpieces for anti-Israel rhetoric. It will therefore be necessary to explore how BDS supporters employ this rhetoric in analyzing this conflict. Further, while this book acknowledges and attempts to do justice to opinions on many sides of this conflict, it opposes the BDS movement as an infringement on open expression and academic freedom that, as such, hampers the search for new knowledge, quashes freedom of association crucial to fostering peace, and undermines the respect for incertitude around complex issues—such as the Israel/Palestine conflict—for which there are no simple right or wrong answers. To paraphrase Kenneth Stern, strong passions, informed by core beliefs but lacking insight into the sacred values of the other side, can lead to intuitive reactions that are counterproductive.[8] *Queering Anti-Zionism* contends that extremists on both sides of this conflict, in their avid pursuit of their versions of the Truth, have done not inconsiderable damage to academic freedom that will require determined, concerted efforts over many years or decades to repair. Indeed, at present, there is no foreseeable end in sight to this crisis. Further, academic freedom has become increasingly endangered by everything from contingent labor, the erosion of tenure, the curtailing of shared governance, and boycotts by professional organizations, to for-profit institutions that pursue revenue not truth, ideological polarization, and the internationalization of higher education.[9]

This book nonetheless respects and seeks to understand the serious claims that BDS supporters make about Israel, but it will not shy away from calling out fallacious arguments or egregious misstatements that treat opinions and unsubstantiated claims as matters of undisputed truth or settled fact. *Queering Anti-Zionism* also opposes blacklists, such as Canary Mission, and anti-BDS legislative and legal actions like those undertaken by Lawfare and others, as well as the now too common accusations of antisemitism and Islamophobia on campus—not because they are sometimes inaccurate or overstated, but because they chill free speech and thus can shut down much-needed dialogue and debate. This book maintains that, for an array of reasons—including substantial funding from outside organizations and nations; the religious and geopolitical context of the dispute; the antidemocratic biases of the left; the disinclination to boycott or sanction powerful, resource-rich, or obscure, violence-wracked nations that practice unspeakable crimes against humanity; and the comparative ease of doing media coverage on Israel/Palestine—this conflict has garnered disproportionate attention on college campuses. In so doing, it has indirectly helped to marginalize public campus discourse about other far more dire human rights abuses, including those perpetrated against women and girls, migrant workers, and ethnic, religious, and sexual minorities throughout the world.[10]

This is not to say that the Israel/Palestine conflict does not matter. Indeed, it matters a great deal. It represents an ideal case study for understanding the nature and persistence of hate in human culture. Learning about this conflict makes us responsible for reflecting on the internal dynamics of this elaborately organized, well-funded, and virulent intergenerational hate, which has claimed the lives of 120,000-plus people over the course of 160 years. We must come to terms with how polarization and partisanship breed one another and become entrenched verities passed down the generations. Indeed, R. Amy Elman asserts that in this conflict the inflicting and receiving of pain in the claustrophobic, bounded confinements of hate have become obsessive sadomasochistic enjoyments to partisans that obviate good judgment and quotidian ethical concerns.[11] We must face the too frequent deleterious influence that the Israel/Palestine conflict has had on open inquiry and the breadth of political speech on campus, and how it has warped our larger understanding of the world and, more specifically, the politics of the Middle East. Moreover, given the persecution too many face in non-Western nations, academic freedom has profound resonance for LGBTQ academics. Their sexualities have become a wedge issue in political proxy wars that use gay and lesbian academics as targets of antiforeigner and antireligious nationalist hate.[12] Finally, academics across the world who publish or even voice unpopular opinions on this conflict can find themselves at the mercy of fierce, countervailing partisan winds, and all too often confront efforts from various quarters to chill their speech and abridge their academic freedom by subjecting them to what Cary Nelson calls "micro-boycotts."[13]

The History of Pinkwashing

The compound portmanteau term "pinkwashing" derives from the seventeenth-century verb "to whitewash," which means to hide crimes and vices, or to exonerate through biased presentation of evidence. The Nazis forced gay male concentration-camp inmates to wear inverted pink triangles to shame them for their "inverse" gender identification. Subsequently, in the ACT UP movement, the pink triangle was repurposed to symbolize political resistance to homophobia, the plight of HIV+ people, and those living with AIDS.[14]

In the 1980s the now-iconic pink ribbon logo became a form of cause marketing that companies used to advertise their support for breast cancer, victims, and charities. These logos became the ideal means to promote products and sell merchandise. However, in a classic case of false advertising, research revealed that many products sold by these companies contained carcinogenic ingredients linked with the increased risk of breast and other forms of cancer. In addition, the focus on mammograms, prevention, and a cure for breast cancer ignored environmental factors, and that poor women of color suffered disproportionately from this cancer. Accordingly, in 1985, the organization Breast Cancer Action (BCA) coined the term "pinkwashing" to characterize this fraudulent and deceptive form of cause marketing.[15] In 2002 BCA inaugurated its "Think Before You Pink" campaign as an impassioned feminist protest against the indiscriminate and disingenuous use of pink ribbon logos to turn profits and, according to Cary Nelson, "hid[e] the way they are actually contributing to cancer through their manufacturing processes."[16]

In reference to the BDS movement, Schulman contends that the term "pinkwashing" emerged informally among activists in the United States in 2010 as a nonce blending of whitewashing and greenwashing, or the marketing of products on the pretense that they were environmentally friendly.[17] However, according to Aeyal Gross, professor of law at Tel Aviv University, the pinkwashing moniker actually originated in Israel in 2001 when left-wing LGBTQ Israeli activists created the group Black Laundry (Kvisa Shchora in Hebrew) to protest the IDFs' crackdown on Palestinians following the Second Intifada. After long struggles for LGBTQ equality in Israel—often conducted against determined opposition from society, the government, and, in particular, Orthodox Judaism—the right-wing government of Benjamin Netanyahu cynically championed LGBTQ rights to advance his own agendas against Iran and the Palestinian Territories at the United Nations.[18] To burnish Israel's image abroad and deflect from the European Union's critique of Israeli human rights abuses of the Palestinians, Netanyahu presented Israel as a gay-friendly, progressive, democratic country that protected human rights, in contrast to other benighted, authoritarian, homophobic Middle Eastern nations.[19] Although the claims he made were factually accurate, and therefore did not constitute pinkwashing, Netanyahu nonetheless opportunistically supported political parties and organizations abroad that discriminate against LGBTQ people. Thus, as Gross asserts, "the term Pinkwashing is not very successful. It causes people to misunderstand the situation," because unlike the use of the term "greenwashing" to describe the false environmental claims, Israel has made real advances in LGBTQ rights.[20] Nonetheless, Netanyahu essentially hijacked the Israeli gay rights movement for his own ends, making it an instrument of foreign policy and projecting the image abroad of Israel as a pro-LGBTQ nation while undertaking expansionist pro-settler and anti-Palestinian and Arab Israeli policies at home.

However, BDS activists like Schulman—in addition to Puar, Davis, Butler, and Spade—paint with a very broad brush and conflate leftist LGBTQ Israelis with a conservative government they oppose.[21] They also deny that "Israel has had real LGBT rights advances." Many in the Israeli gay community who acknowledge Palestinian aspirations and suffering thus find themselves involved in a four-front struggle: against religious homophobes and families of various stripes in Israel, the allegations of pinkwashing from abroad, the conservative Israeli government, and continued political struggles, particularly around transgender issues and asylum rights for gay and lesbian Palestinians. The achievements and histories of LGBTQ Israelis undermine the premises of the pinkwashing allegation. LGBTQ culture and history in Israel have nothing in common with the use of pink ribbon logos in cause-marketing for breast cancer, which rests on fraudulent consumer claims that inflict harm.

Same-Sex Relations in the Middle East

Outside of Israel the accusation of pinkwashing results not only from lack of knowledge or distorted misreading of LGBTQ Israeli politics and history but also from contiguous and interrelated historical developments in Western nations: (1) as Puar, Davis, and Schulman assert, the growing success and cooption of the LGBTQ rights movement in the West, but also, more particularly, in Israel; (2) the escalating fear of and prejudice against Muslims after 9/11 and the War on Terror; (3) BDS activists' unblent opposition to Israel; (4) the critique of assimilationism and militarism that Lisa Duggan characterizes as "homonormativity"[22] and Puar later conceptualizes as "homonationalism"; and (5) the cognitive dissonance caused by queer BDS activists' rejection of Israel on the one hand and Israel's stellar record of human rights for LGBTQ persons on the other.

Queer BDS activists could not accord positive value to anything that originated in Israel because their moral and political convictions, in addition to their sense of social justice, dictate that they reject that country. Also, according to the principles governing the BDS movement,

BDS proponents cannot engage with those who support the existence of the State of Israel. Unfortunately, the resulting lack of dialogue can undermine the stances of BDS proponents, foster selective blindness and reliance on sloganeering, and seriously weaken the force of their arguments. Further, direct debate with opponents not only helps clarify intellectual and moral positions, but can also lead to innovative solutions to entrenched problems. On the other side, pro-Israel extremists fail to acknowledge the arguments of their opponents, downplay the suffering and claims of Palestinians, and resort to legal action, blacklisting, or allegations of antisemitism to chill free speech about Israeli human rights abuses.

For the BDS movement, pinkwashing represents the means to accomplish three ends: (1) denigrate the social advances Israel has made that otherwise would have been lauded, given that LGBTQ people confront considerable violence and adversity in most other nations across the globe; (2) attempt to hurt the Israeli gay tourist economy and tarnish its LGBTQ community, and (3) chill or freeze speech around homophobia and other human rights catastrophes in Islamic nations.[23] While Puar and Schulman make important points about the need to resist Islamophobic demonization, one need not engage in invidious or ethnocentric comparisons to make note of two crucial facts: (1) the situation for LGBTQ people, as well as women and religious minorities in Islamic countries, including Palestine, is dire; and (2) Islamic gays and lesbians can find means and values outside of Western-style identity politics—including polyamory, homosociality, modesty, and the closet—to resist compliance, evade detection, and, in the case of BDS activism, make common, if qualified, political cause with others. To counter the chilling of free speech that accusations of Islamophobia (like those of antisemitism) can cause, responsible parties can petition gay-friendly countries and organizations to pressure homophobic ones to change their practices through diplomacy, advocate for asylum rights for persecuted and endangered gays, and support and publicize Islamic LGBTQ organizations such as alQaws[24] and Muslims for Progressive Values, among others.[25]

Resistance to the status quo matters in preserving and dignifying LGBTQ Muslims' lives, for while juridical punishments are often unevenly and sporadically enforced, they do reflect dominant social attitudes and inform the familial expectations of marriage and the homophobic prejudices that LGBTQ Muslims confront. In the Middle East same-sex relations are illegal; they are punishable by imprisonment in Egypt, Kuwait, Oman, Qatar, and Syria, and punishable by death in Iran, Saudi Arabia, and the United Arab Emirates. In Yemen and Gaza, the punishment varies between death and imprisonment. The West Bank, Lebanon, and Jordan have decriminalized same-sex sexual behaviors, but discrimination, disinheritance, shunning, assault, harassment, kidnapping, honor killings, and even torture remain too common, and have been exacerbated by the occupation and the boomerang effect of allegations of pinkwashing.[26]

If the situation for LGBTQ people in Muslim countries is informed by postcolonialism, corrupt political authoritarianism, social and economic inequities, anti-Western backlash, and Islamism, then a different situation obtains in Israel, which has been the beneficiary of democratic institutions, progressive court rulings, the efforts of gay, lesbian, bisexual, and transgender advocacy groups, and alliances with other human rights organizations.[27] Israel inherited the anti-sodomy "buggery" laws from the colonial code of the British Mandate (which are still in force in Gaza),[28] but consenting adults did not face prosecution under these laws, and the Knesset formally repealed this statute in 1988. Israel banned workplace discrimination against LGBTQ persons in 1992; legalized open military service in 1993; provided same-sex domestic partner benefits in 1995; permitted legal change of names in 1995; reduced the age of consent in 2004; and secured inheritance rights in 2004—the same year the Knesset approved anti-hate crime legislation for LGBTQ persons.

Israel legalized same-sex adoption in 2003; recognized same-sex civil unions performed (as with the case of heterosexuals) abroad in 2008; same-sex civil divorce in 2012; and surrogacy rights for gay male couples (and single heterosexual men) in 2020.[29] National health insurance covers transgender surgery, and there are proposed laws currently under consideration—although still controversial—to eliminate gender markers in national identity cards and to ban conversion therapy. In brief, from 1988, when sodomy statutes were repealed, to 2014, when Tel Aviv unveiled the first memorial to gay and lesbian victims of the Holocaust, to 2016, when the ruling of the National Labor Court in the Meshel case meant that transgender people were to be covered under the Israeli Equal Employment Opportunities Law,[30] Israeli LGBTQ activists have waged a long, hard but largely successful battle for their rights. Furthermore, the future looks promising. In secular schools, although bullying and shunning persist, teenagers learn about treating diverse sexualities equally. The once-marginalized and closeted voices of religious, Mizrachi, Likud, Ethiopian, gender nonconforming, Arab, and transgender Israelis are now coming out and speaking out to create fundamental transformations in Israeli culture, politics, and religion. Negative stereotypes about gay Jews, Christians, and Arabs are steadily eroding.

However, these achievements do not mean that the LGBTQ rights movement in Israel does not face continued tragedies, accusations of pinkwashing from abroad, and the dilemmas of cooption by the state to further its schemes of settlement building and threatened annexation in the West Bank.[31] Some difficulties for the Israeli LGBTQ community emerge from familiar religious fundamentalist sources within Judaism, Christianity, and Islam. For instance, gay and lesbian marital unions remain outside Israeli civil law because the Orthodox Chief Rabbinate of Israel controls marriage, which means that gays and lesbians (as well as heterosexuals) seeking civil marriage must travel outside of Israel. Further, in 2006, Muslim Knesset member Ibrahim Sarsur warned gays that if they dared to approach the Temple Mount during the World Pride parade in Jerusalem they would do so "over our dead bodies." In response, gay rights leader Charles Merrill stated that if Christianity, Islam, and Judaism wanted homosexuals stoned as dictated by their ancient scriptures, then "our gentle innocent blood will be on their hands."[32]

Such innocent blood was indeed shed on August 1, 2009, when a masked man dressed in black and carrying an automatic weapon stormed into Beit Pazi in the Tel Aviv branch of the Agudah, Israel's LGBT Task Force. He opened fire on a group of gay and lesbian teenagers who were meeting in the basement of Bar-Noar (Hebrew for "youth bar"), killing two people and wounding fifteen others.[33] Further, on July 30, 2015, Shiri Banka, a sixteen-year-old high school student, was one of six people stabbed at the Jerusalem pride parade by an ultra-Orthodox Jew named Yishai Schlissel, who had carried out a similar attack on a gay pride parade in 2005. Tragically, Banka, who had gone to the parade to support her queer friends, died of her wounds on August 2.[34]

BDS advocates who excoriate Israel claim, as Miriam Elman remarks, that such murders prove Israel is not that gay-friendly after all. Elman calls such accusations "reverse pinkwashing," and remarks that it amounts to "seeking to use an isolated incident to deny the truth about Israel's gay rights record in order to wash away the violent and pervasive persecution of LGBTQ individuals in Palestinian society."[35]

BDS Advocates on Pinkwashing

Neither these achievements nor these struggles have positive or persuasive meaning for queer BDS activists because Israel violates their core sense of moral rightness, and serves to negate their concerns and alliances as LGBTQ people and feminists. Although they condemn ongoing homophobia in Israel, they do not note that these prejudices remain personal and familial (largely religious) sentiments that do not receive juridical or legislative sanction.

For instance, in *Terrorist Assemblages*, Puar, warning against Islamophobia, whitewashes the homophobia, antisemitism, and sexism to which Palestinians subscribe, but has also, along with others, effectively silenced criticism of Muslim nations for their misogyny, homohatred, and mistreatment of religious and ethnic minorities. Further, in her article "A Documentary Guide to Pinkwashing," Schulman provides a detailed timeline for the pinkwashing public relations campaign. She claims that over the years Israel spent $90 million to attract gay tourists and putatively falsely advertise itself as a progressive, democratic nation that welcomed gay people, particularly in Tel Aviv, which was called "one of the most intriguing and exciting new gay capitals in the world." Schulman writes:

> The goal of pinkwashing is to justify Israel's policies of occupation and separation by promoting the image of a lone oasis of progress surrounded by violent, homophobic Arabs, thereby denying the existence of queer Palestinian movements, or of secular, feminist, intellectual and queer Palestinians. By ignoring the multidimensionality of Palestinian society, the Israeli government is trying to claim supremacy that in their mind justifies the occupation.[36]

But this argument, as James Kirchick asserts in "Pink Eye," amounts to a non sequitur.[37] Merely because one applauds gay rights in Israel does not mean that one denigrates Palestinian culture or erases "the multidimensionality of Palestinian society." Hence, for Schulman and Kirchick, solidarity with some facets of Palestinian society, including Hamas, requires calls for the end of the Jewish state. This naturally entails the demise—through violence or displacement—of the Israeli LGBTQ community, which would represent an act of genocidal homohatred on an unprecedented scale. The Anti-Defamation League (ADL) states that "this reality does not diminish, ignore or 'pinkwash' the Israel-Palestinian conflict, nor does it negate the homophobic attitudes present in some segments of Israeli society, particularly in the ultra-Orthodox sector of Israeli society." Kirchick further remarks that the Israeli record on LGBTQ rights is impressive, despite the homophobia that still plagues some sectors of Israeli society. Touting that record does not, as he remarks, "constitute a covert method of justifying the occupation or racism against Arab citizens."[38]

Queer BDS intellectual activists and others in the BDS movement not only impose an ersatz pinkwashing discourse on Israel in an effort to tarnish its outstanding record on LGBTQ rights but also cynically appropriate and exploit the queer movement. BDSers have also exploited their links to the ecological, racial justice, and disabled rights movements as a way to burnish its progressive credentials. Further, governments across the globe routinely advertise themselves to boost local economies and attract tourists, including nations like China and Russia, which stand guilty of grievous human rights abuses but are not subject to boycott, divestment, and sanctions campaigns that are well-publicized in the media or on college campuses.[39] Finally, Israel could stand accused of homophobic discrimination if it did *not* advertise Israel as a gay-friendly tourist destination. But at least Schulman empathizes with other gay people.[40] In "Citation and Censorship: The Politics of Talking About the Sexual Politics of Israel," on the other hand, Puar contends that Israel has lied to disguise the truth that it is nothing but a nation mired in militarism and invidious conflict with the Palestinians; Israel accomplishes this through projecting homophobia and backwardness onto Palestinians while denying Israeli oppression of queer people and the way Israeli colonialist control of the Palestinian people renders them homophobic by degrading their cultural norms and values. In brief, she appears to claim that Palestinians are homophobic because of Israel and Israeli law, policy, and sexuality discourse. She asserts that

> Israeli pinkwashing is a potent method through which the terms of the Israeli occupation of Palestine are reiterated—Israel is civilized, Palestinians are barbaric, homophobic, and uncivilized. This discourse has manifold effects: it denies Israeli homophobic oppression of its own gays and lesbians ... and it recruits, often unwittingly, gays and lesbians of other countries into collusion with Israeli violence towards Palestine. In reproducing Orientalist tropes of Palestinian sexual backwardness, it also denies the impact of colonial occupation on the degradation and containment of Palestinian cultural norms and values. Pinkwashing harnesses global gays as a new source of affiliation by recruiting liberal gays into a dirty bargaining of their own safety against the continued oppression of Palestinians.[41]

While Puar correctly notes that colonial occupation has manifold dire consequences for civil societies, this fact could not plausibly be the sole reason for homophobia among Palestinians, particularly given the traditionalist cast of the culture, the authoritarianism of the Palestinian Authority (PA) and Hamas, the widespread belief in the normative dogmas of Shafi'i Islam, and the fact that there are numerous nations and communities around the world that are deeply homophobic but not subject to colonialism.[42] Further, Puar would surely be the last to claim that Palestinians do not exercise agency outside of Israel, or bear responsibility for their decision-making processes and actions. It remains unclear how touting the record of Israeli LGBTQ rights involves denying the existence of homophobia in Israel, the ethical obligation to provide more funding for underserved sectors of the Israeli queer community,[43] the fact that Israeli organizations engage in outreach efforts to LGBTQ Palestinian groups and individuals, or the need for independent queer Palestinian organizations such as alQaws.[44] Because Puar backs BDS, Israel is categorically beyond the pale, and she would not engage in transnational LGBTQ solidarity between Israel and Palestine. She concludes with a disquieting non sequitur. She contends that the mere act of regarding Israel as a safe haven for gays amounts to an invidious bargaining for personal safety over the oppression of Palestinian people. Does Puar mean that LGBTQ people should be willing to risk their lives by permitting a dangerous homophobic and authoritarian regime to overtake Israel for the sake of Palestinian liberation? While her exact meanings remain perhaps intentionally unclear, such a regime would scarcely liberate gay *or* heterosexual Palestinians.

The Politics of Queer Palestinian Identity

However, the strong emphasis that Israel places on its positive LGBTQ rights record means that some—including homophobes—can congratulate themselves on the accomplishments in Israeli society on which they hitch a free ride but for which they did not struggle. All the while they opportunistically condemn homophobia in Palestinian and Arab societies. The oppositional binary thinking that characterizes extremists on both sides of the Israel/Palestine conflict can conceal or distort crucial realities, while the antinormalization dicta of the BDS movement forbids civil discourse aimed at frank discussion of the consequences and ramifications of the conflict, which ends up jeopardizing the very people it claims to represent. The BDS movement ignores the lived realities on each side of the divide: the ones acutely victimized by these partisan passions are those who find themselves caught in the middle—such as gay and lesbian Palestinians—for whom societal persecution (especially in Gaza), pinkwashing, and the anti-Palestinian provisions of Israeli asylum law all pose grave dangers and reveal the ethical lacunae of partisans on both sides, not to mention the human costs of the conflict. Whether seeking, as BDS advocates, to quash open speech around Palestinian homophobia or, as pro-Israel partisans, to advertise Israeli gay rights to discredit Palestinian society, both sides fail to contemplate the grievous harms their practices, prejudices, and discourses inflict on others.

One disquieting truth is that many Palestinian gay men face potential abuse, torture, shunning, humiliation, kidnapping, and lethal violence at the hands of PA security forces, members of their own families, and armed militant groups.[45] Some might empathize with and even publicize this state of affairs to seek advantage or advertise their nationalistic moral credentials. In the face of such persecution, however, some gay Palestinians, thought to number around two thousand at any given time,[46] seek refuge in nearby LGBTQ-friendly Tel Aviv where, rather than being welcomed, they face discrimination, resort to criminal activities, and *secrecy*. They do not suffer as gay men but rather as *Palestinians*, an identity they must keep in the closet to avoid detention by Israeli security authorities. If captured, they are regularly sent back to Palestine, where they can face cruel fates: at best, accused of acting as collaborators with the Israelis and subject to abuse, and at worst, death at the hands of other Palestinians.[47]

Some BDS supporters either implicitly or explicitly join in this view that the gay Palestinians who seek asylum in Israel are anti-BDS collaborators who betray the national Palestinian cause. Gay Palestinians who seek refuge in Israel at the very least find themselves bearers of inconvenient truths about unspeakable realities. Thus queer BDS advocates do not bring up this issue in their otherwise blistering critiques of Israeli pinkwashing and so reveal that they really do not care for the plight of LGBTQ people but rather seek to cynically manipulate them.[48] For instance, in his documentary *Pinkwashing Exposed* (2015), Dean Spade excoriates an Israeli gay documentary called *The Invisible Men* (dir. Yariv Mozer, 2012). The latter film, which concerns persecuted gay Palestinians escaping from their families and hiding in Tel Aviv, assails the anti-Palestinian prejudices of putatively gay-friendly Israeli society, not to mention the checkpoints, barriers, and other exhausting and demoralizing indignities visited on stateless Palestinians daily.[49] However Spade makes no mention of the lived experiences of these gay Palestinians nor does he even call for a gay *Palestinian* to direct a film on this subject matter. Rather he insists, both implausibly and quizzically, that this documentary constitutes propaganda used to disguise the "immense homophobia in Israel and the United States," a claim that is particularly bizarre given that the film does not concern the United States at all.[50]

Thus one side erases Palestinian homophobia and the men who flee, while the other applauds its pro-LGBTQ laws and policies but prohibits gay Palestinians from claiming asylum status because of their national origin.[51] For these reasons and others, many LGBTQ Palestinians, as Franke remarks, "bristle when the Israeli government purports to speak on their behalf and look after their interests, driving a wedge between their gay-ness and their Palestinian-ness. Israel expresses an interest in their welfare only so long as their interests are framed as gay. To the extent that they identify as Palestinian, Israel's helping hand cruelly curls into a fist."[52] Further, knowing that gays are despised in the PA, the Israeli police and military apparatus target Palestinian gays for blackmail, thus turning many into informants. This in turn feeds the hatred and mistrust of gays in the PA, and the perception that they are collaborators. The PA police accordingly also seek to ferret out every homosexual and secure him as their agent and informant, while the fact that Palestine lacks large urban centers to which gay Palestinians might escape and blend in makes flying under the radar all the more difficult. Checkpoints and geographical segmentation also hamper and complicate gay Palestinians' efforts to organize politically. Gay and lesbian Palestinians are unwilling scapegoats for their sexuality and national identity; caught in the crosshairs of the Israel/Palestine conflict, they face some of the more odious forms of persecution for sexuality difference in the world.

However, LGBTQ Palestinians, in defiance of these circumstances, have developed increasingly visible and viable forms of political resistance and community-based organizing aimed at battling Palestinian intolerance on the one hand and Israeli occupation on the other. Began in 2001 as a community outreach project of the Jerusalem Open House for Pride and Tolerance[53] to address the needs of queer Palestinians living in East Jerusalem, alQaws has expanded since 2001 and hosts social and political activities in Jerusalem, Jaffa, and Ramallah, in the West Bank. Further, Isha L'isha or Woman to Woman, an organization founded at the Haifa Feminist Center, not only hosts meetings and organizes lectures, events, and educational programs, but also maintains an active archive of the personal stories of Palestinian lesbians and feminists.[54] Finally, organizations like alQaws have garnered support despite opposition. In August 2019 the PA tried to disband the group, claiming that it went "against and infringe[d] upon the higher principles and values of Palestinian society."[55] But the PA rescinded its ban in the face of protests that garnered the support of US Congressional representatives Ilhan Omar and Rashida Tlaib. As Omar stated, "LGBTQ rights are human rights and we should condemn any effort to infringe upon them."[56]

Zionism, Arab Nationalism, and the Origins of the Israel/Palestine Divide

Understanding the origins of the problem that has led to accusations of pinkwashing and the imperiling of gay and lesbian Palestinians necessitates a brief consideration of historical developments that began in the late nineteenth century, when Zionist, or Jewish nationalist ambitions to create a Jewish homeland in historical Israel, began to threaten Arab leaders in Palestine.[57] Jewish acquisition of lands for settlements from wealthy Arab owners led to the eviction of *fellaheen* from the lands they had cultivated and caused the Arab population to be dispossessed. Local residents also saw European immigration as a peril to the cultural make-up of the Levant. But Jewish immigrants continued to arrive because of Middle Eastern expulsions, European pogroms, anti-Jewish legislation, economic hardship, and antisemitic persecution.[58] Palestinian nationalism arose in response to this growing Zionist movement, which escalated with the ongoing rise of antisemitism, as well as through a desire for Arab self-determination in the Levant.[59] After the Nazis rose to power in Germany, the Jewish population in Palestine doubled, which caused relations with Palestinian Arabs to further deteriorate.[60]

In 1921 the grand mufti of Jerusalem, Amin al-Husayni, became the leader of the Palestinian Arab movement and stirred antisemitic religious hatred against the Jewish settlers. The first major uprising against the Jews, the 1921 Jaffa riots, caused the Jewish settlers to organize the Haganah, the prototype of the IDF, as a defense force.[61] Several Arab riots and insurgencies ensued, which prompted the British Peel Commission to propose a two-state solution in 1937. Arab leaders rejected the proposal and refused to share land in Palestine with the Jewish settlers.[62] In May 1939, the British government changed course and proposed a one-state solution in Palestine, establishing a quota that limited Jewish immigration and placing restrictions on Jews purchasing land from Arabs. These policies remained in effect throughout World War II and the Holocaust, when many more European Jewish refugees attempted to escape illegally to Palestine.[63]

During the 1936–39 Arab revolt in Palestine, Arab leadership and the Nazis established ties that led to cooperation between the Palestinians and the Axis powers during World War II. In 1941 the grand mufti declared a holy war against Britain and asked Hitler to oppose the establishment of a Jewish national home in Palestine. Hitler promised he would eradicate the Jewish settlements after the Germans had gained victory in Europe. He organized a joint Palestinian-Nazi military operation in the Levant, which caused relations between the British and the Palestinian leadership to disintegrate.[64]

In May 1947 the UN General Assembly once again proposed a two-state solution for Israel/Palestine, as experience had shown that both people could not live together peaceably in one state. Although neither side liked the plan, the Jews accepted it, while the Arabs rejected it, arguing that it violated the rights of the Arab majority in Palestine. The Palestinian leadership, like the Arab League, also objected in principle to the establishment of a Jewish state because they perceived Jews not as a nation but only as a religion.[65]

In May 1948, one day prior to the end of the British Mandate, David Ben-Gurion declared the establishment of the State of Israel. The formal declaration asserted that Israel would "ensure complete equality of social and political rights to all its inhabitants irrespective of religion, race or sex; it will guarantee freedom of religion, conscience, language, education and culture; it will safeguard the Holy Places of all religions; and it will be faithful to the principles of the Charter of the United Nations."[66]

The termination of the British Mandate and the establishment of Israel caused the immediate eruption of the 1948 Arab-Israeli War, wherein the armies of Jordan, Iraq, Syria, Egypt—and soon thereafter Lebanon—invaded or intervened in Palestine. While Arab commanders ordered villagers in isolated areas to evacuate for military purposes, no evidence indicates that the Arab military leaders called for them to leave their dwellings. In fact, they urged Palestinians to stay in their homes. Assaults by Israeli military forces on major Arab centers as well as expulsions led to the exodus of large portions of the Arab/Palestinian populations. In addition, the earlier flight by the Palestinian elite and the psychological effects of Jewish atrocities (stories about which both sides promulgated) also played important roles in the Nakba.[67]

In the violent chaos of these historical processes, by the time Israel was established as a state, around 750,000 Palestinians had either fled or been removed to the West Bank, Gaza, or neighboring Arab countries, where they have become semi-permanent refugee populations under the supervision of the United Nations Relief and Works Agency for Palestine Refugees in the Near East (UNWRA).[68] Jordan, the exception to this rule, granted citizenship to Palestinians until it withdrew from the West Bank in 1988.⁶⁹ In the meantime Israel—which defined the Arabs/Palestinians as a hostile domestic demographic that had instigated deadly riots, worked for the overthrow of Israel, and whose numbers, more important, jeopardized the status of Israel as a Jewish state—passed a controversial law barring the return of Palestinian refugees to Israel.⁷⁰ Soon thereafter, in 1950, the Knesset passed Israel's Law of Return, which gave Jews around the world the right to return to Israel and become citizens. The Israeli government sent some of these new Jewish arrivals to live in former Palestinian villages, gave these towns Hebrew names, and thus set into motion the erasure of Arab/Palestinian heritage from Israel.⁷¹ In the context of World War II and the 1948 Arab-Israeli War, there were enormous transfers of Jewish and Palestinian/Arab populations within Israel, Europe, and the Middle East. Soon after Israel declared nationhood, Arab nations violently expelled around 850,000 Mizrachi Jews from their ancient pre-Islamic abodes, where they had suffered under Jim Crow–like *dhimmi* laws,⁷² but now also lost their nations, homes, and economic livelihoods simply because they were Jewish.⁷³ Approximately 140,000 homeless European Jewish survivors of Nazi persecution and refugees from the Nazi concentration camps arrived in Israel, some of them smuggled in before the creation of the Israeli state.⁷⁴ Finally, as previously mentioned, during the Nakba around 750,000 Palestinian Arabs were expelled from or fled their homes in Palestine.

BDS Activism, Counter-Activism, and the Third Narrative

As the foregoing narrative of the origins of Zionism and Arab nationalism makes clear, the Israel/Palestine conflict, which involves the exigent claims of migrants, immigrants, refugees, and both Jewish and Arab displaced persons, is complicated and does not admit to facile solutions. But these facts are elided in BDS activism, which has become a central part of social justice advocacy for a number of American professors, professionals, and students—located mainly, if not exclusively, in ethnic, gender/sexuality, and Middle Eastern studies programs.⁷⁵ Their activities should not be overly exaggerated to produce an image of American universities as rife with anti-Israel animus.[76] Nevertheless, this movement originated in Britain and was popularized by the Palestinian activist Omar Barghouti in July 2005. BDS has over the years gained considerable and, more recently, alarming traction on college campuses. Barghouti regards academic freedom as less vital that other liberties and has accused Israel of practicing apartheid to drive home his justification for BDS. He states,

> The claim most parroted by these self-styled progressives in numerous well-publicized columns in the mainstream Western media was that academic and cultural boycotts stifle the free expression of ideas, hamper cultural dialogue, and infringe on academic freedom. Other than the hypocrisy of anyone who supported blanket boycotts of apartheid South Africa in the past and now moralizes about the "intrinsic" danger of boycott against Israel, there is a disturbing bias in this claim, because it regards only Israeli academic freedom as worthy of any consideration or concern. In addition, it invariably privileges academic freedom as superior to other freedoms.[77]

Barghouti's demotion of academic freedom in favor of vague "other freedoms" are borne out in the tactics of the BDS movement on college campuses. They have used student governments and professional organizations to pass pro-BDS resolutions, sometimes using ethically questionable methods to accomplish their ends: They have disinvited or shut down through the heckler's veto pro-Israel speakers or events; they have harangued audiences with anti-Israel speeches; they have used classroom and publication venues to promulgate anti-Israel viewpoints; they have assaulted or threatened pro-Israel Jewish students or vandalized their property; they have refused to write letters of recommendation for qualified students who want to study in or about Israel; they have denied Israeli academics funding, publication, hiring, and participation in collaborative projects; they have shunned and publicly humiliated pro-Zionists for expressing their political views; they have engaged in boycotts against individuals who are Israeli or known to be or suspected of harboring pro-Zionist views; they have quashed pro-Israel publications or failed to observe professional standards of fact-checking and peer review in anti-Israel publications; and they have urged progressive speakers to refuse to address Zionist Jewish student groups whom they accuse of Nazi-like human rights abuses.[78]

Beginning in May 2021, however, anti-Israel—as well as anti-Western and anti-democratic—activism on college campuses exploded into a full-fledged conflagration, coinciding with the bombing campaign between the IDF and Hamas that was then occurring. Although Hamas, an authoritarian terrorist organization that brutalizes women, religious minorities, and LGBTQ people, started the bombing campaign, Israel was systematically blamed and pilloried, and anti-Israel petitions were launched across US college campuses. The BDS movement wanted far more than simply to chill free speech or boycott Israelis or Israeli universities. They attacked the academic freedom of their opponents. On some campuses, they assailed those who were reluctant to join in the anti-Israel fervor by signing petitions or making invidious statements claiming that Israel was an apartheid state that was, in many cases, guilty of genocide and, of course, systematic racism. These missives demanded, among other things, that courses on the Israel/Palestine conflict be taught exclusively from a Palestinian perspective: a frontal assault on academic freedom in the name of putative "social justice."[79] Further, according to Martin Kramer, BDS advocates desire to expel Jews from the university positions they or their comrades wish to occupy. Kramer argues that the academic boycott movement does not intend to boycott Israeli institutions of higher education—which would be an impossible task given their profound interdisciplinary, international networks—but rather to isolate, stigmatize, and, eventually, decimate Jewish academics, whom they regard as "over represented."[80]

For their part, pro-Israel forces have also used student governments and professional organizations to defeat pro-BDS resolutions; disseminated blacklists of pro-BDS or pro-terrorist parties through sites such as Canary Mission; resorted to accusations of antisemitism to chill the speech of their opponents; brought legal actions against universities for alleged antisemitic bias or failure to protect pro-Israel Jewish students and groups from discrimination, harassment, or intimidation; and, above all, availed themselves of legislative means aimed at shutting down BDS activism and imputed antisemitic biases on campuses. In brief, partisans on both sides exercise their academic freedom, but also regularly jeopardize, abuse, or violate the academic freedom of their opponents.

In the meantime, university administrators, who hear vociferous complaints from both sides about alleged lack of fairness, balance, and inclusivity, all too often are ineffective, equivocal, or timid. Many have campus cultures that promote safe spaces, disinvitation of controversial speakers, boycotting of ideologically troublesome professors, trigger warnings, or other implicit or explicit practices aimed at assuring students and professors that they deserve to be shielded from viewpoints they find challenging, objectionable, morally noxious, or even traumatizing.[81] These policies have vigorous supporters. They argue that, among other things, advocates of free speech are racially and socially privileged, distort these issues on campus, and imperil the freedom of students and professors who want controls on free speech free-for-alls. Such practices arose in ethnic, sexuality, and gender/women's studies programs to protect students from toxic racist, sexist, or homophobic environments that, they allege, hamper their ability to learn effectively.[82]

However, the free speech policies instituted recently by the University of Chicago, and widely adopted elsewhere, do much to halt the mischiefs associated on campuses with the Israel/Palestine conflict.[83] The letter from the University of Chicago administration sent to incoming students each year reads in part:

> Members of our community are encouraged to speak, write, listen, challenge and learn, without fear of censorship. Civility and mutual respect are vital to all of us, and freedom of expression does not mean the freedom to harass or threaten others. You will find that we expect members of our community to be engaged in rigorous debate, discussion, and even disagreement. At times this may challenge you and even cause discomfort.

> Our commitment to academic freedom means that we do not support so-called "trigger warnings," we do not cancel invited speakers because their topics might prove controversial, and we do not condone the creation of intellectual "safe spaces" where individuals can retreat from ideas and perspectives at odds with their own.
>
> Fostering the free exchange of ideas reinforces a related University priority—building a campus that welcomes people of all backgrounds. Diversity of opinion and background is a fundamental strength of our community. The members of our community must have the freedom to espouse and explore a wide range of ideas.[84]

These policies mean that pro- or anti-Israel students or professors cannot organize campaigns to disinvite, harass, or shout down speakers, or claim that opponents should be silenced on the grounds that they are triggering, traumatizing, or morally odious. In addition, these free-speech practices discourage resorting to subterranean methods of shutting down or chilling speech as opposed to engaging in open public debate that can educate the public.

On the other hand, the BDS movement—which abides by the rule of free speech for me but not for thee—upholds, in part through student groups like Students for Justice in Palestine (SJP), its own rights to academic freedom while denying the same to its pro-Israel opponents. According to this logic, Zionists commit such heinous crimes against humanity that they do not have any more right to disseminate their views than do Nazis or Holocaust deniers, and therefore should be denied public fora.

The BDS movement developed from two preceding models: (1) in 1945 the Arab League Council voted to discontinue commercial relations with Zionist Jews in pre-state Israel;[85] and (2) in 2001, at the UN's World Conference Against Racism in Durban, South Africa, certain NGOs—engaging in egregious antisemitic acts such as distributing copies of the notorious antisemitic conspiracy-theory book *The Protocols of the Elders of Zion*, and singling out Israel among all the nations of the world for condemnation—characterized Israel as an apartheid racist state that engaged in war crimes, including genocide and ethnic cleansing.[86] The so-called Durban Strategy that emerged from the conference ignored other nations and contemplated the isolation of Israel as a pariah state.[87] Also known as the Durban Conference, this meeting set the ideological and organizational foundation for the current efforts of the BDS movement, which was also encouraged by the gradual erosion of the Oslo peace process begun in 1993, the eruption but subsequent demise of the Second Intifada, the collapse of the Camp David peace talks, the construction in 2002 of what the Israelis called the security barrier and the Palestinians the apartheid wall[88] (which Israel had built because of terrorist suicide-bomber attacks in the early 2000s),[89] the death of Yasser Arafat, the fifty-year-plus occupation of the West Bank, and, above all, the repeated failures of diplomatic efforts aimed at resolving the conflict through a two-state solution.

The BDS movement, which took root principally in Durban, has five central aims: (1) to delegitimize, de-normalize, and isolate Israel; (2) to reject peace initiatives aimed at resolving the conflict through a two-state solution; (3) to forbid dialogue and cooperation between Palestinians and Israelis; (4) to end the existence of Israel as a Jewish state putatively founded on settler colonialism, apartheid, and racist Zionism; and (5) to stop the military occupation and colonization of the West Bank. As Barghouti, the founder of the Palestinian Campaign for the Academic and Cultural Boycott of Israel (PACBI), said of the two-state peace initiative, "Good riddance! The two-state solution for the Palestinian-Israeli conflict is finally dead. But someone has to issue an official death certificate before the rotting corpse is given a proper burial and we can all move on and explore the more just, moral and therefore enduring alternative for peaceful coexistence between Jews and Arabs in Mandate Palestine: the one-state solution."[90] In her book *Parting Ways: Jewishness and the Critique of Zionism* (2012), leading queer philosopher Butler follows Barghouti in an elaborate proposal for this one-state solution. Her answer to the dilemma has been critiqued on various grounds, including concerns, based on historical dynamics both inside and outside of Israel/Palestine, that one state would not lead to peaceful coexistence but, rather, to internecine civil war, sectarian violence, and the destruction of civil society.[91] However for

Butler, as for Barghouti, the spool of history must be unwound because Israel, founded as a democratic Jewish state, committed the presumed original sins of apartheid, Zionism, and settler colonialism.[92]

Using the successful boycott, divestment, and sanctions movement against South Africa, which did practice apartheid, as an inspiration, the BDS movement falsely treats Israel as on par with the former South Africa.[93] It urges "international cultural workers . . . and cultural organizations, including unions and associations . . . to boycott and/or work towards the cancellation of events, activities, agreements, or projects involving Israel, its lobby groups or its cultural institutions."[94] The BDS movement directs its followers to battle against Israel culturally and educationally using the following means:

1. Refrain from participating in any form of academic and cultural cooperation, collaboration, or joint projects with Israeli institutions;
2. Advocate a comprehensive boycott of Israeli institutions, including suspension of all forms of funding and subsidies;
3. Promote divestment and disinvestment from Israel by international academic institutions;
4. Work toward the condemnation of Israeli policies by pressing for resolutions to be adopted by academic professional and cultural associations and organizations; and
5. Support Palestinian academic and cultural institutions directly without requiring them to partner with Israeli counterparts.[95]

Intended to isolate Israeli cultural and educational institutions, these measures mainly end up hurting Arab Israeli or American students and individual Israeli academics. Indeed, many or most people who support BDS do so because it seems like the only game in town. The majority of such casual BDS advocates remain understandably angered over violations of Palestinian human rights by the Israeli government and frustrated that any critique of Israeli policies results in accusations of antisemitism. They oppose the expanding settlement blocs in the West

Bank and East Jerusalem, the security barrier/apartheid wall, the discrimination against Arab Israelis, the siege of Gaza, the occupation of the West Bank, and the repeated failures of the peace process, which they perhaps naively tend to blame on the more powerful nation—the Israeli Goliath facing off against the Palestinian David.

However, a closer look at the BDS founding documents show that they contemplate what Barghouti calls the "euthanasia" of Israel. They do not want a return to the 1967 borders but to 1947—before the founding of Israel and, soon after, the Nakba in the context of the large-scale Arab invasion of Israel. Further, the anti-normalization policies of BDS foreclose cooperation, collaboration, or joint projects with Israeli institutions, abridge academic freedom for Israeli—and now Jewish American—scholars and others who have professional ties with them, and make Israeli academics political representatives of their government, with whose policies they might well disagree. The BDS movement has created approaches to Israel that, to draw but one false and misleading analogy, would amount to boycotting Chinese scholars and cultural representatives, as well as Chinese institutions of higher education, because the Chinese government runs an unconstrained surveillance state that has interred, tortured, or involuntarily sterilized more than a million Uighur Muslims,[96] and has decimated the culture of Tibetan Buddhists. Finally, other than calling for the dissolution of the Israeli state, the BDS movement has no policy recommendations for improving the actual lives or situations of Palestinians or Israelis, or for resolving the conflict. Their forbidding of cooperation between Israelis and Palestinians not only imperils the peace process but also, to take one example, does injury to Arab Israeli university students who study in Israel, and who are therefore criticized or boycotted by the BDS movement for cooperating with the enemy.[97] As the Palestinian academic Sari Nusseibeh has observed,

> Bridging political gulfs—rather than widening them further apart—between nations and individuals thus becomes an educational duty as well as a functional necessity, requiring exchange and dialogue rather than confrontation and antagonism. Our disaffection

with, and condemnation of acts of academic boycotts and discrimination against schools and institutions, is predicated on the principles of academic freedom, human rights, and equality between nations and among individuals.[98]

Thus, as this statement makes clear, there are alternatives to BDS that avoid pro-Israel partisanship and *hasbara* (i.e., pro-Israel propaganda). The Third Narrative is an organization of scholars that backs the two-state solution as the only viable vehicle for achieving long-term peace for both peoples, and it opposes various forms of BDS and anti-BDS activism and boycotting alike. It vigorously supports academic freedom as an important tool for understanding and resolving the conflict and condemns *all* efforts to abridge the speech of scholars on *all* sides of this debate, as well as binary approaches to the conflict that demonize either of the parties and that diminish or distort their histories and aspirations. The mission statement of the Third Narrative reads,

(a) We respect the humanity of Israelis and Palestinians alike, and believe that all political analysis of the Israeli-Palestinian conflict must be grounded in empathy for both peoples.
(b) We believe in two states as the only way to avoid perpetual conflict, and recognize that since both peoples require national self-expression, the struggle will continue until this is achieved.
(c) We believe the Israeli occupation of the West Bank not only deprives Palestinians of their fundamental rights, but is also corrosive to Israeli society and is incompatible with the democratic principles upon which the State of Israel was founded.
(d) We accept the obligation to actively oppose violations of human rights, but cannot condone the use of violence targeting civilians as a tool to address grievances, or to promote strategies that would undermine the future viability of each nation.
(e) We strongly oppose the rhetoric used by both sides which demonizes and dehumanizes the other, or distorts the history and national aspirations of each people, to promote violence and hatred.

(f) We reject the all-too-common binary approach to the Arab-Israeli conflict that seeks to justify one side or the other as all right or all wrong, and sets out to marshal supposed evidence to prove a case of complete guilt or total exoneration. Scholarship and fairness require a more difficult and thoughtful approach. As academics we recognize the subjective perspectives of individuals and peoples, but strive to apply rigorous standards to research and analysis rather than to subsume academic discipline to political expediency.

(g) We reject all attempts to undermine or diminish academic freedom and open intellectual exchange, including those cases associated with the Israel-Palestine debate. Academic boycotts and blacklists are discriminatory per se and undercut the purpose of the academy: the pursuit of knowledge. Likewise, we are against legislative and other efforts by domestic or foreign interests that seek to diminish the academic freedom of those scholars who might propose, endorse, or promote academic boycotts, even if we strongly disagree with these tactics.[99]

Queering Anti-Zionism operates under no illusions that ideological partisans on either side of this issue, who are wedded to what they perceive as a Manichean struggle between Good and Evil, intend to stand down, embrace pedagogies that do justice to various sides of the Israel/Palestine conflict, or cease efforts to recruit students to become proxy warriors in their ideological battles. This holds quite true for LGBTQ university students. All too often they arrive having suffered rejection, social isolation, suicidal ideation, harassment, or ostracism, and having had sometimes fierce encounters with familial or social homophobia, sexism, and transphobia. Even if they come from more supportive and accepting backgrounds, they nonetheless confront ingrained societal biases, and do so often feeling uncertain and vulnerable. They seldom walk through the doors of the university equipped with self-assured expertise about the intricate geopolitical realities of the Israel/Palestine conflict. Rather, pro-BDS or, sometimes, pro-Israel groups or academics approach them promising acceptance, inclusion, and the exhilarating pleasures of moral superiority through oppositional black versus white thinking. LGBTQ students remain dependent on the good faith representations of others who too frequently elide salient complexities and differences and offer them much longed for belonging and common cause with others in intersectional alliances, where they can find, however rationally improbable, in Israel, a safe and only vaguely known object onto which to project homophobia through lambasting Zionism. Finally, they can end up lending their support to causes that are inimical either to their ethics or to their political interests as gay people in an international context, but which they put aside either because they are unaware of the specifics or because of some vague sense of a greater good that transcends LGBTQ concerns.

In writing *Queering Anti-Zionism*, I therefore hope that many who claim to care about the welfare and multifaceted education of our students—as well as about our institutions of higher education—choose to promote empathic understanding and substantive knowledge rather than imperiling the mission of the university by attacking academic freedom, undermining open inquiry and dissent, abusing the social and intellectual vulnerabilities of our students, or chilling free speech.

1
SARAH SCHULMAN'S QUEER ADVENTURES IN ISRAEL/PALESTINE

From Empathy to Shunning: Schulman's Journey into BDS Ideology

Sarah Schulman wrote her influential *New York Times* op-ed on pinkwashing in the wake of an educational sojourn she took to Israel, Palestine, Europe, and North America that radicalized her and inaugurated her professional advocacy of the BDS movement. This activist tour of self-discovery led to the publication of her part-memoir, part-travelogue, part-essayistic pastiche, *Israel/Palestine and the Queer International* (2012). As befits the subject matter and structure of this salmagundi, the book meanders in paratactic fashion. Her well-intentioned endeavors to write clearly for the cause of social justice and to communicate with a broad general audience unfortunately results too often in oversimplification, misrepresentation, strategic silences, and false equivalences.

In her introduction, Schulman describes her background as a Jewish lesbian who "grew up surrounded by Holocaust survivors."[1] While establishing her credentials around rejecting antisemitism, as well as living with the sequelae of the cataclysmic event that revealed to the world the necessity of founding the State of Israel, Schulman approaches Jewish culture, like she approaches Israel, from a white American perspective, and incorrectly assumes that the vast majority of Israeli Jews are white. She assails Israel for having compelled European Jewish refugees to learn Hebrew rather than continue to speak Yiddish. The Israeli government did in fact decide, after much debate, to adopt modern Hebrew as one of two national languages (the other being Arabic), and an important reason was that the newly minted Israelis should leave behind the shame, passive victimization, persecution, and degradation they associated with the *galut* (exile). However, she does not mention that the Mizrachi and Beta Jews from the Middle East, Asia, and Africa, who comprise around 40 percent of the Israeli Jewish population, would not feel comfortable with Yiddish as a language that did not reflect their non-European Jewish heritage. Hebrew, the Semitic language of the Hebrew Bible and most of the liturgical literature, represented the common culture of Jews worldwide. Also, Schulman makes the false claim that Israel killed Yiddish (a language she associates with Jewish ethics, liberalism, and non-dominance). In fact it was the Nazis and American assimilationism that nearly exterminated the *mame loshn*, or the Yiddish mother tongue. Yiddish has enjoyed a renaissance as a living language in Israel,[2] as well as among ultra-Orthodox Jews, whose cultural conservatism and homophobic views Schulman unsurprisingly finds unacceptable. Except for those leftists with linguistic nostalgia, Yiddish does not necessarily have a politically liberal demotic pedigree.

Elucidating the processes whereby she came to oppose Zionism, Schulman describes how her family—whose pernicious homophobic shunning she chronicled eloquently in the *Ties That Bind* (2009)[3]—fervently supported Israel. Thus associating Israel with masculinized dominance, rejection of the liberal, learned world of the European Yiddish *galut* and familial homophobia, Schulman also identifies herself as a "Diasporic Jew," a designation that, quoting Isaac Bashevis Singer, means that she would muddle through the world but never command it. Further, in 1982 she dated a Christian lesbian from a left-wing organization who denounced the IDF for the massacre in Sabra and Shatila—which Israel had countenanced but which had been the direct work of Christian Phalangist troops during the Lebanon civil war.[4] Her awakening about nationalist Zionist military aggression comported with her experience of the "cruel homophobia" of her family, and she understandably concluded that her family was "wrong about a lot of things."[5]

Thus, her emerging anti-Zionist stance dovetailed with the anti-gay prejudices of the family that shunned, demeaned, and disavowed her, principally through the humiliating mechanism of sibling favoritism. Despite her identification with the pacifism of Singer, who had very complicated, subtle, and multivalent views on Israel, her wholesale rejection of Israel appears to emerge not as much from independent, self-reflective, and mature judgment as from an injured emotional reaction against the family that ostracized her.

Her experiences as a professor underscore her views on antisemitism and homophobia, which she connects to Islamophobia. Either disavowing or choosing to ignore Islamic nationalist and immigrant politics, perhaps to avoid even the appearance of Islamophobia, she presents antisemitism as an entirely Christian European and American Christian fundamentalist social malaise.[6] Hence she informs her reader that she finds it harder to come out as a Jew than as a lesbian with her reflexively antisemitic Eastern European immigrant students and sees "Europeans' histrionic paranoia and acting out against Muslims . . . as historically consistent"[7] with their antisemitism. The framework of her argument does not enable to her acknowledge that, in Western Europe, Muslim immigrants perpetrate most of the hate crimes against European Jews,[8] just as the prejudices some of them harbor reflect attitudes in their home countries, the historical collaborations that Islamic nations had with Nazis, and contemporary Islamist anti-gay, anti-woman, anti-religious minority, and anti-Israel opinions.[9] Furthermore, Schulman misrepresents the historical record by claiming that Europe bears sole responsibility for causing the conflict between the Palestinians and Israelis by putatively having forced World War II Jewish refugees who were not Zionists into the arms of Israel. The hostilities between the two groups in the British Mandate predate World War II by many decades, and most refugees went to the United States or Israel to escape the antisemitic violence and persecution they encountered when they attempted to return to their European homes.[10] Many Jews who chose to relocate in Israel over the United States (or elsewhere) identified as Zionists who wanted to rebuild the Jewish nation, and were not, as Schulman claims, forced into the Zionist embrace. Also, the US and UK quotas were still in full force, and the legislative bodies of these states did not want to have these refugees enter.[11]

Defining herself as a kind of cosmopolitan wandering Jew who lives with and celebrates difference, she nonetheless does not allow Zionist Jews, who believe in the national self-determination of Jews in the land of Israel, to differ from her or live within their own definitions of Jewishness. Rather, in a striking instance of ideological intolerance, she defines them as an insupportable threat to her preferred exilic definition of Jewish identity. She objects to Zionism because Jews have traditionally been a "minority living with other cultures that are dominant in size and reach."[12] Her view that Jews were therefore kept from "dangerous power" makes sense, particularly since they were, for the most part, prohibited from serving in the military in Europe and, certainly, in Muslim countries. From these observations she discovers what she regards as the source for the shifts in Jewish self-identification since the founding of Israel. Jews have taken up arms, have their own nation to defend, and thus have become more bellicose. The transformation is consequent on leaving the diaspora and having "our own nationalist state where we make the rules and dominate other people," which she regards as an "alien paradigm shift" that had profound "consequences on Jewish self-perception."[13] Schulman taps into a very marked antisemitic discomfort among some Jews about wielding power.

Holocaust Trauma and Israel as a Rogue State

For Schulman, the United States supports Israel because Israel's creation in 1948 enabled the United States to establish a military footprint in the region, an assertion which flies in the face of the fact that the United States has no military installations in that country. With Mizrachi and, later, Russian and African Jews fleeing their countries, Israel acquired a total Jewish population of approximately 74 percent, but Schulman improbably claims that Israel had "imposed and transported anti-Muslim and anti-Arab sentiment."[14] Schulman, in pursuit of her views, picks and chooses her evidence, and does not mention that Mizrachi Jews during that period were escaping from the antisemitic animus that had become normative and virulent in the countries they had inhabited as *dhimmis* or legal inferiors for millennia. Indeed, Jews represented the first examples of what has become the successive waves of expulsion or destruction of religious minorities throughout the Middle East and Muslim Africa, which has reached near genocidal proportions today.[15]

Throughout her book Schulman engages in widescale patterns of disavowal, misinformation, and false inference. For instance, she does not mention how the grand mufti of Jerusalem, Haj Amin al-Husayni conspired with the Nazis to massacre the Jews of pre-state Israel who lived on land they had purchased from the Ottoman Empire.[16] She also returns to her concern with American military and Jewish state power, wondering if America supports Israel because it identifies with and wants to protect Jews or "just because it needs a military base in Israel from which to conduct wars and control resources."[17] Further, she claims that the relationship Israel has to the United States, Europe, and the Palestinians results in "a lot of instability, false fronts, fear, and pretending. Israel exists simultaneously as a colonial settler state in relationship to Palestinians, and as a semicolonized project of the Christian West, the very people who caused the Jews' suffering to begin with."[18]

The Evangelical and Christian Zionists who support Israel are mainly American and were not, unlike European Christians, implicated in the Holocaust, although they propound and export homophobic animus. And while Jews had an ongoing historical footprint in the Levant, there was a massive swapping of refugee populations—Palestinian and European/Mizrachi Jew alike—before and during the 1948 Arab-Israeli war. More than 800,000 Palestinians became displaced in the Nakba,[19] while Arab governments in Algeria, Egypt, Iraq, Libya, Morocco, Syria, Tunisia, and Yemen, who have never acknowledged the harms they inflicted, displaced almost one million Mizrachi Jews after the Israeli government accepted (and the Palestinians rejected) the plan to partition British Palestine to create two states.[20] Schulman puts forward a plausible perspective about how the United States and Israel have a "conflicted" relationship, but the ties between the two nations are mainly ones based on intelligence sharing, economic and intellectual exchanges, technological innovations, and shared democratic institutions.[21] Schulman claims that Israelis established and have defended their nation through military means as part of the sequelae of postgenocidal trauma: "Impossible to overstate are the long-range consequences of the trauma of genocide on the European Jewish psyche and how this has been expressed through Israeli culture and policy. Through this process African Jews, Sephardic Jews, and especially Arab Jews have been created as implementers of the consequences of a trauma they did not experience. Yet their own authentic historic trauma of displacement and Israeli racism is never discussed."[22] The trauma of the Holocaust indeed has long-term, intergenerational consequences. But Schulman, herself the child of Holocaust survivors, appears to be a pacifist, and suffering such an unspeakable horror does not necessarily make people more warlike. Even in the face of persistent Holocaust denial, Schulman provides no proof of how the Shoah negatively influenced "Israeli culture and policy," which depends on the unsubstantiated opinion that Israel relishes going to war. Moreover, while she correctly points out that Israeli prejudice against Mizrachi and African Jews was ignored for a long time, it has—along with their traumatic experiences of displacement, threatened destruction, and dispossession—become recognized in Israeli society more recently, although much work remains to be done.[23] But Jews, according to Schulman, have a hard time facing the truth about Israel because Europe has not accounted for its legacies of antisemitism, which omits that Germany paid significant reparations to Israeli Holocaust survivors in 1952 and that other European nations, although far yet for accoumting for their legacies of antisemitism, yearly commemorate the Holocaust.[24]

She claims that the policies of Israel "do not make the world a safer place for Jews or anyone else" because "Israel has not acted responsibly towards the Palestinians and, like the United States, has deteriorated into a 'rogue state' that causes pain and inflicts suffering from a 'delusional place.'"[25] While Schulman correctly notes that Israeli Jews need to treat Palestinians better—by withdrawing from the West Bank, ending military actions against Gaza, reducing racism against Israeli Arabs, and providing reparations for displaced Palestinians—these faults do not necessarily make Israel a rogue nation that operates from delusion. The Israelis and Palestinians are engaged in a complicated and multifaceted historical conflict that does not lend itself to sloganeering or facile accusations on either side.

In addition, successive waves of Jews who have immigrated to Israel seeking refuge from antisemitic persecution and egregious economic hardship would not agree with her conclusions that the existence of Israel has made their world less safe, and this would be even more true for the Mizrachi and European Jewish refugees who came to Israel before and after the 1948 war. For them and others, Israel has saved their lives and provided them with refuge from resurgent waves of antisemitism across the globe, particularly in Western and Eastern Europe, and, earlier, in Africa. In the Middle East, they had been ethnically cleansed by the very Muslims whom Schulman does not see as problematic for her as a Jew, mostly because she has ideologically committed herself to avoiding all appearances of Islamophobia, in part because, for her, the West alone is blameworthy.[26] Should Jews risk a repeat performance of the Holocaust or mass forced deportation and dispossession in the *galut* as a vulnerable minority? History has an engrained habit of repeating itself unless prevented from doing so. Without Israel as a Jewish nation both willing and able to defend itself, another genocide or violent persecution could readily occur again.

Providing no context for the causes that prompted Israel to engage in Operation Cast Lead—the Israeli invasion of Gaza that occurred in 2008, after its unilateral withdrawal from those territories in 2006—Schulman says that this invasion prompted her to engage in direct action protest.[27] In 2008 Hamas and other terrorist organizations began to fire thousands of mortar launches and Grad rockets into southern Israel, which eventually sparked an IDF operation to halt this aggression and end weapons smuggling into Gaza. Aerial bombardment targeted weapons caches, police stations, and other official installations, which was followed by a ground campaign. Despite efforts to limit civilian casualties, approximately 1,400 Palestinians died, which led some BDS proponents to characterize the operation as genocidal, even though Hamas's use of Palestinian civilians as human shields was well documented by several sources.[28] This kind of heightened and inaccurate accusation has succeeded in making the charge of genocide nearly meaningless through reckless abuse. Israeli public air-raid shelters cut down on civilian deaths in southern Israel but gave many children severe cases of post-traumatic stress disorder.[29] Meanwhile, the BDS movement decried the disparities between Israeli and Palestinian death tolls as proof that Israelis had committed atrocities.

During her protest against Israeli actions in Gaza, Schulman feels disconcerted when she sees pro-Hamas signs among the protesters—until she reaches for false analogies to reassure herself:

> The first truth was that I did not know or understand enough about Hamas outside of what was fed me on American television to evaluate intelligently. I certainly did not know what Hamas meant to Palestinian people. Second, I realized that I have spent my life marching in coalition with people . . . even people who opposed my basic existence. I have marched in the same gay pride parade with gay Republicans for decades, and I once marched with Hasidic and Orthodox Jews in Brussels when a synagogue was bombed, even though I knew that they opposed my freedom and existence as a lesbian. . . . So the only reason that sharing a common outrage with Hamas at the killings in Gaza disturbed me more than all the other religious fundamentalists I had had some moment of common ground within the past was my own prejudice.[30]

Perhaps Schulman could have done primary research into both the IDF military actions in Gaza and the policies of Hamas before concluding that nothing more than uninformed personal prejudice and American mass media reports had made her distinguish Hamas from others with whom she differed over politics and homophobia. For while she might have political differences with gay Republicans, and while Hasidic and

Orthodox Jews might oppose her rights as a lesbian, they, unlike Hamas, would not kill her for her lesbianism[31] or, for that matter, hunt her down and take her life for her Jewishness.[32] Reluctant to complicate or investigate her claims, Schulman, a gay and feminist activist, ends up defending the terrorist organization responsible for instigating the Gaza war and brutally oppressing gays and women. In the meantime, like other BDS proponents, she pillories Israel for defending itself against Hamas's brand of asymmetrical warfare.

However, Schulman does not *want* Israelis to defend themselves against Hamas or other bad actors. Rather—although she refuses to state it directly—Schulman wants Jews either to leave Israel or to once again become a blameless if persecuted minority in the Middle East and elsewhere. Since the latter options are obviously unattractive, she takes up her own version of pinkwashing New York City by advertising it as the "best place in the world for Jews" because "you can be culturally normative without keeping other people down and still be at a healthy remove from identifying with the army, the cops, or thinking you can win the presidency."[33] The patent absurdity of suggesting that 6.9 million Jewish Israelis, nearly half of them non-Western, and the vast majority of them lacking means or legal standing to emigrate even if they wanted to, solve the problem of Jewish Israeli existence by relocating to a city of 8.54 million New Yorkers does not merit commentary. When she considers the actual practical consequences of her beliefs, she either elides salient realities, misstates the facts, or engages in frivolous speculation.

Journey to Tel Aviv

Schulman begins her journey into transforming her political philosophy in earnest, starting with her claim that the BDS movement intends to "change Israeli policy through economic and cultural pressure."[34] But this innocuous-sounding phrase actually means, in the lexicon of the BDS movement,[35] delegitimizing and de-normalizing Israel, in addition to instituting a Palestinian right of return, which would cause the demise of Israel as a Jewish state. Schulman glosses over the goals of BDS and also offers no concrete steps toward resolution of the conflict; once she returns to New York City, she demands the end of dialogue aimed at creating peace between Israelis and Palestinians.

Schulman is invited to give the keynote address at the Annual Lesbian and Gay Studies and Queer Theory Conference at Tel Aviv University but remains undecided how to respond, given the BDS academic boycott of that university. But she desires to help gay people while honoring her political commitments. She had just published the *Ties That Bind*, in which she "called for third-party intervention" and "made very explicit my belief that when people are victimized and ask others to intervene, those others should help them."[36] Wishing to do something helpful but uncertain of herself and her knowledge, Schulman decides to proceed anyhow. Much like Butler in calling for BDS against Israel, Schulman sincerely believes she has the best interests of the Jewish Israeli and Palestinian people at heart and, more particularly, feels frustrated, like so many others, at the lack of progress on resolving major issues surrounding the conflict. Those who oppose her suffer from Holocaust trauma, have become blinded by Jewish nationalist commitments, or, like Netanyahu, are cynical deceivers. There are no complexities in her black-and-white views that the Jewish Israelis are colonial oppressors and the Palestinians are indigenous victims suffering at the hands of once-virtuous Jews gone rogue.

A case in point illustrates her black-and-white views. In Germany during her preparation phase, she becomes annoyed at the anti-Muslim rhetoric of two gay German men. However, her conviction, formulated without evidence, that Muslims are not threatening to her while Christians pose dangers, simply reverses this binary opposition and does not advance further into insight into or understanding of the situation—either the one facing the two men or the dynamics of homophobic prejudice in Europe. She does not acknowledge the truth that both right-wing Christians and Muslims, depending on occasion and context, can be hostile to gays and Jews.[37] And although she claims she opposes making comparisons, she nonetheless proceeds to compare a World War II film about the Jewish Warsaw Ghetto uprising to one about the aftermath of Operation

Hot Winter in Gaza. But no matter how affecting the images of suffering in Gaza are, the comparison between Gaza and the Warsaw Ghetto lacks merit. The Polish Jews during World War II were an unarmed minority group subjected to the most heinous hatred, whereas in Gaza, Hamas started a war to which the IDF responded after thousands of rockets had landed in southern Israel. In one case, around 13,000 Jews died at the scene, while most of the remaining 50,000 were captured and sent to the Majdanek and Treblinka death camps. In the other, approximately 1,000 civilians perished under very different circumstances, with many of them used as human shields.[38]

Once Schulman arrives in Israel, she hears from one contact that people in the West Bank are "just beginning to deal with what it means to be queer in a place not all that friendly toward them/the idea." The contact wonders if Schulman "can offer them some historical perspective of your work back in the day fighting similar battles." She decides that she can provide her "knowledge of how to be effective" and feels much pride at the example of Butler, who has "the integrity to be so out as a lesbian" while assuming the role of a leader in the BDS movement.[39] In her opinion, Butler represents the Jewish ethical ideal that existed before Jewish people acquired a state of their own, and she feels that the Jews of the *galut* like Butler, have traditions that gear them to oppose "'state violence and state racism.'"[40] Preparing to speak in Israel, Schulman counters the argument that Israel is judged by a higher standard than other countries. She insists that Israel and the United States are in fact judged by a lower standard, given both nations' histories of oppressing people, occupying their land, taking away their futures, and destroying their human potential. While this might arguably be the case with the United States, which has engaged in foreign military adventurism for many decades, one wonders why she does not become exercised over or even mention nation-destroying incursions into Tibet, the Islamist genocide of Christian Sudanese in Africa, the Russian invasion of Crimea and Eastern Ukraine, the Indian-Pakistani destruction of peace in once multi-ethnic Kashmir, the genocide and land confiscation of Rohingya Muslims in Myanmar, the displacement of more than eleven million civilians in Syria, and the deliberate starvation and genocide of Houthi Muslims in Yemen, to name but a few examples. But Schulman, who retains a singular, and even narcissistic, focus on the Jewish people and her need for them to maintain high ethical standards, honestly believes they have betrayed their traditions and harmed the Palestinian people. Because the latter are victims, she does not hold them responsible for their bad choices, or egregious violence, or tragically misguided leadership. The Jewish Israelis, in contrast, are responsible for feckless leaders like Netanyahu who stoke Israeli Jewish fears to win elections, expand settlements, and, most recently, to threaten to annex portions of the West Bank. Indeed, if one examines the consequences of continued conflict dispassionately, Schulman and other BDS proponents work to exacerbate enmities and worsen conditions for both Israelis and Palestinians by fanning the flames of the conflict.

The Jewish Embrace

At this juncture Schulman makes a startling and revealing statement. She says that outside her opposition to Israel, she does not have an engaged Jewish identity at all. Having "nothing to prove" and having never "belonged to a Jewish organization," she proudly asserts that she has "avoided contemporary Jewishness almost entirely."[41] Nonetheless, despite her indifference to all things Jewish, which somehow makes her more unassailably or authentically Jewish, she believes she has particular insight into the Israeli "conundrum" because, as an American, she is a "citizen of a country that consistently violates international law, defies standards of human rights, and financially supports oppressive regimes (including Israel) while regularly killing civilians in different places on earth without justification or reason."[42] As far as violations of international law are concerned, judicial bodies have held Israel culpable in creating settlements in the occupied or disputed territories. Some might hold that almost all of the two hundred member nations of the United Nations have at some point or another broken international law—a fact that makes singling out Israel suspect. However Israel should nonetheless be asked, as Schulman asserts, to account for its decision-making processes without resort to comparisons.

Schulman turns to *Muzzlewatch*, the official e-letter of Jewish Voice for Peace (JVP), which documents how "human beings who try to transform supremacy ideology are met with degradation, diminishment, indifference, dismissal, distortion, and outright persecution."[43] She notes that she herself has experienced this odious treatment, including, she ventures to claim, persecution as a lesbian writer. This overly broad characterization not only abuses the serious import of these terms but also blows her career-related difficulties as a lesbian writer out of proportion even as she fails to take any responsibility for them. This exaggerated use of the word persecution illustrates the outsized and, indeed, histrionic and untempered character of her discourse in general. Identifying herself with *Muzzlewatch*, she claims that she and *Muzzlewatch* "expose their persecutors,"[44] and, wandering off topic, she wants to do the same with those publishers who have rejected her work, or, as she elsewhere claims, the playwright Jonathan Larson, who she believes plagiarized her novel in his musical about AIDS, *Rent*.[45] In the meantime the JVP, which she regards as a persecuted organization, has become increasingly radical over the years; it not only blames Israel for American racism, genocide, and Islamophobia but also disrupts peaceful pro-Israel activities on university campuses and elsewhere.[46]

The Palestinian Embrace

Schulman now turns to the most important mission of her trip: She wants to ask her Palestinian hosts to "openly acknowledge queer support for the boycott"[47] rather than to have her hosts accept her and her Palestinian queer friends' activism on the condition of remaining quiet about their sexuality. She receives a letter praising her for condemning the "Israeli apartheid" and the "inhuman siege that has rendered Gaza the world's largest open-air prison."[48] Although impressed by this letter, which bristles with exaggerated or false claims and propagandistic sloganeering against Israel, Schulman still wants her Palestinian hosts to recognize queer support and acknowledge Palestinian LGBTQ organizing. She has a conversation with her hosts, who raise familiar concerns about how homosexuality imposes "Western values on Palestinians, who already have enough problems."[49] However, having decided that she wants to develop a political partnership with Palestine, Schulman transforms herself into what she calls a "citizen of the queer international."

> Then there is the word "international," well known to communists of all stripes as an identity to strive for, in which nationalist boundaries would be defeated by larger similarities among workers, where the bonds should lie. "The Internationale" was the theme song of world communism. . . . In his book, *Desiring Arabs*, Joseph Massad, a professor at Columbia University and a Palestinian, describes the "Gay International" as a Western apparatus imposing concepts of homosexuality on Palestinian sex between men. All these factors converged on my use of the "queer international," a worldwide movement that brings queer liberation and feminism to the principles of international autonomy from occupation, colonialism, and globalized capital.[50]

Schulman sets forth an ambitious goal that, at first glance, seems admirable and transcendent. The use of the moniker "queer international" in this context plays semantic games with the broad accusations that Massad makes in *Desiring Arabs*, an ungenerous apologia for prejudice against those gay Middle Eastern men who identify as gay or homosexual, and who therefore commit the presumed crime of imposing Western colonialist values on the Middle East. As James Kirchick notes, "State repression against gay people happens on a frequent basis across the Middle East. Massad, however, who claims to be a supporter of sexual freedom per se, is oddly impassive when confronted with the vast catalogue of anti-gay state violence in the Muslim world. Massad . . . does acknowledge that, 'gay-identified' people exist in the Middle East, but he views them with derision."[51]

In endorsing Massad, Schulman abandons the politics of outness she embraced as an ACT UP activist and, with that, LGBTQ people, whom she vowed to support in *Ties That Bind*. Moreover, she has made sweeping statements about her support for gay and feminist rights in her aforementioned manifesto, but when asked about honor killings and the status of women in Palestine during her trip, she replies that "right now, that is not my job."[52] Schulman defines herself as a feminist, but if protesting against honor killings and the debasing of women's status is not her job, one must ask to whom this job belongs.

Schulman next travels to Tel Aviv, a city that respects and gives full rights to LGBTQ people and does not countenance honor killings. She nevertheless takes the occasion to remark that Tel Aviv looks like a theater set—an observation that will enable her to contrast attractive appearances with unsatisfactory realities for LGBTQ people in Israel. She meets a few disaffected lesbians who express their grievances around lesbian invisibility, army service, and the impossibility of having a healthy lesbian relationship in Israel, among other things. She avoids other Israeli LGBTQ organizations, does not visit the Holocaust memorial to gay people, and, in general, stays away from everything that could place gay Israelis in a more balanced and positive light. Further, her miniscule sample of lesbians is not an accurate representation of overall feelings of life satisfaction among LGBTQ people in Israel. In the 2018 UN World Happiness Report, Israel ranks number 11, just behind New Zealand and Sweden.[53] This suggests that Schulman has not spoken with a representative swath of LGBTQ Israeli people, and therefore comes to biased conclusions designed to comport with negative preconceptions of Israeli queer life and culture that delegitimize Israel rather than accurately portray a multivalent and largely content reality.

Schulman visits Palestine where, in profound contrast to Israel, she meets with queer Palestinian activists who she describes as engaged, sophisticated, determined, and well educated. They discuss American celebrity and intellectual figures who could serve as spokespeople for Palestinians, as well as the opposition Palestinian queers confront in attempting to join ranks openly with heterosexual boycott groups such as the Palestinian Campaign for the Academic and Cultural Boycott of Israel (PACBI). Although she initially has an unsuccessful meeting with

Barghouti, who denies the existence of gays and only accepts her help on the condition that she keep her sexual orientation in the closet, he later decides to be more accepting. In the meantime, she suffers first-hand the harassments and difficulties of Palestinian life in contending with checkpoints and the barrier wall. She visits the well-appointed Israeli settlement towns and the poor and decrepit Palestinian villages, and she comes to the conclusion that arrangements between Israeli Jews and Palestinians in the West Bank come close to de facto apartheid: "Two separate systems by which one group dominates and controls the other through brutality, denial of rights, and lack of liberty. They have separate roads, separate water, separate experiences. One has autonomy, protection, and opportunity. The other does not."[54]

Schulman correctly notes the dire economic and political conditions for Palestinians in the West Bank, but she inaccurately blames them exclusively on the Israelis, instead of noting that Palestinians also suffer from the corruption of the PA and poor management of public resources donated by non-governmental organizations (NGOs) and the European Union (EU). She decides to bring three Palestinian queer activists to the United States to put a human face on their struggle. She finds Puar's conception of homonationalism (or the purported acquisition of racist sentiments against Muslims and immigrants that occurs among some LGBTQ people who have acquired rights in Western nations) helpful as an organizing tool, mainly because it enables her to distinguish bad queers who support Israel from good gays who do not.[55] After Schulman discusses the losses and wins she experiences in broadcasting the news about the BDS movement to a North American gay audience, she returns to Haifa to speak with Isha L'Isha about media censorship and distortion. According to this organization, the Israeli state creates a binary opposition between "us" and "them" that "constructs a national Jewish self-perception as moral, humane, cultured, and peace-seeking while constructing the stereotype of the Palestinian as the complete opposite."[56] Schulman claims that "In all matters, people who face and deal with problems, who negotiate, reach toward resolution. To do this seriously, one must view one's opponent as an equal partner in creating change.

Since the media and educational systems do not present a complex image of Palestinian society, it becomes impossible for Israelis to work with Palestinians to create change."[57]

Schulman asserts that she wants Israelis and Palestinians to view each other as equal partners in creating change, yet she treats the Palestinians not as equals but rather as victims who can do no wrong, whereas the Israelis are the opposite. She correctly notes that Israelis have an obligation to see past fear-ridden stereotypes and state ideologies, but the Palestinians also have these obligations. Without mutual recognition there can be no negotiation across differences—only games of Manichean black-and-white victimology and oppression. The Palestinian media is also a minefield of stereotypes, antisemitic canards, glorification of violence and martyrdom, and distortion, bias, and hatred.[58] Yet Schulman believes that "those most disenfranchised from power" are the "most ecumenical and inclusive ... the most creative and most open to a world in which *all* people's needs are addressed."[59] While this statement does describe some Palestinians and, in addition, some Israelis, disenfranchisement per se does not automatically confer virtue on anyone, any more than power or authority automatically confer vice.

The Return to Amerika

Traveling to Berlin to visit Butler among others, Schulman endorses numerous false—and potentially dangerous—dichotomies. She notes with approval that, rather than spotlighting the conflicts between LGBTQ people and Muslims, Butler "suggested that the German LGBTQ community focus instead on increases in right-wing violence and homophobia within the church."[60] Why not hold Muslims accountable, too? In truth, the danger emerges from both the right wing and Muslims, and to politicize the situation by picking one over another risks not only further violence but also a fundamental misunderstanding of facts that could well endanger gay people victimized by, or threatened with, hate crimes and harassment. Facts are potentially dangerous, and Schulman and Butler distort them. But, happy at the bridges being created between the Palestinian queer and the boycott movements, Schulman remarks that in every case her side had achieved success, and that the Knesset was considering anti-BDS legislation to control the flow of people into the country, which the Israeli courts have subsequently and correctly rejected. In other words BDS propaganda and the consequences of the asymmetrical warfare conducted in Gaza, which made Israel look like a criminal perpetrator, continued to claim Palestine as a victim.[61]

Returning to New York City, Schulman meets a Palestinian American filmmaker and her two Palestinian lesbian comrades. With tragic irony, they discuss the queer Palestinian movement "in the context of the revolution exploding in Egypt,"[62] unaware that that revolution would die, and that Abdel Fattah el-Sisi would not only engineer a successful coup against the democratically elected Mohamed Morsi[63] but also placate Islamist right-wingers by instituting a major crackdown on the Egyptian LGBTQ community.[64] In this unfortunate context, they also meet with Joseph Massad, whose book had castigated the very Egyptian gay people that General el-Sisi would persecute in the future.[65] Schulman once again returns to his work, about which she gives a laudatory report:

> "Western male white-dominated" gay activists, under the umbrella of what he terms the "gay international" have engaged in a "missionary" effort to impose the binary categories of heterosexual/homosexual onto cultures where no such subjectivities exist, and these activists in fact ultimately replicate in these cultures the very structures they challenge in their own home countries. . . . The categories *gay* and *lesbian* are not universals at all and can only be universalized by the epistemic, ethical, and political violence unleashed on the rest of the world by the very international human rights advocates whose aim is to defend the very people their intervention is creating.[66]

Making a sharp distinction between sexual practices and identities in the West and Middle East, and castigating the former as putatively foreign to Islamic cultures, Massad argues that it is invasive to demand people come out of the closet who wish to maintain sexual privacy. This is true in the West as well, and it is not advisable or ethical to out people unless they are in a position to do harm to other LGBTQ people. However, it is patently ridiculous, no matter what culture one is considering, to label as gay or lesbian all men and women who practice same-sex sex. Yet why object so stridently to crafting a cultural space for those who wish to identify themselves as gay or lesbian, and what role does cultural shame and taboo play in maintaining these supposedly neutral and natural cultural processes? Massad's angry book constitutes a denunciatory screed against all things Western and putatively colonialist. Did young men thrown off rooftops or tortured and mutilated by ISIS for moral depravity identify themselves as Western homosexuals, or were they publicly exposed while practicing "Islamic sodomy" in private?[67] How do such distinctions matter ethically or practically? Nevertheless, the lack of Palestinian statehood has an obvious impact on the lives of LGBTQ people, and Schulman's Palestinian gay friends explain that "Western ideas of the gay trajectory were not always helpful or applicable to Palestinian queers."[68] Because of political oppression, personal shame, and the taboo against extramarital sex of any variety, Palestinian queers focus on ending the occupation and keep their sexual activities private, or known only to a few trusted persons. At last, the sexual "diffusion" of Middle Eastern gays, as least according to Mossad, makes political organizing and fights against AIDS nearly impossible. After all the triumphs of Schulman and her queer Palestinian comrades, she suffers what she calls a backlash. The United States government denies Barghouti a visa, her Palestinian queer friends return home, and Schulman encounters Michael Lucas, the pro-Israel producer of a gay porn film called *Men of Israel* (2009). Lucas threatens to organize an economic boycott against the New York Lesbian, Gay, Bisexual, & Transgender Community Center if it does not ban Siege Busters, a pro-Palestinian group dedicated to organizing a freedom flotilla to break the siege of Gaza during Israel Apartheid Week. Since Schulman now identifies LGBTQ issues as Palestinian issues, she stridently objects. She makes the not very coherent point that "our beloved center . . . [is] using Palestine as a turning point in the shift from community accountability to solid corporate mold."[69]

She insists that Israel does not represent and never has represented all Jewish people, and Schulman no longer tolerates Jewish Zionists who do identify with Israel. Schulman moves to the hardline BDS position that refuses all dialogue with pro-Israel parties: "Israel's borders themselves are shifting and changing and must themselves be understood as weapons, as tools of occupation. . . . Dialogue can solve nothing until colonialism is reversed. Doing business with Israel, as it stands, ratifies inequality."[70] By stating that dialogue can solve nothing until "colonialism is reversed," Schulman, like Butler, supports a Palestinian right of return, an elimination of the 1948 borders, and a dissolution of Israel as a Jewish state. Schulman insists that she wants to be an ethical Jew, and contends that she has nothing in common with Zionist Jews or their supporters, whom she now classifies as "nationalists, racists, and liars."[71] She identifies with her queer Palestinian friends and "their faith in change, their willingness to go out on a limb because they have their eyes on the prize, the commitment to the big picture, and to active cooperation with others beyond personal aggrandizement," which she here implicitly associates with advocacy of their LGBTQ identities.[72] For reasons Schulman never explains, outside the dubious claim that the Palestinians are indigenous whereas the Jewish Israelis are settler colonialists, the Palestinians have a right to Palestine, but not the Jews to Israel. In brief, Schulman enjoys the very American privilege—which an increasing number of Jews do not—of feeling so blithely safe in her Jewishness that she need not concern herself with protecting herself from antisemitic violence or dispossession. Rather, she explicitly claims that Jews in Israel have played the role of colonial settlers who have occupied Palestine and engaged in apartheid and ethnic cleansing.

Aftermath

Schulman once again happens to encounter Lucas in New York City. She cannot resist the temptation to engage in an egregious *ad hominem* attack. Lucas, whom she describes as looking like "Zoolander," has skin pulled tight and swollen lips, and looks like a cross between "Faye Dunaway and Cher."⁷³ Schulman does not act graciously with those who frustrate her will, and she subsequently accuses a man of malice for refusing to host any gay group meeting in the Community Center that uses the term "apartheid" or "injustice." She also rebukes a woman she encounters who brings together Jewish Israeli and Palestinian artists, saying she "had never experienced art as useful for peace." Finally, she chides Jewish students who want to engage in "dialogue" with Palestinians.⁷⁴

In the whirlwind mash-up she creates in *Israel/Palestine and the Queer International*, Schulman succeeds in communicating to the reader one consistent, reliable fact: her transformation from someone who believes in dialogue across differences to someone who has such a hostile assurance of her own ideological rightness that she refuses to countenance divergent viewpoints. In her earlier work on familial homophobia, the *Ties That Bind*, Schulman had argued passionately that "human beings deserve, by virtue of being born, acknowledgment, recognition, interactivity, and negotiation."⁷⁵ After her immersion in BDS, Schulman rejects this humanizing insight. This change of perspective became evident the year following the publication of *Ties That Bind* at a two-day conference Schulman convened at City University of New York (CUNY) in April 2013 titled "Homonationalism and Pinkwashing." When she addressed the carefully selected partisan audience as the keynote speaker, Schulman denied a request from the audience that she include another "keynote speaker from the other side."

After a pause, she shouted out to thunderous applause: "Like there's two sides!"⁷⁶

2

JASBIR PUAR, OR, ZIONOPHOBIA IN HOMONATIONALIST TIMES

The Queer Science of Jasbir Puar

In February 2016 Jasbir Puar, a Rutgers University professor of women's and gender studies and an influential leader in the BDS movement, gave a stridently anti-Israel lecture at Vassar College titled "Inhumanist Biopolitics: How Palestine Matters." Due to its incendiary claims, and the predictably emotion-laden positive and negative responses to them, Puar became somewhat of an overnight academic luminary—an intellectual lightning rod in debates over academic freedom on the one hand and the campus politics of fulsome public expressions of antisemitic bias on the other. Defenders praised the quality of her scholarship and affirmed her right to incite controversies in her exercise of academic freedom,[1] while detractors accused her of resorting to an antisemitic blood libel dating from the twelfth century which stated that Jews ritually sacrificed Christian children at Passover to obtain blood for unleavened bread.[2] Assertions for and against Puar have been ferocious if, at times, grounded in reasonable argument. In a 2018 interview, however, she exhibited a certain lack of insight into the criticisms against her. She championed academic freedom but also offered that "the more one ascribes value to Palestinian lives, the more vociferous the accusations of anti-Semitism."[3] Ironically, Puar did not so vigorously defend academic freedom when it came to others' requests to open-access to information, for she demanded that the Vassar lecture not be recorded and threatened legal action against anyone who would make existing audio recordings of her lecture public. Furthermore, she canceled a scheduled lecture at Fordham University, "The Biopolitics of Debility in Gaza," because the university administration, which supported her right to express opinions with which it disagreed, insisted on recording and making publicly available her lecture.[4] Finally, for her efforts, her advocates stated that she received numerous death threats, which ended up having the incidental overall effect of burnishing her credentials and celebrity among anti-Israel and BDS activists.[5]

The controversies stemmed mainly from four principal, memorable claims she made at Vassar; three of which she later rearticulated at much greater length in her 2017 book, *The Right to Maim*: (1) Israel harvested for scientific experimentation the organs of Palestinians killed during terrorist acts and violent demonstrations; (2) Israel deliberately withheld adequate nutrients from Palestinian children so that they suffered stunted growth; (3) Israel undertook an intentional policy of shooting not to kill or wound but rather to permanently maim Palestinians, a stratagem that Puar characterized as "practices of bodily as well as infrastructural debilitation, loosely effaced in concerns about 'disproportionate force' [which] indicate the extension of perhaps the perversion of the 'right to kill' claimed by states in warfare into what I am calling the 'right to maim'";[6] and (4) Israel exposed Palestinian children in Gaza to more violence than that suffered by any other children anywhere else in the world.[7]

Before delving into her theoretical arguments about homonationalism and pinkwashing, in addition to what she characterizes as the eugenicist racist biopolitics of Israeli Jewish gay and lesbian assisted reproductive technologies (ART)—which stand at the center of this LGBTQ-focused chapter—we must evaluate these allegations that Israel engages in organ harvesting, stunting, and maiming of Palestinians. Doing so will explicate how Puar uses her concept of assemblages—which she adapts from Gilles Deleuze and Felix Guattari's *A Thousand Plateaus: Capitalism and Schizophrenia* (1987)—as a rhetorical style of thought, and will help illuminate an engrained penchant for false cause, hyperbole, nonce inference, and, consequentially, conspiratorial fantasies that color her entire oeuvre and, to paraphrase her, drive her project about power, about bodies, about resistance, and about politics. As Cary Nelson expresses the matter, "Puar has turned personal susceptibility to conspiracy theories into an academic principle: rumor-based research."[8] This results in an "argumentative free fire zone; anything goes so long as it discredits Israel, a country that she considers wholly without redeeming impulses."[9]

If we set aside the emotion-laden denunciations and commendations her work has elicited, a more careful and dispassionate analysis of her oeuvre reveals inadequate or seriously distorted standards of evidence, the suppression of and failure to engage with opposing points of view, conclusions drawn without supporting documentation, uselessly (rather than necessarily) near-incomprehensible prose, all-encompassing assemblage-style parataxis, indifference to proof of correlation or cause and effect, and a willingness to allow her anti-Zionist political convictions to drive every aspect of her agenda, almost to the point that this work might more accurately be characterized as propaganda in the genre of speculative fiction rather than objective scholarship.

Indeed, in her Vassar lecture she applauds this segue from proven facts to ungrounded speculation, as she endeavors to stretch "the speculative into the now." As she notes, she attempts to offer different narratives of occupation, apartheid and settler colonialism that partake in unusual or generally avoided genres of storytelling to solicit less amenable or expected avenues of solidarity affiliations. So, this is a project that seeks to invite new participants in the global quest for Palestinian liberation. It's a solidarity project to open up political discourse, genres that might affect different entities into a relation to solidarity that might otherwise appear untenable.[10]

Puar regards what she calls storytelling and political discourse as attractive and viable means to draw new followers to the cause of Palestinian liberation whose "relation to solidarity" might otherwise appear untenable. This paragraph becomes emblematic of how Puar, like Schulman, Davis, Spade, and Butler, enjoins her potential supporters to discard the multifaceted historical facts and complexities of the Israel/Palestine conflict and deliver the usual suspect charges in encapsulated form—the occupation, racism, settler colonialism, genocide, and apartheid—to those for whom the complicated realities of the conflict, which require discernment and hard work to untangle, might deactivate their enthusiasm for the struggle, or necessitate their familiarization with works in a tradition of scholarship (whether pro- or anti-Zionist) that are reliable, serious sources of information. However Puar, in unmooring herself almost as entirely from ascertainable facts as from the recognized body of scholarship on the conflict, ventures much further into fanciful conspiratorial machinations than do these other BDS intellectuals.

The Organ-Harvesting Allegation

Unlike other responsible scholars in the field of the Israel/Palestine conflict, Puar does not seek to examine, much less comprehend, the real-world dynamics of this subject matter. In terms of her allegations of Israeli organ harvesting, she feels no apparent need to possess, or acquire, even the basic knowledge of transplantation biology required to understand how organ harvesting works. Rather, she spins out anti-Zionist theories in a specialized thought experiment wholly divorced from any major strands of scholarship around topics concerned with the Israel/Palestine conflict. There are, moreover, basic facts that Puar has so mangled and manipulated as to be disingenuous at best and to engage in seriously irresponsible putative scholarship at worst.

Puar alleges that Israel has long trafficked in and countenanced the harvesting of organs from Palestinians killed in violent confrontations for use in medical experimentation. The actual record reveals that during the Second Intifada Yehuda Hiss, the chief pathologist at the Abu Kabir Institute of Forensic Medicine in Tel Aviv, broke the law by harvesting without permission the few body tissues that can be sterilized—skin, heart valves, inner-ear bones, and corneas—from cadavers during autopsies and had them transferred to medical facilities. As Cary Nelson notes, "No tissue, however, can be fully sterilized without causing damage to it."[11] Notably, Hiss never harvested major organs for transplantation, and the items he did harvest were employed to support the work at his hospital, and not for personal gain.[12] A large host of nations have put implied consent laws in place which would have made Hiss's actions legal, but Israel has no such legislation. Other Israelis, including ultra-Orthodox Jews, who regard such harvesting as a grave and insupportable offense against *halakha* (Jewish religious law) and as a desecration of the dead, reported him.[13] During an interview, Hiss referred to the cadavers as "Orientals," which Puar used to support her contention that these cadavers were Palestinian; but at that time, during the Second Intifada, Ashkenazi Jews used this moniker mainly (if not exclusively) to refer to Mizrachi Jews, not Palestinians. Perhaps, particularly during the period of the Second Intifada, some cadavers were Palestinian, but to claim that Palestinian cadavers stand at the center of this narrative constitutes nothing less than what Nelson calls "a colossal error and at worst a deliberate falsehood or a paranoid fantasy."[14]

Puar claims that Hiss harvested the organs of Palestinians killed in terrorist acts or violent demonstrations, but this is factually impossible, as such individual bodies are contaminated by bacteria and arrive at pathology labs too late for organ harvesting. Had Puar conducted research, she would have run into this inconvenient truth and been forced to withdraw her narrative—or, alternatively, willfully ignore the evidence. Worse still, she leaps from the juridically prohibited actions of one pathologist, who was held legally liable for harvesting corneas, skin, heart valves, and inner-ear bones, to claim that Israel, the country that prosecuted him, somehow countenanced, supported, or colluded in these illegal acts. While, after her Vassar lecture, she first claimed that "some speculate" that "Palestinians held in morgues were mined for organs for scientific research," by her March 2016 essay in *Jadaliyya* she was reporting that "the fraught history of organ mining practices from both IDF soldiers and Palestinian bodies during the 1990s is well documented."[15] Puar decided to recommit to her anti-Zionist ideological convictions, twist the Hiss narrative beyond recognition, and thus hold fast to the blood libel, which historically has frequently led to mob violence and has occasionally caused the decimation of entire Jewish communities.[16] Finally, Puar claims that Israel has never offered an explanation for its practice of holding the bodies of Palestinians killed in violent actions. But Israel publicly announced that it did so to prevent funerals from turning into vengeful demonstrations, which had been the cause of incitement to further violence in the past, and which Israel wished to avoid repeating to save Israeli and Palestinian lives.[17]

The Stunting Allegation

Puar has also charged that Israel purposefully stunted the growth of Palestinian children, especially in Gaza, by depriving them of necessary nutrients. Stunting, which occurs when children are too short for their age, does not emerge immediately but takes a few years to manifest. During the Second Intifada (2000–2005), which caused considerable strain on Palestinian health and infrastructure, the Nutrition Department in the Ministry of Health in the PA became concerned about the impact on public health of the ongoing social chaos. Puar wants her audience to believe that Israel restricted food imports to maintain them in a debilitated, barely functioning state and, by implication, to sadistically abuse Palestinian children to mete out punishment for the violent uprisings.

But this grimly phantasmatic supposition is incorrect. The Palestinian Economic Policy Research Institute (MAS), an autonomous non-profit group based in Ramallah, concluded that, "although Gaza strip has even been subject to a blockade, it has never experienced a serious shortage of food owing to the flow of goods through Israeli crossings."[18] Food insecurity in Palestine occurs mainly at the household level because of poverty and lack of access to adequate food available on the market. Despite a high reliance on food imports, which occurs throughout the Arab world, Israel has maintained regular, reliable food deliveries to Palestinians. No serious or informed parties have ever claimed that Israel withholds food from Palestinians.

Thus if the stunting of Palestinian children cannot be attributed to Israel withholding necessary food nutrition, then it can be ascribed to other principal if not exclusive factors: (1) the food insecurity attendant on poverty, and the consequent inability to purchase food available at the market; and (2) consanguineous marriage, the rate of which hovers at around 40 percent of the population, as Palestinian research repeatedly has shown.[19] Consanguinity means marriage between first or second cousins,[20] which is traditionally permitted in Islam and relatively common in many Arab nations, if now often discouraged for health reasons.[21] Palestinian public health officials have proposed education to discourage consanguineous marriage, particularly since this form of marital union is linked to children's reduced cognitive abilities, higher instances of childhood stunting, birth defects, and other adverse mental and physical sequelae.[22] But, not surprisingly, Puar makes assemblage-style claims but offers no proof or examples, however misconstrued or distorted, to back up her charges that Israel stunts Palestinian children.

However, other critical health issues that seriously affect children, particularly related to infrastructure and the Israeli/Egyptian blockade designed to staunch the flow of arms and terrorists, exist in Gaza, which experts predict will become uninhabitable in the near future.[23] The aquifer in Gaza is contaminated and depleted. Periodic IDF bombing raids cause death, injury, or trauma to Palestinian children, as does their use as human shields by Hamas. Unemployment and dependence on public assistance run very high. A desalination plant to provide drinking water is required. Raw sewage runs into the Mediterranean. The electric grid desperately needs repair.[24] But these and other problems cannot be addressed as long as Hamas and other terrorist organizations persist in conducting intermittent but costly military campaigns against Israel. Hamas wishes to conquer Israel, because they regard Israel as holy Islamic land stolen from Palestinians by Israeli Jews.

And yet the Mediterranean coast represents an important economic and employment opportunity for Gaza, but one that would require committed demilitarization for it to succeed. At present no investors would risk having their hotels and other buildings destroyed if Hamas used them as staging grounds for military operations. In brief, peace through compromise on both sides would address Gazan Palestinian food insecurities based on poverty, environmental hazards, endemic warfare, and unemployment while improving the social conditions required to conduct public health campaigns against consanguineous marriage and other medically adverse practices. But Puar, like other BDS advocates, does not support peace initiatives that would materially improve the lives and health of Palestinians, but rather insists on metaphorically poisoning the waters by casting blame entirely on Israel, and therefore ignoring peaceful solutions to the problems.

The Maiming Allegation

A similar contempt for empirical evidence, and cause and effect, as well as the resort to malevolent fantasy and disregard for actual Palestinian lives (as seen in the organ-harvesting and stunting accusations) informs Puar's contention that Israel deliberately maims Palestinians. In fact Israel, seeking to reduce deaths from violent confrontations between Palestinians and the IDF, issues orders not to shoot to kill, often at great danger to its own soldiers. When someone with a Molotov cocktail runs toward a soldier, it is much less dangerous for the soldier to shoot to kill the attacker than to shoot at the attacker's extremities in an effort to halt but not kill the person. Puar concludes that Israeli forces—in the fog of war, where bullets fly through the air and bodies are assailed through eye-stinging, smoky hazes—has an intentional policy that it actively pursues and encourages to purposefully maim Palestinians. As Nelson explains, "Puar insists maimed bodies are not an accidental, unintended form of collateral damage; they are a necessary and deliberate part of Israeli policy. Israel does not want Palestinians to be able to recover fully from their wounds; it wants them permanently maimed."[25]

In her Vassar lecture, Puar made the seemingly contradictory claim that Israel stunts and maims Palestinians to disable as many of them as possible, while keeping them alive as a kind of defanged threat to the security of the nation. Puar offers no proof for such a perverse agenda, and no evidence in the forms of an IDF or other military or civilian manual containing such commonsense-defying directives. But in the putative logic of her assemblages, connections operate that do not require proof or evidentiary linearity. Further, according to Puar, Israel does not avoid shooting to kill from humanitarian motives; rather, it relishes, in perverse erotic fashion, the display of visibly disabled and incapacitated Palestinian bodies. In *The Right to Maim* she also claims that Israel disables to deprive Palestinians of the power to resist (although the Israelis fail in this endeavor) and also to profit from the services it must give the disabled which, in turn, render the Palestinians dependent on the ongoing Israeli military occupation. Puar appears unable to prevent herself from ascribing a malevolent will to control and a malicious intent to exercise complete power to everything Israel does. For her, Israel is irremediably inhuman: It embodies a biopolitical machinery of pure demonic design.

Claiming, without supporting evidence, that Palestinians in Gaza and the West Bank have among the highest rates of disability in the world, Puar contends that most Palestinians and Israelis would prefer to die rather than face the ignominy of being disabled:

> For many on both sides of the occupation, it is better to "die for your country"—in Palestine you become a martyr—than to face a life with a body that is deemed disabled. The consequence of believing that disability is worse than death is simple: "not killing" Palestinians while rendering them systematically and utterly debilitated is not humanitarian sparing of death. It is instead a biopolitical usage and articulation of the right to maim.[26]

In her extreme expression of the BDS credo that Israel, by definition, can do no right, Puar, in a stunning non sequitur, here actually claims that the IDF avoids shooting to kill from an "articulation" of a "right to maim" that basically makes maiming worse than inflicting death. Remarkably, she believes that, even when acting to save lives, Israel is culpable for sadistic, morally odious behavior. Moreover, Puar offers no proof that there exists in Israel a "culture" or "cult" of death that makes dying for your country preferable to becoming disabled—a claim that flies in the face of laws that protect and provide financial support for disabled persons in Israel.²⁷ In contrast, martyrdom enjoys great prestige in Palestinian culture for many reasons, chief among them the fervent will to reclaim lands and lost prestige.²⁸ Dying a violent death in confrontation with Jewish Israelis—particularly if one manages to take some of those lives as well—confers honors and financial benefits on the family of the martyr and represents something indeed preferable to facing "a life with a body that is deemed disabled."²⁹ Puar insinuates—but declines to state outright—a dynamic whereby IDF soldiers shoot to maim so they can revel in their power to deny Palestinians the honor attached to martyrdom.

Homonationalist Assemblages

Puar includes a gay- and lesbian-focused chapter in *The Right to Maim* titled "Disabled Diaspora, Rehabilitating State: The Queer Politics of Reproduction in Palestine/Israel." She begins her discussion by lambasting an erotically charged Israeli commercial featuring interethnic gay and lesbian characters, "In Israel, Love Has No Boundaries."³⁰ Puar employs the pinkwashing rhetorical claims that Israel simultaneously legitimizes and deflects attention away from its military occupation of Palestine through manipulating its record of human rights for gay and lesbian Israelis, so that it functions as propaganda that obscures or legitimizes the occupation of Palestine.

> Resonating within a receptive field of globalized Islamophobia significantly amplified since September 11, 2001, this messaging relies on a civilizational narrative about the modernity of the Israelis juxtaposed against the backward homophobia of the Palestinians. As such, pinkwashing has become a commonly used tag for the cynical promotion of LGBTQ bodies as representative of Israeli democracy. More generally it is the erasure of hierarches of power through the favoring of the "gay-friendly nation" imagery. It is a discourse about civilizational superiority that relies on a transparent and uninterrogated "Palestinian homophobia" that is contingent on the foreclosure

of any questioning of "Israeli homophobia." Besides making Zionism more appealing to (Euro-American) gays, part of the mechanism at work that benefits Israel is a disciplining of Palestinian queers into legible subjects.[31]

For Puar, nothing that Israel says or does (or indeed fails to say or do) in relation to the Israeli LGBTQ community is unrelated to the Israel/Palestine conflict. Hence an advertisement that engages in the ordinary shaping and idealizing rhetoric of public relations campaigns everywhere cynically uses Israeli LGBTQ bodies to represent Israeli democracy and, simultaneously, constitutes an unexamined discourse about Palestinian homophobia that forecloses discussion of Israeli homophobia. Here as elsewhere, however, neither Palestine nor Israel present exceptions, nor are they exceptional. Her critique that Israel shows no love for the Palestinians is ironic given that her writing gives abundant proof that Puar scarcely loves Israel. Although Puar notes the absence of any consideration of Palestine, it is surprising that she would expect otherwise, particularly from an advertisement that focuses especially on the eroticized transcendence of racial differences in an Israeli national context that does not engage Palestinian subject matter.

In *The Right to Maim* Puar makes a disquieting point about LGBTQ sexuality that she had explored extensively in her earlier work, *Terrorist Assemblages: Homonationalism in Queer Times* (2007). Opposing identity politics, and expressing reservations about intersectionality theory, she proffers instead the concept of assemblages as what she terms "a series of dispersed but mutually implicated and messy networks, [that] draw together enunciation and dissolution, causality and effect, organic and nonorganic forces."[32] But this bringing together of elements that have no ascertainable or reliable cause and effect relationship, and which are based on free associations that can include or correlate practically anything, means that all things in any given assemblage mixture can be held to have significant relationship with any other thing to which Puar wishes to connect it. Facts and conjecture intermix freely—a state of affairs that leads down an avenue to unimpeded, dystopic, conspiratorial theorizing about Israel. In brief, these assemblages liberate Puar from the constraints of identity politics and intersectional bodies, and provide an intellectual free-for-all dressed up in nearly indecipherable theoretical prose. The rhetoric of assemblage basically provides Puar with the liberty to make connections as she pleases and claim hypothetical causalities and almost random but somehow significant sequences at will. In addition, she pointedly rejects intersectionality analysis because it is bound to identities and, more particularly, to bodies—none of which have privileged status other than those Palestinian bodies that Puar claims are victimized by Israel. Unlike other bodies, they are traditionally bounded and saturated in symbolic power. This contradiction between the negligible meaning of bodies in general in her writing and the intensely inflected meaning of Palestinian bodies victimized by Israel in particular shows the contradictory theorizing at the heart of her entire project. She grants and withholds signification and importance at will, depending on her political ideological purposes.

Thus she asserts that, in the Middle East, sexualities are assemblages rather than Western-style identities or bounded bodies. She notes that in the "Middle East" there is "a healthy skepticism about the universalizing of LGBTQ discourses," because "knowledge of the complexities of sexuality in the region is far more nuanced."[33] According to this view, LGBTQ people in the Middle East (outside of Israel) do not refer to or conceive of themselves as gay, lesbian, bisexual, or transgendered—not because doing so invokes the dangers of imprisonment, corporal punishment, disfiguration, disinheritance by family, shunning, maiming, or killing but rather because their knowledge of sexuality differences as non-Western constitutes a more subtle and nuanced assemblage. While one can readily imagine how sexualities transmute and reformulate themselves in multiple contexts, her claim about assemblages nonetheless raises fascinating questions that Puar never answers regarding how Middle Eastern queers perceive themselves in complex and ever-shifting political, religious, social, and historical milieux. In the absence of identity politics or even bounded bodies, however, it is nonetheless valid to ask not only how they find one another or make common cause to protect themselves from persecution, familial disapproval, and homophobia, but also what happens to those Middle Eastern queers who elect to choose a more Western-style identity politics? One fears, according to the logic of Puar's arguments, that they are abandoned, shunned, or subjected to interpersonal and state violence because of how they elect to express their sexual desires and subjectivities. Further, this queer sexuality assemblage would appear ill-equipped—particularly since Puar never exactly describes how it behaves or how it signifies—to have the power to protect these Muslim sexualities from health- or violence-related challenges. How would such an assemblage fight against AIDS or sexually transmitted diseases, which require avowal of an identity, not to mention a body under assault?

In contrast, Israel, according to Puar, has succeeded all too well in adopting the Western-style democratic identity politics that have helped LGBTQ Israelis organize themselves and achieve extensive civil rights protections. Alas, they have therefore, according to her, become incorporated within the state project of homonationalism. By "homonationalism," in this instance, Puar means the racialization of gays and lesbians who are selectively normalized and incorporated within a national body politic that deems them worthy of protection because it can use them for ulterior purposes.[34] Indeed, according to Puar, Israeli LGBTQ politics has made the country

> a pioneer of homonationalism, as its particular position at the crosshairs of settler colonialism, occupation, and neoliberalist accomodationism creates the perfect storm for the normalization of homosexuality through national belonging. The homonationalist history of Israel illuminates a burgeoning of LGBTQ rights and increased mobility for gays and lesbians during the concomitant increased segregation and decreased mobility of Palestinian populations, especially post-Oslo. . . . The advent of gay rights in Israel begins around the same time as the first intifada, with the 1990s known as Israel's "gay decade" brought on by the legalization of homosexuality in the Israeli Defense Forces, workplace antidiscrimination provisions, and numerous other legislative changes.[35]

66   Chapter 2

In this zero-sum game formulation, Puar had also argued, in *Terrorist Assemblages*, for a quasi-causal assemblage-style relationship between the temporally simultaneous rise of Islamophobia and homonationalism in the post-9/11 cultural sphere. She contends that anti-Muslim sentiment, and wide-scale perceptions of Muslims as homophobic and sexist, had led to a reaction formation in which Western gays and lesbians had become normalized and acquired rights. Equitable treatment of gays and lesbians who sought social acceptance within neoliberal state institutions like marriage and the military was inversely related to growing prejudice against Muslims as, so to speak, anti-gays. In brief, sexuality across social domains matters, and because Muslims were bad, LGBTQ people must be good, or at least serviceable and subject to appropriation by the neoliberal state.

Even as LGBTQ and Muslim sexualities are joined at the hip, so too does she represent the increased mobility of LGBTQ Israeli populations as intrinsically correlated with the decreased mobility of Palestinians. However Puar, in this assemblage, by default provides no proof for any causal relationship between these nonce associations, which therefore amount to false cause. In the 1990s, in fact, restrictions were placed on Palestinian movement because of the violence of the First Intifada (1987–93). Some advances in LGBTQ rights in Israel, which also chanced to take place in the 1990s, occurred for wholly unrelated reasons that Puar fails to consider or even to rationally refute. In the 1990s Israel joined the urgent international response to the AIDS epidemic.[36] With that came increased queer activism and organization in democratic states, as well as calls to come out of the closet to save lives; this in turn helped catalyze, in Israel and elsewhere in Western countries, both short- and long-term legislative victories. None of this had anything to do with the effects of the First Intifada on Palestinians—or on Jewish Israelis—and pursuing this point constitutes an effort to find LGBTQ content in political contexts where it is at best negligible.

Puar proffers this unsubstantiated claim about the inverse relationship between Israeli gay and Palestinian mobility to drive home her larger points about Israelis' rehabilitated capacities following the founding of the State of Israel and concomitant Palestinian debility and disability. And, although she claims to be strictly antiprogressive and antiteleological in her thinking, she nonetheless asserts that the homosexual question (i.e., How well do you treat your homosexuals?) has replaced the woman question and the Jewish question. With the Jewish and the woman questions putatively resolved or, more accurately, conveniently sequestered or left behind, the missionary narrative *au courant* concerns white gays and lesbians who, according to Puar, "sav[e] brown homosexuals from brown heterosexuals."[37] This dismissively sardonic statement discredits international LGBTQ solidarity movements that perform the important work of monitoring severe abuses against LGBTQ people across the world, advocating for them at the United Nations, and addressing policies around AIDS and other health crises affecting LGBTQ people.[38] Her remarks also minimize the value of Western calls for queer people to come out of the closet. Such calls were memorialized by ACT UP in the logo "SILENCE = DEATH," which recognized that not claiming a gay identity could have deadly consequences, as it compromised gay people's powers to speak openly, and therefore advocate politically, for the health and life of their communities. Moreover, given the relationship among social beliefs, strict religious dogmas, and homophobic attitudes, the decline, particularly among younger people, of adherence to organized religion has been yet another real, as opposed to imputed, cause for the decrease in homophobic animus since the 1990s.[39] Finally, as more LGBTQ persons came out of the closet, they increasingly became recognized as complex, ordinary persons; accordingly, gay people, who exist everywhere, became accepted within their communities and cultures as real, valuable, and connected persons who thus acquired social capital.[40]

Puar expands on these and other related claims with the contention that the Israeli occupation of Palestine has made Israeli men masculine again. It resolved the homosexual and Jewish questions for cis-gendered, gender-conforming homosexual (and heterosexual) Israeli Jewish males who have presumably been capacitated after their debilitation as an historically persecuted minority in Europe (particularly during the Holocaust) and in the Middle East (after the forced dispossession and fleeing of Mizrachi Jews following the founding of the State of Israel). However, one must ask the far more plausible question as to whether the enervating, persistent struggle between the Israelis and Palestinians does not impose far more severe limitations—through PTSD, wounds and injuries, exposure to endemic violence and hatred, sheer exhausted demoralization, and steep economic expenditure—on robust human flourishing on both sides.

Puar correctly notes the costs of war through "suicide bombings, shootings, drones, border skirmishes, and missile attacks."[41] She also observes that "food and medicine rationing" as well as "restrictions on access to medical care"[42] cause debilitation of Palestinian populations, but inaccurately blames Israel alone for this particular situation.[43] Puar omits to mention that both Israel and Egypt control the borders in Gaza in order to staunch the flow of terrorists, arms smuggling, and Hamas attacks on Israel through the use of tunnels, missile and rocket launches, and, more recently, incendiary balloons—a novel form of ecological warfare that causes considerable damage to Israeli farms, fields, woodlands, and fauna. Although she declines to say so directly, her entire discourse assumes that military action on the part of Palestinians is, as per the doctrines of BDS, justified as a means to end the occupation, by which she signifies the elimination of Israel.

Pronatalist Policies and Racialized Jewish Israeli Gay and Lesbian Parenting

Puar thus considers the disabilities and debilitations stemming from the Israel/Palestine conflict, particularly in Hamas-controlled Gaza. She then turns to pronatalist policies in Israel, which capacitate Israeli gay and lesbian Jews in a putatively racialized homonationalist fashion, and which she regards as the single most pernicious manifestation of pinkwashing. She notes that marriage equality has not taken hold as an activist agenda in Israel in the manner it has in other democracies. In fact, as Puar acknowledges, this is true because the Orthodox rabbinate controls marriage, and there is no civil marriage—for homosexuals or heterosexuals—in Israel. In the face of this impasse over same-sex marriage, the legalization of surrogacy has become the major rights issue for gay Israelis, who were for a long time forced into the considerable expense and inconvenience of using overseas agencies.[44] But in 2020 the Israeli supreme court found this form of discrimination illegal; it gave the Knesset one year to implement full rights to surrogacy for gay and single heterosexual men, which had already been extended to single women.[45] From the observations that Israel is a very pro-natalist state and that Jewish Israeli gays and lesbians, like Arab Israelis and Palestinians, seek to become parents and, often enough, have large families, Puar arrives at a newly expanded and far more sinister characterization of pinkwashing than seen in the work of other BDS activist academics:

> To be gay in Israel is not only to be Jewish (and not Palestinian and in many cases not even Arab), not only to be able-bodied (and not disabled) but also to be parents, to reproduce the national body politic along racial and rehabilitated lines. Thus, I would argue that the most pernicious thing that the discourse of pinkwashing accomplishes, along with keeping activated a discourse about Palestinian homophobia, is effacing the fact that the state's interest in homosexuality is superseded by its interest in the reproductive capacities of bodies engaged in Israeli pronatalism. This capacitation of reproduction serves the goals of the occupation in a much more endemic manner, through the biopolitics of population reproduction and the cultivation of a racially elevated Israeli body politic—not quite as simple as the "demographic" issue might initially seem. Pinkwashing, and the subsequent attention to the sexual regulation of homosexuality whereby the field of sexuality is completely taken up by the question of orientation, obscures intense forms of control being enacted at the level of reproduction across homo-hetero divides.[46]

The first statement is incorrect, as there are childless and disabled lesbian and gay Jews, Arabs, and Christians (and other minorities) in Israel as elsewhere. From the fact, however, that many Israeli gays and lesbians do choose to have children in a very pro-natalist culture that seeks to maintain a Jewish majority population, Puar concludes that the Israeli government takes interest in them only to the extent that they can become parents, and thus reproduce the state "through the biopolitics of population reproduction" or, in more demotic terms, the birthing of children. In focusing on the traditional definition of pinkwashing as Israel's putatively dishonest abuse of its sterling record on LGBTQ human rights to conceal or whitewash its struggles with the Palestinians, Puar now claims that anti-Israel critics are missing the most salient issue: Israeli Jewish gays and lesbians take part in the national project of birthing Jewish children who will increase the number of Israeli Jews, and who will therefore grow up to struggle against the Palestinians when they join the IDF. Yet the same phenomenon exists on the Palestinian side, where having large families is seen as a heterosexist necessity that considerably exacerbates homophobia, since, unlike in Israel, LGBTQ Palestinians are not perceived as potential parents who can conceive children through ART. However, even in giving credence to these supposedly dire proclamations, which assume no end in sight to the conflict, Puar has done nothing more than to attempt to cynically instrumentalize the motives of the Israeli government and criminalize Israeli Jewish gays and lesbians for the simple human act of bearing children. At last, Puar claims that controlling "bodily capacity at multiple vectors—national discourse, disability, ART, pronatalist ideologies—entails that pinkwashing is part of a larger assemblage, the goal of which is to modulate debility and capacity across manifold populations."[47] In more direct terms, Israel "modulates debility" through encouraging heterosexual and homosexual adults to have children, who ordinarily do not have the debilities of the elderly. Lost in this lengthy and strained attribution of sinister motive to the entirely ordinary human phenomenon of bearing children in Israel is that Arab and other minorities partake in these practices as well.

Middle East Human Rights and Israeli Treatment of Gazan Children

Before moving onto the conclusion, I would like to return to an earlier claim Puar made: that Israel has exposed Palestinian children in Gaza to more violence than that suffered by any other children in the world. This contention matters because the basic premise for the existence of the BDS movement revolves around the charge that Israel stands as the single most important political issue, as well as the most grievous source of human rights abuses in the world. However, facts on the ground do not substantiate what amounts to an obscenely irresponsible assertion. This claim undermines how we judge and measure the relative seriousness of other violations—even those considered only in Israel's neighborhood in the Middle East.

For instance, the bombing of Yemen by a Saudi-led coalition has, since 2015, caused more than 85,000 thousand Houthi Yemenite children to die of malnutrition because of an imposed blockade. Experts say Yemen has become the worst humanitarian crisis in the world, with the UN reporting that 14 million people could soon be on the brink of starvation.[48] Further, countless numbers of children die daily in the Syrian civil war, which has killed many thousand Palestinians. Their wide-scale deaths, which have occasioned few if any protests, have involved the use of chemical weapons and mass bombings of innocents by Bashar al-Assad and Vladimir Putin, who seem interested not in the fate of children but rather in jockeying for geopolitical power.[49] ISIS has revived unspeakable forms of torture, including crucifixion, beheading, burning of genitals, use of pincers on women's breasts, and hurling men suspected of same-sex intimate behavior from rooftops,[50] and has severely abused children by recruiting and indoctrinating them to serve as soldiers in its caliphate.[51] In Afghanistan, more than 3,000 children died in 2018 alone from bombing campaigns carried out by Taliban, Afghan National, and US forces.[52] Finally, Save the Children, which notes that one-fifth of the world's children live in conflict-wracked nations, lists the following as the worst and most dangerous places in the world for children: Afghanistan, Central

African Republic, Democratic Republic of the Congo, Iraq, Mali, Nigeria, Somalia, South Sudan, Sudan, Syria, and Yemen.[53]

The BDS movement shows no signs that it plans to investigate, condemn, or take action against these and other horrific international human rights abusers, or to subject those who commit these wrongs to boycott, divestment, and sanctions actions. Indeed thus far the response has been *silence*—a silence that gives considerable pause about the ethical judgment and strategic blindness of the BDS movement, which also lacks policy recommendations for peace between Israel and Palestine other than calling for the nation of Israel to disappear because of the pressure exerted by the anti-normalization campaign. The BDS movement has endeavored, thus far with success confined mainly to cultural venues and the humanities, to transform Israel—which is an internationally well-connected hub of technological, medical, economic, environmental, and military development and innovation—into an isolated pariah nation.

However, all this is not to say that Palestinian Gazan children do not suffer because of the Israeli/Egyptian blockade, military actions by the IDF in response to bombings by Hamas and associated terrorist organizations, and other causes in which Israel might be construed as playing a role in the death, injury, or psychosomatic trauma of Palestinian children. According to Defense for Children International, the IDF has killed approximately 355 Gazan Palestinian children, a number that does not include the approximately 700 per year taken into Israeli custody for interrogation and imprisonment for suspected involvement in terrorist acts.[54] In addition, as B'Tselem reports, the conflict with Israel disproportionately affects Palestinians. In 2008 and early 2009, Israel invaded Gaza as part of Operation Cast Lead, which caused only 13 Israeli deaths but ended with well over 1,000 Palestinians killed and the devastation of the Gaza Strip. Israel launched extended bombing campaigns in Gaza in late 2012 which killed dozens of Palestinians. While Israeli strikes targeted Hamas and other militant groups that fire rockets into Israel, a local UN office estimated that 77 percent of people killed in Gaza up to that point were civilians, including 30 children. A separate UN agency estimated that 70 percent of the killed were civilians, including 27 children.[55]

Tragically, particularly after no fewer than twelve unsuccessful attempts over the decades to conclude a peace agreement by trading peace for land, both Jewish Israeli and Palestinian children are taught to expect that conflict will be a part of their future. As Laurel Holliday remarks in *Children of Israel/Palestine*, two "ethnically distinct peoples . . . lay claim to the very same sand, stone, rivers, vegetation, seacoast, and mountain" and "grow up feeling that they are destined for conflict with their neighbors."[56] Children prepared for a future of warfare, who learn pervasively negative stereotypes about their neighbors, have already been primed for psychological damage, including anxiety, depression, PTSD, and substance abuse. Not surprisingly, advocates for both sides have made repeated and sometimes substantiated allegations of abuse against the other side, and in 2015 Human Rights Watch (HRW) took the responsible course of action by asking the UN to place Israel and Hamas on its "List of Shame" over their violations of the rights of children.[57]

Conclusion

Although the adventitious assemblages Puar concocts occasionally hit the mark unintentionally as in her remarks on homonationalism and the surprisingly favorable position that gays, lesbians, and bisexuals have swiftly acquired in Western nations in recent decades, most of what she blends together in her intellectual Mixmaster reflects her anti-Israel ideological convictions and, as she herself admits, her resort "to a somewhat polemical deployment of empirical information."[58] In pursuit of her BDS activist agenda, Puar has allowed her passions for her brand of political justice to overrun her better judgment, and she's shown herself willing to demonize her opponents, disregard standards of proof and evidence, jettison plausible cause and effect, and not consider, or answer, possible objections to her contentions.

Because Puar has expressed fantasy-based allegations and conspiracy theories against Israel, she has faced fierce criticism that alleges that her work gives voice to pervasive antisemitic bias. Unfortunately, and perhaps tragically, her willingness to engage in speculative fictions relating to presumed Israeli machinations regarding organ harvesting, stunting, maiming, Jewish Israeli homonationalist parenting, and Israel as the worst violator of the human rights of children in the world has inevitable, unpropitious, and perhaps unintended consequences. Respectable scholars could not take her seriously, or commend her densely incomprehensible prose, which does not earn a right to its difficult nature or bear up under sustained analysis of its logic, strategies, and assumptions.

Israel has many legitimate responsibilities—which justice requires that it address and ameliorate—for the ways it treats the Palestinians. They are a people who have remained stateless, economically disadvantaged, chronically underemployed, and mired in endemic internal and external violence, military occupation, and restricted movement through security check points for altogether too long; at the same time, they watch their homeland steadily eroded by the construction of more and more Israeli settlement blocs. However Puar does not engage substantively with these and other real and complicated wrongs, for which the Palestinian leadership also bears responsibility. Rather, one confronts in her a biased and one-sided prosecutor who can be taken seriously only by those who are not only ignorant of the facts but also predisposed to drawing unreflective conclusions because they already despise Israel and everything that nation represents. Standing, perhaps by choice, outside the normative conversations about the Israel/Palestine conflict, Puar does not teach or communicate effectively: She indoctrinates, misinforms, and incites hatred.

Yet despite her wall-to-wall conspiracy theorizing, blood libel, mischaracterization, distortion, and stunning disregard for fact and evidence, Puar has been rewarded with promotion and a prestigious book award. In 2018 she was given the National Women's Studies Association (NWSA) Alison Piepmeier Book Prize for *The Right to Maim*, which the association characterizes as a "groundbreaking monograph in women, gender, and sexuality studies that makes significant contributions to feminist disability studies scholarship" and marks "a paradigm shift in thinking fully about the global politics of disability and capacity" that has "much to teach us about contemporary disability politics."⁵⁹ This fervent defense of her scholarship speaks eloquently about the manner in which egregious falsehoods are becoming mainstreamed and rewarded, as well as to the ever more urgent necessity to clearly and forcefully counter them to protect the integrity of the public intellectual square.

3

ANGELA DAVIS

ISRAEL AS THE QUEER INTERSECTIONAL OUTSIDER

The First Intersection: Alabama and the USSR

Once upon a time, in a land far, far away, Angela Yvonne Davis—a young intellectual, but even then an academic political celebrity and famous communist militant—visited the Soviet Union and East Germany, where she warmly greeted and shook hands with the autocrat and sponsor of state terror Erich Honecker.[1] Although she has praiseworthy lifetime achievements, including her antiracist and feminist activism, her groundbreaking publications, and her work with death penalty and prison abolition, Davis has also, ironically, in the past favored prison sentences for Soviet dissenters, whom she labeled "common criminals,"[2] applauded the 1968 Soviet invasion of Czechoslovakia, and gave implicit assent to the repressive anti-ethnic minority and antidissident policies of the Brezhnev era.[3]

Like other anti-Israel BDS public intellectuals studied in *Queering Anti-Zionism*, Davis has made erroneous political judgments with assured conviction and enthusiasm. She has regarded terrorists and autocrats as embodying idealistic, well-intentioned, or justified political systems while evincing insufficient knowledge of relevant sociopolitical realities of the nations they govern to arrive at such conclusions. She has nostalgic memories of the Soviet Union, and she romanticizes Islamism. She has overestimated the political underpinnings of human flourishing and meaningful living. She has allowed her passions for advocacy for the disadvantaged and oppressed to sideline academic standards of evidence and fact. She has, through lack of knowledge, self-deceiving imagination, or biased perception, admired attributes that such terrorists and autocrats did not possess. She has rejected critical aspects of modernity, Western democratic institutions, and even reformist iterations of socialist capitalism. And, finally, like some others, Davis has nurtured a wishful longing for and abiding belief in many of the revolutionary agendas once invested in Soviet communism, including its antisemitism and politically expedient relish for anti-Zionism.

In her case, Davis, born in 1944 in Birmingham, Alabama, has provided such eloquent witness to the egregious racism of American society that she might, perhaps, have more than adequate reason for her pro-Soviet stances. For the young Davis, looking for a cause that could command devotion and hope anything might have seemed preferable to the societal wrongs of the United States: institutionalized racism, the Vietnam War, the histories of slavery, racial segregation, the near-genocide of Native America, the military-industrial complex, nuclear weapons, second-class citizenship for women, and the persecution of queer people. She might be excused, in the face of what she knew too well of her native country, for championing the communist ideology of a foreign and putatively classless society that promised to obviate racial animus by leveling differences among people. But how did her anti-American views on the one hand and pro-Soviet stances on the other comport logically with what Eric Heinze calls her "absolute moral condemnation of systematic, state-directed ethnic discrimination"?[4] That becomes a much harder question to answer, since Davis has not eschewed the historical lacunae in her thinking, and has, instead, continued to repeat her contradictions under different guises across the course of her lifetime.

In 1973, when she took her celebrated trip to the Soviet Union one year after her acquittal on charges of conspiracy, murder, and kidnapping (stemming from her earlier role in purchasing the weapons involved in the deaths of four people), Davis could not have been entirely unaware but must have chosen to consciously rationalize or minimize her knowledge of the crushing force of Soviet ethnic cleansing and repression of millions of minority and outsider groups in the name of triumphant class struggle. Jews, Roma, Muslims, Chechens, Balkans, Georgians, Baltic peoples, Ingush, ethnic Ukrainians, homosexuals, political dissidents, and religious adherents were but some of those who were oppressed—or who perished—before and during this time. Davis, herself a lesbian, embraced authoritarian Soviet leaders[5] and, like others studied in this book, frequently jettisoned concerns for the fates of LGBTQ people and women in the service of the evidently greater political goals of anti-imperialism and anti-Zionism. Rather than disguise their crimes, moreover, these antinationalist, pro-Sovietization dictators proclaimed that they sought "the elimination of national customs and culture in the creation of a homogenous Soviet nation" of modern workers liberated from the anti-internationalist constraints of capitalist, superstitious, tribal, and nationalist beliefs.[6] For Nikita Khrushchev, among others, opposition to communism, like the practice of homosexuality, constituted a mental illness that required treatment in one of the innumerable *psikhushka*, or psychiatric prisons, scattered throughout the Soviet Union.[7] For Davis, as Heinze notes, there was no apparent "contradiction in applauding one of history's most imperial, most trans-continental, most crudely modernist machines of ethnic and national discrimination . . . and cheerleading for it in the name of anti-discrimination."[8] In *Détente, Democracy and Dictatorship*, Aleksandr Solzhenitsyn excoriates these discrepancies, wryly observing that

> in our country, literally for one whole year, we heard nothing at all except about Angela Davis. There was only Angela Davis in the whole world and she was suffering. . . . Well, they set her free. Although she didn't have a rough time in this country, she came to recuperate in Soviet resorts. Some Soviet dissidents—but more importantly a group of Czech dissidents—addressed an appeal to her: "Comrade Davis, you were in prison. You know how unpleasant it is to sit in prison, especially when you consider yourself innocent. You now have such authority. Could you stand up for these persons in Czechoslovakia

who are being persecuted by the state?" Angela Davis answered: "They deserve what they get. Let them remain in prison." This is the face of communism. This is the heart of communism for you.[9]

In part, Davis's disavowed self-contradictions, as manifested in her cordial relationship with Honecker and others, emerged from her naive belief that East Germany had, unlike democratic West Germany, dealt successfully with its fascist past. The mere fact that it had become a communist state proved it had left Nazism behind. But Davis, because of her ideological communist commitments, could not have allowed herself to know (or perhaps would not have cared) that, from its beginnings, East Germany practiced antisemitism and anti-Zionism, and had later on after the war suppressed knowledge of and investigation into the Holocaust.[10] Moreover, for its part, the Soviet Union had never stopped minimizing or erasing the Holocaust and persecuting Jews, and it maintained its official anti-Zionist and antisemitic policies from the 1950s through the demise of the USSR in 1991.[11] The "Zionism Is Racism" and "Zionism Is Fascist Nazism" slogans continued in force, particularly at the Durban Conference, among those antisemitic ruses used by numerous authoritarian regimes that engage in serious abuse of human rights and feign surprise at the racism they opportunistically discover in the Jewish state. For these reasons, as Heinze remarks, the Soviets employed Davis not to teach about but rather to stifle all critical interrogation of and teaching about racism and ethnocentrism within the USSR: "'Education about racism became *nothing* but education about racism *in the US*."[12] For Davis, in contrast, the Soviet Union had to educate the United States about the falseness of its stance of moral superiority vis-à-vis the USSR, and the kind of equitable economic system required to obviate systemic bigotry, despite that nation's own persecution of minorities. In this unequal equation of the romance of communism, the bitter realities of the Soviet Union were elided in this presumably equal educational exchange. For Davis racism was nothing more—or less—than an organized system of class oppression practiced exclusively by the US and its Western-style allies.

Back to the USSR: Anti-Zionism and Intersectionality Theory

Today Davis is an out lesbian and a distinguished professor emerita of the history of consciousness at the University of California, Santa Cruz, whose history reveals how much or how little consciousness changes as a function of time. In brief, in the name of squelching imperialistic racism articulated in the sloganeering rallying cries of communist solidarity, Davis once countenanced murderous Russian ethnocentric repression. Moreover, as revealed in her recent collection of interviews and lectures, *Freedom Is a Constant Struggle: Ferguson, Palestine, and the Foundations of a Movement* (2015), and the short video that features her, *When I See Them I See Us: Intersectional Struggle & Transnational Solidarity with Palestine* (Black-Palestinian Solidarity campaign, 2015) Davis continues to embrace anti-Zionism—the major strand of Soviet-era ideological propaganda that has transcended Cold War aporias to reemerge in the twenty-first century as pro-BDS advocacy.[13]

Davis continues to embody the leftist intellectual spirit of 1975. Just eight years after the shocking victory of the IDF in the Six-Day War, which turned a left-wing not pleased to witness Jewish triumphs instead of defeats, the UN General Assembly passed the nonbinding Resolution 3379, spearheaded by the Soviet Union, which characterized Zionism as "a form of racism and racial discrimination."[14] Meanwhile the Soviets and other nations that signed onto the resolution continued to engage in systematic forms of ethnocentric oppression and suppression of political dissent.[15] Although the UN General Assembly revoked this resolution in 1991, in part because of the advent of the Oslo Accords, Davis, as well as Puar, Spade, Butler, and Schulman, have doubled down on their anti-Zionist, internationalist, and pro-communist statist beliefs. In her recent work Davis has lodged against Israel the kinds of charges of Zionist racism, fascism, and apartheid that sound very familiar to those acquainted with the history of the Soviet Union in the twentieth century. Davis has been hyper-focused on the comparatively mild forms of racism attendant on Zionism while turning a blind eye to every other form of severe racism practiced in the world, including those involving state-sponsored violence and persecution.

Davis has engineered this return to Soviet-era anti-Zionism through an opportunistic abuse of intersectionality theory. This misuse of theory has, in turn, enabled her to become an informal spokesperson for Black Lives Matter (Black Lives Matter), as well as the inspiration for a new global movement, for which she fancies herself the leader, that intersects events in Ferguson, Missouri, with those in Israel/Palestine. She launched, along with prominent African American and Palestinian activists, a media campaign that aspires to show how both groups share a common cause rooted in racism and apartheid (which she equates with segregation) by using deceptive slogans, misleading images, and simplistic rhetoric. Her video *When I See Them I See Us* opens with a seated, serious-looking Davis holding a sign reading, "Racism is systemic. Its outbursts are not isolated incidents."[16] Since national identity and religious conflict, rather than racism, lie at the heart of the Israel/Palestine conflict, Davis misstates, for the purpose of fabricating connections, to press home her anti-Zionist agenda at the expense of Blacks, the first intersection she announces in her video.

Where and how does Davis misapply the valuable tools of intersectionality theory, which has its roots in the powerful nineteenth-century works of Sojourner Truth and her famous speech, "Ain't I a Woman"? As articulated by contemporary legal scholar Kimberlé Crenshaw, who coined the term, intersectionality theory states that experiences of multifarious oppressions are connected to one another through embodiment and lived experience, and must be explored holistically to accurately capture social realities and redress wrongs suffered by multiply disadvantaged persons. For instance, a Black, female, disabled lesbian cannot be accurately viewed as someone who is Black plus female plus disabled plus lesbian, but rather through an intersectional analysis of how these compounded disadvantages affect her overlapping and variable embodied experiences with access and accommodation, sexism, homophobia, and racism. Thus an intersectional analysis often takes the form of an analytical narrative that considers what needs to change to assist Blacks, women, lesbians, and disabled people across the board.[17] In other words, if you consider the disadvantages suffered through this aggregate of experiences, you can redress ableism, sexism, racism, and homophobia individually as well.

In her seminal 1989 article, "Demarginalizing the Intersection of Race and Sex: A Black Feminist Critique of Antidiscrimination Doctrine, Feminist Theory and Antiracist Politics," Crenshaw examined three legal cases—*DeGraffenreid v. General Motors*, *Moore v. Hughes Helicopter*, and *Payne v. Travenol*—which concerned employment discrimination against Black women. The legal outcomes were unsatisfactory because "dominant conceptions of discrimination condition us to think about subordination as disadvantage occurring along a single categorical axis,"[18] whereas Black women stood at the intersections of race and sex, and thus had multiple disadvantages. Crenshaw enjoined legal scholars and social activists to perform intersecting analyses of oppression to avoid the situation in which Black women and others "can receive protection only to the extent that their experiences are recognizably similar to those whose experiences tend to be reflected in antidiscrimination doctrine," with its single-axis focus.[19]

In the name of antinationalist, internationalist, and, most important, anti-Zionist struggles, Davis has opportunistically misapplied intersectionality theory by combining phenomena so fundamentally and significantly dissimilar as to produce inaccurate and therefore distorting pictures of relevant realities. They do not result in the illuminating knowledge that rich intersectionality theory can produce, and therefore do not help anyone gain accurate knowledge that deepens insight and helps redress problems. In her youthful egregious blunders with the Soviet Union, Davis intersected the concrete realities she knew of racism, classism, sexism, and nationalism in her home nation, the United States, with her abstractly intellectualized or utopian fantasies about antisexist, antiracist, anticlassist, and antinationalist practices in a foreign nation, the Soviet Union. The result—in which her intersections were uninformed by close analytical observation, historical context, political knowledge, experiential understanding, or cross-cultural insight—was nothing less than a disastrous miscalculation, based on disavowal or minimization or wishful thinking in the service of the greater ends of an international communist solidarity. Davis acts like someone who has decided what to believe in advance of undertaking substantive research that might challenge preconceived conclusions. She abandoned her own academic freedom to discover truth wherever it took her, for her ideological dreams, and did not gain new and, as sometimes proves to be the case, discomfiting or complicating knowledge. As a Black, feminist, lesbian communist, she ended up making inopportune comparisons and endorsing some of the worst antidissident, anti-ethnic minority, homophobic, and racist abuses in the twentieth century.[20]

As Sohrab Ahmari notes perceptively about the abuses of intersectionality theory as deployed against Jewish people:

> Precisely because it is a theory of generalized victimhood, intersectionality targets the Jews—the 20th century's ultimate victims. Acknowledging the Jews' profound claims to victimhood would force the intersectional left to admit the existential necessity of the State of Israel. But the intersectional left is not prepared to do so because, under intersectionality's rules, all the outcomes are predetermined. Israel has been prejudged an outpost of Western colonialism.[21]

Hence there is an ironic tragedy in Davis's often reflexive antinationalist and pro-communist desires to intersect multiple global struggles against oppression without adequate knowledge of the contexts of her analyses.[22] When Davis speaks about what she does know, as a Black, lesbian, radical intellectual, the results have been among the most trenchantly multivectored studies of racist, classist, homophobic, and sexist oppressions in the United States. For instance, in her classic volume *Women, Race and Class* (1981), Davis reveals, far ahead of her time, how the antislavery movement gave birth to women's rights; how racism inflected—and damaged—suffragism; how the legacies of slavery shaped the construction of a new womanhood; and, how the relations among rape, racism, and the myth of the Black rapist functioned to suppress

Black political activism. Davis, in lucid prose filled with documentation, evidence, and penetrating knowledge, explains that,

> in the United States and other capitalist countries, rape laws as a rule were framed originally for the protection of men of the upper classes, whose daughters and wives might be assaulted. What happens to working-class women has usually been of little concern to the courts; as a result, remarkably few white men have been prosecuted for the sexual violence they have inflicted on these women. While the rapists have seldom been brought to justice, the rape charge has been indiscriminately aimed at Black men, the guilty and innocent alike. Thus, of the 455 men executed between 1930 and 1967 on the basis of rape convictions, 405 of them were Black.[23]

Intersecting Ferguson, Missouri, and Palestine/Israel

Davis, resting her far-flung analyses on uncertain foundations, intersects the nationalist and religious parameters of the Israel/Palestine conflict, which constitutes an armed struggle between Israeli Jews and Palestinian Arabs over land both parties historically claim as theirs, with the struggles of unarmed Black citizens against the depredations of ethnocentrism and police brutality that are rooted in slavery and institutional racism. The specific incidents Davis uses include Israel/Palestine violence in the context of war, on the one hand, and the rise of Black Lives Matter, on the other. The latter was occasioned by the deaths of two unarmed Black citizens of the United States. Both the deaths of the two Black citizens and the war in Israel/Palestine happened to occur in 2014. As the subtitle of her book indicates, Davis desires to transform these disparate but temporally contiguous intersections into *Ferguson, Palestine, and the Foundations of a Movement*. The question inevitably becomes what motivates Davis to make this forced and inopportune intersectional comparison, and how it contributes to misunderstanding each situation in a detrimental fashion that disserves and misrepresents both.

To understand how Davis assembled the components of this work, it will be necessary to briefly reconstruct the events that transpired in Ferguson, Missouri, in 2014 and 2015, along with the roles that Davis and others allege the IDF, Israeli police, and Palestinian protestors halfway across the world played in occurrences that, she argues, inform one another in foundational ways. The result is a classic case of false analogy, baseless cause, and false premise. These intersections matter because, partially on their account, Black Lives Matter adopted a platform that engaged in Holocaust inversion, charged Israel with practicing South African apartheid, and accused Jewish Israelis of committing genocide against the Palestinians.[24] Davis also succeeded in alienating pro-Zionist Jews who had always played seminal roles in social justice movements in the United States, giving them the non-choice of abandoning their Zionist allegiance to Jewish national self-determination in Israel or embracing unremittingly harsh views of the Jewish state in order to remain in her movement.[25]

This task is simplified by the fact that Jews do not fit the movement's traditional definition of marginalization, because antisemitism misconstrues Jews as powerful, influential, conspiratorial, and privileged, and therefore as outside the circle of the authentically oppressed. Thus if Jews defend themselves or Israel, then they cannot be included in intersectional coalitions, the latter of which, in reflexively antisemitic fashion, erase the determinants of antisemitic discrimination. For these reasons antisemites and anti-Zionists are easily able to infiltrate and hijack intersectional movements, and to demonize Jews as advantaged or conspiratorial white people who exist at the very apex of societal privilege.[26] In brief, with the help of an egregious abuse of intersectionality theory, Black Lives Matter contravened the historically pro-Zionist stance of most major Black American advocacy groups, organizations, churches, and the Civil Rights movement led by Martin Luther King, Jr.[27] As Black critic Chloe Valdary noted, to "protest police brutality against a minority on the one hand and promote the disenfranchisement of another historical minority on the other—namely the Jews—is philosophically inconsistent and morally bankrupt."[28]

Police brutality against Black citizens is exactly what occurred on August 9, 2014, in Ferguson, Missouri. Michael Brown, 18, and his friend Dorian Johnson, 22, left a convenience store where surveillance video showed that Brown had committed the minor crime of stealing some cigarillos. The store owner nonetheless called the police. When police officer Darren Wilson arrived at the scene, Brown and Johnson were walking away from the store, down the center of a two-way road. According to witnesses, an altercation between Wilson and Brown ensued. Brown attacked Wilson in his vehicle in an apparent effort to wrest control of his police gun from him. After Wilson shot Brown in the hand, Brown fled on foot with Johnson. Wilson ran after the unarmed men, and Johnson hid behind a car. According to Wilson and several witnesses, after a pursuit Brown stopped, turned around, and charged Wilson—but, significantly, at a very considerable distance. Despite this, Wilson did not withdraw, call for backup, drive away, or otherwise seek to deescalate the situation. Rather, he continued to fire shots until he killed Brown.

On November 24, 2014, a grand jury composed of nine whites and three Blacks failed to indict Wilson. Protests and riots, some violent, ensued, causing property damage and, more important, serious physical injuries. The FBI also later concluded that there was no evidence that Brown had raised his hands and said, "Don't shoot," although protesters later made extensive use of "Hands up, don't shoot!" as a rallying cry against racist police violence. On March 4, 2015, the US Department of Justice, under the direction of Attorney General Eric Holder, also found that Wilson had acted in self-defense. Forensic evidence in the form of DNA from Brown that was found on Wilson and in his police car cleared Wilson. In addition, credible witnesses corroborated Wilson's account, whereas investigators found incriminating witnesses not credible.[29]

As President Barack Obama remarked at the time, no one might ever know the complete truth about this tragic death by apparent misadventure or mischance. But the clash between an unarmed Black citizen and an armed police officer had taken place in a town where the police force had regularly used egregious racist language, racial profiling, and profiteering against the Black community it putatively served.[30] The rage over the killing of Michael Brown acted as the flashpoint in the long-simmering racial abuses by the Ferguson police department. Ferguson depended financially on fines and other charges levied by police officers and selectively used against Black citizens.

Significantly, no notable person other than Angela Davis connected the protests that ensued in Ferguson with the violent clashes that occurred between Israelis and Palestinians in the same year, half a world away. The latter had begun with a series of revenge killings on the Palestinian and Israeli sides, and then, after a heavy barrage of rocket attacks launched by Hamas from Gaza into southern Israel, an IDF military operation in Gaza designed to quell the violence that lasted more than fifty days. In addition, the Israeli police and the IDF shot down armed Palestinian youths because during this time and at other times the latter attempted and often succeeded in killing Jewish civilians—using knives or automobiles as battering rams to do so.[31]

What Dominic Green has aptly called the "intersectionality of fools"[32] was made manifest because the violent riots in Ferguson and actions in Israel, respectively, were framed by Angela Davis in her book *Freedom Is a Constant Struggle* and the video *When I See Them I See Us* to create a misleading similitude between the recurring shootings or killings of unarmed Black men in the United States, on the one hand, and the deaths of armed Palestinian protestors in Israel/Palestine, on the other. Her text and the video juxtaposed images, but they were shorn of vital historical, cultural, and political contexts, and created misleading analogies that led to two false conclusions: (1) The IDF were indiscriminately killing Palestinian civilians in Gaza through a murderous and senseless bombing campaign; and, (2) as with unarmed Black men in the United States, the Israeli police, armed with rifles with rubber bullets and tear gas, were gunning down innocent Palestinian youth because of Netanyahu's policies of constructing settlements in East Jerusalem and the West Bank.[33]

Designed to promote common cause and create linkages in the American imagination, the connections Davis makes between Ferguson and the West Bank/Gaza not only are ethically and practically untenable but also show how Davis instrumentalizes the Civil Rights movement for her own BDS ends—just as Schulman instrumentalizes LGBTQ rights, Puar Middle Eastern studies, Spade disability studies, and Butler Judaic studies. As Yoav Fromer remarks, the comparison between Ferguson and Israel/Palestine is not simply unfair and inaccurate, but also insulting. Policemen in American cities were not killing Blacks because they were "attacking innocent civilians with knives, or shooting parents in front of their children, or using cars as battering rams, as they are in Palestine. The entire point of the Black Lives Matter movement is that the victims are *innocent*."[34]

In addition, the allegation that colonialism informed both situations is misleading. Classical colonialism, grounded in the competition of world powers of different historical eras for control of resources and markets, as well as in imperialistic fantasies of national grandeur and racial or religious supremacism, set out to civilize a putatively backward or unenlightened world. Colonialism oppressed native peoples, stripped their lands of riches, extracted tribute from them when possible, and in some places, like South Africa and the Congo, to name but two examples, committed mass atrocities. Colonialism was about conquest, domination, and exploitation.

But might Israel constitute an instance of settler colonialism, and if true, does that not delegitimize Israel and the Zionist project? However the motives differed, and the Jews of from the Diaspora went there not to subjugate a racially inferior population but because, as Maxime Rodinson says, "It was the life preserver thrown to them."[35] Indeed, the 1947 UN partition plan recognized the rights of both Jews and Arabs, and represented a solution to the conflict that British and Turkish imperialism had helped to create in that land. The Jews accepted the partition plan; the Arabs, for complicated reasons, did not. Yet in the Israeli-Arab War (1947–48), the British imperialists supplied the Jordanians with significant armaments while the Britain communists congratulated "the new Jewish State of Israel" and said that, "the interests of the Arab peoples lie in co-operation with the new Jewish state against Imperialism for the freedom and peace throughout the Middle East."[36] The 1947–48

Israeli-Arab War and 1967 Six-Day War displaced large numbers of Palestinians and created a refugee crisis that persists because Arab nations refused to assimilate or grant citizenship to Palestinians. On the other side of the conflict, the literal physical survival of a people, the Jews, was at stake—a people who, in the mid-twentieth century, had been faced with attempted extermination in Europe by a genocidal regime and with mass deportation and dispossession by Islamic powers in the Middle East.

Representing Israel as an apartheid and racist state purposefully misconstrues the function of the West Bank settlements and the barrier wall—both of which are far from popular in Israel. While some extremist settlers regard Judea and Samaria as biblical inheritances of the Jewish people, most have the far more realistic view that the more limited settlements serve as a buffer zone. Should Israel return the West Bank to the Palestinians, it could turn into another Gaza; Israeli population centers could be threatened with mass violence from advanced weaponry that could be even more precise and seriously destructive than the rockets Hamas fires into far inside southern Israel. Misrepresenting the situation and falsely substituting racial animus as the cause for the conflict instead of the very real security and other considerations belies the real nature of the problem in Israel. Like the BDS movement, this mischaracterization makes arriving at solutions all the more difficult. Using power to subjugate populations deemed racially, ethnically, or religiously substandard constitutes the character of colonialism. In addition, however, as Fromer remarks, using force to protect civilians from lethal violence is what all modern states do when necessary for self-defense.[37] Finally, in characterizing the Israel/Palestine conflict as based on racial difference (in an attempt to make it familiar to American audiences), BDS thoroughly erases the demographic realities: almost half of Israeli Jews are nonwhite people from Africa, Asia, the Middle East, or South America.

The divergence in tactics, contexts, and ethics negates Davis's self-serving claim that Palestinians share common cause with Blacks. Martin Luther King, Jr., who was a Zionist,[38] helped undo Jim Crow through nonviolent resistance modeled on the examples of Mahatma Gandhi,

Henry David Thoreau, and other peaceful protesters. King's efforts succeeded because he occupied the moral high ground and exposed the hate and violence informing southern bigotry. Although not all organized actions for justice can avoid violence, civil rights prevailed because it had a message of love, justice, and social healing that people could hear and respect.

These distorting misapplications of intersectionality theory become evident not only in the video *When I See Them I See Us* but also in Davis's volume of lectures, essays, and interviews, *Freedom Is a Constant Struggle*. Here Davis compares the militarization of the American police to the Israeli police, and complains that the Israelis, who are experts in counterterrorism, have trained US police departments in inappropriate responses to mass violence.[39] The Israeli police's training differs greatly from the kind of disproportionate, thoughtless, and provocative militaristic response the Ferguson police had to an unarmed civilian; the shooting of Michael Brown showed the police's lack of experience, good sense, and discipline. This opportunistic comparison also disregards the fact that the Israelis train American police forces to respond to incidents of terror involving bombs and explosives, as well as major actual or threatened loss of life, such as occurred on 9/11, not to circumstances such as those surrounding the fatal shooting of Michael Brown.

Acknowledging that intersectionality theory has been about "bodies and experiences"[40] across the dimensions of race, class, gender, ability, and sexuality that Crenshaw had analyzed, Davis announces her intention to transfigure Crenshaw's work through (re)conceptualizing it as "the intersectionality of struggles." In other words, as she earlier did with the United States and the USSR, Davis wants to connect social movements that take place across different histories, languages, geographies, cultures, and oft-hidden back contexts and realities in which, frequently enough, victims are also the oppressors, or where the situations are too complex to accommodate simple black-and-white dichotomies.[41] However, like someone wanting to short-circuit the educational process, Davis stands ready to credit everything she wants to believe and ignore contradictory, complicated, or ambiguous facts through which might she gain knowledge that would threaten her preconceptions.

Davis glancingly admits that a lack of contextualized knowledge might be a hindrance, but then proceeds to treat this point as one that concerns only the need to find the right or, more accurately, the simpler kind of descriptive language to use rather than acquiring the appropriate forms of contextualized knowledge:

> My experience has been that many people assume that in order to be involved with Palestine, you have to be an expert. . . . The question is how to create windows and doors for people who believe in justice to enter and join the Palestine solidarity movement. So that the question of how to bring movements together is also a question of the kind of language one uses and the consciousness one tries to impart. I think it's important to insist on the intersectionality of movements. In the abolition movement, we've been trying to find ways to talk about Palestine so that people who are attracted to a campaign to dismantle prisons in the US will also think about the need to end the occupation in Palestine.[42]

In essence Davis declares that one needs to find forms of what might be termed bridge language that can connect movements together no matter how much they do or do not share, or how little activists do or do not know about them. She premises that all anti-imperialistic, antiracist, anticolonialist, and antinationalist struggles are essentially the same across the world. Perhaps there are nuances, but they do not affect the larger picture. Hence Davis resorts to distorting images, false comparisons, and logical lapses to make her intersectionality analyses fit. Worst, she works against preparing people for the work of actually resolving the Israel/Palestine conflict, which does require close historical, political, and cultural knowledge, an informed sense of context, and an appreciative tolerance for complex thinking, moral ambiguities, overlapping realities, and competing narratives.

The situation in Israel/Palestine is marked by such contradiction, ambiguity, and national/religious enmities. By choosing violence and rejectionism, for instance, many Palestinians have played a role in perpetuating the cycle of discord. Despite efforts to promote nonviolence, some Palestinians have instead continued to choose armed struggle and to espouse eliminationist rhetoric, in part because some regard the Levant as sacred Muslim territory. In 2014 alone, just as Black protesters, most of them peaceful, were demanding that police end their violence, Palestinian youth publicly celebrated the killing of Israeli citizens. They have shouted out the rallying cry of the Hamas charter to "hunt down the Jews" and reclaim all of "Palestine."[43] Unlike Black Lives Matter, which has focused on police brutality and called for reform in civil society, some Palestinian youth chose to attack innocent, unarmed women, children, and the elderly simply because they were or were thought to be Jewish. For their part, Israeli Jews have not in recent times responded by redoubling their efforts to secure peace. Feeling more threatened than bravely innovative, they have created tentative plans to annex the West Bank—a move that, if undertaken, would undermine a two-state solution, increase violence, and give more impetus to the BDS movement. The Israeli government has expanded settlement blocs to people who regard Judea and Samaria as sacred Jewish territory, and paid inadequate attention to Israeli Arabs and the need to close social gaps in housing, wages, opportunity, and education.

Misapplying Intersectionality Theory and Trafficking in Africans in the Sinai

Objecting to the opportunistic instrumentalization of the Civil Rights Movement to force a comparison between Israel/Palestine and the struggles of Black citizens against police brutality, Valdary angrily insists that

> *my* people have always been Zionists because *my* people have always stood for the freedom of the oppressed. So, you most certainly do not get to culturally appropriate *my* people's history for your own. You do not have the right to invoke *my* people's struggle for your shoddy purposes and you do not get to feign victimhood in our name. You

do not have the right to slander *my* people's good name and link your cause to that of Dr. King's. Our two causes are diametrically opposed to each other. Your cause is the antithesis of freedom. It has cost hundreds of thousands of lives of both Arabs and Jews.[44]

Davis, in her historical instrumentalization of intersectional analyses to link the struggles of Blacks against racism and police brutality on the one hand to the Israel/Palestine conflict on the other, has, not surprisingly, supported Hamas, a terrorist organization that threatens and manipulates journalists, kills Israeli citizens, and sacrifices Palestinian civilians as human shields for military and propaganda purposes.[45] But just as Davis turned a blind eye to systemic racist oppressions during the Soviet era, so too does she ignore Hamas's record of race-based human trafficking in the Sinai to enable their jihad,[46] through which they contemplate attacks on Western culture and genocide against the Jewish people. The final consequences of misapplying intersectionality theory are, in essence, ethically abhorrent. Davis, who claims to want to end the oppression of unarmed Black citizens in the United States, ends up backing an authoritarian terrorist organization that, in order to get the funds to fire rockets into Israel, engages in organ and human trafficking of Africans in the Sinai.

4
DEAN SPADE'S BDS ACTIVIST MALPRACTICE

Disrupting the Creating Change LGBTQ Conference

In January 2016, at the Hilton Hotel in Chicago, LGBTQ activists and their allies convened for the twenty-eighth annual Creating Change Conference, organized by the National LGBTQ Task Force. The diverse international meeting included groups and individuals from many nations, including those that persecute queer people, engage in quasi-genocidal wars, countenance sex trafficking, violate international laws, and commit egregious human rights abuses against women and girls, religious minorities, migrant guest workers, and political dissidents. Despite the presence of people from such nations, Dean Spade, associate professor of law at Seattle University School of Law, and the Muslim Alliance for Sexual and Gender Diversity, among others, singled out for vociferous opprobrium members of only one national identity: Jewish Israelis. These Israelis happened to strenuously oppose many of the foreign and domestic policies of their nation, particularly its relations with Palestinians, but unlike all the other conference participants, they were transformed into political embodiments and representatives of their government, and held personally liable for its policies. In contrast, Saudi Arabian participants, for instance, were not assailed for their government's malevolent abuse of gays and women, racist exclusionary policies, and economic mistreatment of migrant guest workers.

This attack, led by Spade, occurred during a scheduled session called "Beyond the Bridge." Sara Kala-Meir and Tom Canning, two queer left-wing Israeli leaders from the Jerusalem Open House for Pride and Tolerance, who happened to have helped the Palestinian queer rights organization alQaws in its founding, were the presenters. The San Francisco–based North American LGBTQ rights organization A Wider Bridge, a nonprofit (501c3) whose mission includes strengthening bonds between Jewish and Israeli gays worldwide, hosted this talk by Jerusalem Open House.[1]

Although A Wider Bridge is a nonpolitical, nonprofit organization that does not have ties to the Israeli government,[2] Spade and his allies protested, arguing that the task force needed to exclude Jerusalem Open House and A Wider Bridge from participation in the conference because of their imputed involvement in Israeli government-sponsored pinkwashing. It was a charge for which Spade had no intention of providing evidence—he had none—since his tactics consisted of bullying, shunning, name-calling, and intimidation rather than reasonable debate and the adducing of evidence and fact. Further, Spade and his allies disrupted the above organizations to show support for BDS and Palestinians who they alleged were oppressed by Zionist occupation and state-sponsored racism, not to mention the high crimes of genocide and apartheid.[3] One reporter, Hannah Elyse Simpson, noted that under the logic of pinkwashing, LGBTQ Americans have no right to celebrate marriage equality while Guantanamo Bay still held detainees without due process. "Only Israel," she observed, "plus any organization that originates from—or even does business—there gets held to an unreasonable standard."[4]

During the conference, Roberta Kaplan, the attorney who successfully argued *United States v. Windsor* (2013) before the US Supreme Court on behalf of lesbian rights activist Edith Windsor, which sought to invalidate the Defense of Marriage Act (DOMA), came to the defense of Jerusalem Open House and A Wider Bridge, along with many others from within and outside the Jewish community. The National LGBTQ Task Force, which had initially bowed to pressure from Spade and his allies, reversed its decision to cancel Jerusalem Open House's presentation. The task force's executive director, Rea Carey, explained, "We want to make it quite clear that the Creating Change Conference will always be a safe space for inclusion and dialogue for people with often widely different views.... It was not at all our intention to censor representatives of the Jerusalem Open House or A Wider Bridge at Creating Change and I apologize that our actions left people feeling silenced."[5] Over the voices of the objectors, who insisted that the Creating Change Conference was siding with the forces of pinkwashing, settler colonialism, racism, apartheid, and genocide, the organizers proceeded to schedule a reception for Jerusalem Open House and A Wider Bridge.

More than one hundred people attended—or rather, attempted to attend—the reception.

The same BDS activists, including Spade, who had initially insisted that the Task Force cancel the Jerusalem Open House and A Wider Bridge presentation, ignored the repeated attempts that conference organizers made to provide spaces for peaceful dialogue about pinkwashing and the Israel/Palestine conflict. Instead, they morphed into a threatening and disruptive crowd of approximately two hundred people who packed the hallways—banging drums, waving banners, and impeding entry to the reception and even unrelated nearby events. They shouted out slogans calling for the destruction of Israel: "From the river to the sea, Palestine will be free!" and "We're going to challenge these Zionist racist motherfuckers!"[6] Rather than addressing the need to end the occupation of the West Bank or cooperate to create peace, they called for the elimination of Israel. Despite this, Tyler Gregory, director of programs for A Wider Bridge, attempted to speak about the intersections among the Israeli LGBTQ community and those around the world. However, he was soon shouted down by a screaming, hate-mongering conference attendee whose rant was captured on video.[7] The protestors not only blocked those who wanted to attend the reception from entering, but also held as virtual prisoners those already inside the conference room. Several protestors commandeered the stage, while the two presenters from Jerusalem Open House, fearing for their safety, had to be escorted out of the building by police.

The tragic ironies of this disruption emerged from the fact not only that many Arab Israeli and Palestinian LGBTQ people depend on

Jerusalem Open House for support services—including counseling and job placements[8]—but also that the organization and its leaders were still terrified and reeling from the trauma, which had occurred only six months earlier, of the stabbing death of Shiri Banka in Jerusalem during the Pride Parade there.[9] However Spade and his cohort, dehumanizing their opponents, caring nothing for the facts or the perspectives of those on the other side, exhibited extreme anti-Israel animus. They helped create what journalist Jonathan Capehart called an "inflection point in the LGBT rights movement. A point of pride for Creating Change is that attendees are encouraged to be their whole selves" and to "have that identity recognized and respected." Spade and his group grossly violated that principle.[10]

Three years later, on January 24, 2019, the Creating Change Conference once again became the site of fervent anti-Israel protests inspired by Spade. Some attendees demanded the destruction of Israel as a Jewish state, and others gave vent to frustrations with the occupation of the West Bank, racism against Israeli Arabs, the interminable nature of the conflict, and American financial support for Israel.[11] For close to fifteen minutes, these protestors commandeered the stage at the plenary session, chanting anti-Israel slogans and eliciting sustained applause from the audience, but also making a mockery of the conference principles of diversity and inclusion.[12] In 2019 the task force made no effort to stop the protests, provide a space for alternate perspectives, acknowledge the breach of safety the protestors caused for many Jewish LGBTQ attendees and their allies, or take meaningful steps to prevent such incidents from happening again in the future. These actions contradicted the policies of Creating Change, which declares on its website that it "discourages the disruption of conference sessions, plenary sessions, meetings or exhibits that result in attendees not being able to fully participate in learning and educational opportunities available at Creating Change. We ask that this core principle of free exchange of ideas be respected as essential to the mission and spirit of the Creating Change Conference."[13]

The LGBTQ Task Force probably should have specified that disruptions would be prohibited, not merely discouraged, to preserve the free speech rights of all. Unfortunately, Spade and his cohort took advantage of this loophole. Indeed, the use of such ideologically rigid stratagems, including sloganeering, propaganda, and fake or exaggerated claims, characterize the anti-Israel BDS activism of Spade. From his video, *Pinkwashing Exposed: Seattle Fights Back* (2015), to his article, "The Right Wing Is Leveraging Trans Issues to Promote Militarism" (2017), to his book, *Normal Life: Administrative Violence, Critical Trans Politics, and the Limits of Law* (2011), Spade resorts to misrepresentation and misinformation when it comes to Israel, viscerally attacking all those who do not comport with his unbending ideas about social justice, including his conviction that Israel incarnates evil.

Exposing *Pinkwashing Exposed*

Spade's feature video, *Pinkwashing Exposed*, narrates how a small but determined contingent of Palestinian solidarity and queer BDS activists, led by Spade (who directed the film), initially succeed in convincing the Seattle LGBTQ Commission to cancel, at the last moment, a scheduled panel by representatives of Israeli LGBTQ organizations. According to the synopsis of the video placed on his website, the Israeli consulate funded what Spade called the pinkwashing tour featuring Israeli gay and lesbian activists: "Local queer Palestine solidarity activists exposed the 'Rainbow Generations' tour as pro-Israel propaganda and got some of the events, including the tour's centerpiece event hosted by the City of Seattle's LGBT Commission, cancelled. A significant backlash ensued involving the Seattle City Council and Seattle's leading LGBT and HIV organizations."[14]

The coalition group visiting the Pacific northwest, the Association of Israeli LGBT Educational Organizations, included Israeli Gay Youth, Hoshen (the Israeli version of the Human Rights Campaign), and Tehila (the Israeli version of PFLAG). A Wider Bridge sponsored their Rainbow Generations program, and these groups had come to Seattle to share their experiences and expertise around issues involving LGBTQ youth, including suicide, conflict with families, and equality for LGBTQ parents and children.[15] A Wider Bridge reported that the LGBTQ Israeli coalition had done fine work during its US tour. For instance, in Los Angeles the delegation had consulted with leaders of the Trevor Project to collaborate on how to help LGBTQ teenagers in crisis. They met with PFLAG to share their programs for counseling parents on how to understand and assist their queer children. They visited the Los Angeles LGBT Center to discuss issues related to HIV testing, prevention, and care. Finally, in San Francisco, the delegation greeted diverse LGBTQ and Jewish groups, including those working for queer inclusion in various faith-based communities. The conversation in San Francisco focused especially on the unique challenges faced by LGBTQ people in minority communities, both in Israel and in the United States.[16]

Although Spade claimed that the six Israeli presenters were paid by and represented the Israeli government, they were in fact selected by Israeli LGBTQ nongovernmental organizations and A Wider Bridge, and they came to the United States voluntarily. In addition, individual programs were cosponsored by organizations including LGBTQ synagogues and groups, the New Israel Fund, and the National Council of Jewish Women. While StandWithUs, a nonpartisan and nonprofit organization dedicated to promoting Israel and Jewish concerns worldwide, cosponsored several events in Seattle, they provided no funding for the tour.[17] A Wider Bridge partners with many cosponsors across the political spectrum, and as Arthur Slepian, the former executive director explained, that organization does not act as a surrogate for the Israeli government:

> We are clear about our own mission and objectives. We do believe in Israel's right, like every other country, to conduct public diplomacy, whether as an antidote to demonization, to encourage trade and tourism, or for other legitimate purposes. We take pleasure in the fact that among the multitude of things that Israel chooses to promote about itself . . . it devotes a small amount of attention to its LGBT community.[18]

While averring that the Israeli consulate had sponsored some events—but provided no financial backing for the tour—Slepian dispensed with the claim that A Wider Bridge was a puppet of the Israeli government.

However, the agitprop emerged in Spade's film *Pinkwashing Exposed*, which indulged in substantive falsifications to paint a black-and-white Manichean view of the Israel/Palestine conflict—with Israelis as the cartoonish villains and Palestinians as the hapless victims of injustice. Interweaving select snippets from the commission hearing proceedings, pictorial representations, letters and newspapers, footage from Israel, interviews with a small cohort of Palestinian, Jewish Voice for Peace,[19] and queer and transgender activists, including Spade, the film attempts to prove that, in Spade's baseless words, Israel constitutes nothing more than an "apartheid regime," in addition to a "settler colonial state founded on the genocide of the Palestinian people."[20]

To prove these odious charges of genocide and apartheid (which, if true, should have been referred for adjudication to the UN and the International Court), and the somewhat more plausible if still very tenuous one of settler colonialism, the film engages in seven principal stratagems: (1) It shows close-up footage of the IDF bombing of Gaza homes and buildings without any context revealing that these air strikes were defensive responses to Hamas rocket attacks in southern Israel, and attempts to discourage known terrorists from further violence; (2) it includes footage of Palestinians who have been killed or disabled putatively because of these Israeli bombing strikes but does not show Jewish Israeli victims of Palestinian terrorism, including suicide bombings, stabbings, and use of automobiles as rams; (3) it uses doctored and edited pictorial and photographic representations to claim that the "Brand Israel" pinkwashing campaign arose in direct causal response to the "tarnished image"[21] of militarism and violence Israel acquired after the Second Intifada (2000–2005); (4) it represents the public response to the actions of Spade and his allies as nothing other than the most shrill, abusive, and invective-laden hate mail, and no missives containing reasoned argumentation or substantive objections; (5) it claims that an Israeli queer documentary *The Invisible Men* (dir. Yariv Mozer, 2012), which concerns persecuted gay Palestinians escaping from their families and hiding in Tel Aviv,[22] constitutes propaganda used to disguise the "immense homophobia in Israel and the United States";[23] (6) it implicitly justifies the BDS refusal to engage in normalized interactions with Israel-associated organizations by arguing that "propaganda is not dialogue";[24] and (7) it uses four putatively historical maps of the Levant from 1946–2005 that, as Shany Mor notes, "are egregiously [and] almost childishly dishonest."[25] The title of these representations—"Palestinian Land Loss"—are placed in scare quotations to distance (probably for legal reasons) the producer from possible accusations of misrepresentation, especially given that these fictitious maps are designed to forward the thesis that Israel, like the United States, Canada, Kenya, Argentina, and Australia, is a Western-style colonial settler state that encroached on and committed genocide against the indigenous population it displaced.

The first map, dated 1946, is the most historically and substantively misleading. The green area represents the territory not under Israeli sovereign control, and does not demarcate land possessed by Arabs or some state of Palestine that never had any historical reality in any period. After Ottoman rule took back possession from Egypt (1834–1917), the Palestinian Arabs (*al-ʾfilistiniyyum al-ʿarab*) were subjects of the Ottoman Empire, as were the Jews who lived there who had purchased their land from the Ottoman Empire. Indeed, nearly all the land had no legally recognized owner after the collapse of the Ottoman Empire following World War I. While the Jews were escaping antisemitic persecution in Europe (and later, the Middle East and Africa) and working to creating a Zionist Jewish homeland, the Palestinian Arabs were becoming increasingly fearful of Zionist incursions. They rejected the Balfour Declaration (1917) because they charged it did not grant them national or political rights, and they believed it disregarded an earlier agreement they had with the British. The British waged war against the Turks in the Levant and established what was intended to be the temporary period of the British Mandate (1923–48). The core component of the Mandate Period was to establish Jewish and Arab territories, respectively. Further, the first map makes no distinction between private property and sovereign land, and it erases the political context. This map appears based on

Dean Spade's BDS Activist Malpractice   103

the National Jewish Fund private land purchases (see blue areas) made through the Ottoman Empire. Further, in 1917, the British government issued the Balfour Declaration, which proclaimed British support for the creation in Palestine as "a national home for the Jewish people."[26] After 1939, and in response to Arab objections, the British—who ruled the area as the British Mandatory government established by the League of Nations to create a Jewish National Home—halted Jewish immigration to what Jews called *Eretz Yisrael* (the Land of Israel), even as the beginnings of what would become the Holocaust threatened,[27] because they did not wish to further antagonize the Palestinian Arabs and surrounding Arab nations.

The second map, dated 1947, represents a United Nations partition plan that the UN General Assembly adopted that year as Resolution 181, but which was never implemented. The plan contemplated the creation of two states: one Arab (green) and one Jewish (blue), upon the termination of the British Mandate period. However, the Palestinian Arab leadership, which just two years earlier had been allied with Nazi Germany—and with whom they threatened, perhaps in rhetorical excess, the extermination of Palestinian Jews[28]—rejected the plan, even as the Israeli Jews accepted it. Arab attacks (ultimately unsuccessful) on Jewish population centers ensued, and Israel declared its independence as a nation. The surrounding Arab nations then attacked Israel and promised the Palestinian Arabs that they would expel the Jews. Although some Palestinian Arabs stayed, between 700,000 and 800,000 fled in fear or were driven out by the Israeli forces, in what came to be known as the Nakba, a traumatic refugee crisis that persists until today.

When the war ended in 1949, the map looked glancingly like the third one, labeled 1967, although major distortions persist. The map shows where Israeli and Arab armies stopped fighting in 1949—lines which held until 1967. The green areas called the West Bank and the Gaza Strip were never Palestinian in the sense that Palestinian political entities controlled them. When an armistice was declared in 1949, Egypt had annexed Gaza, and Jordan the West Bank. Neither were Palestinian territories, although Arab Palestinians lived there. As a people, the Palestinians emerged in distinct form in 1964, with the creation of the Palestinian Liberation Organization (PLO). But simply because Palestinian national identity followed Zionist Jewish identity does not mean that the former is any less real or legitimate. In the 1967 War, when Arab nations, with the exception of Jordan, again invaded, Israel assumed control of the Sinai (from Egypt) and the Golan Heights (from Syria). Subsequently, in a land for peace deal negotiated under Anwar Sadat, Israel returned control of the Sinai to Egypt in 1979.[29]

As Mor explains, "The first three maps . . . confuse ethnic and national categories (i.e., Jewish and Israeli, Arab and Palestinian), property and sovereignty, and the Palestinian national movement with Arab states that ruled over occupied territory for a generation." They are "masterpieces of shameless deception."[30] The final map, usually marked as either 2005 or the indefinite present, purports to show the outcomes of the Oslo Accords (1993),[31] which, under Oslo II (1995), for the first time granted Palestinians control over areas in the West Bank, and created complex administrative and security zones. Negotiators contemplated a five-year interim arrangement to be followed by a final status agreement that would have established a Palestinian state. As in 1947, when the Arab Palestinians rejected land for peace, however, this agreement failed: The Palestinian leadership turned down a state based on 90 percent of the West Bank and all of Gaza. Under Yassar Arafat, they proceeded to break promises not to engage in armed struggle again, and undertook campaigns of suicide bombings and other violent acts against Israeli civilian populations.[32] In the meantime, the Israelis withdrew from Gaza in 2005. In 2007, after a brief civil war with Fatah, Hamas assumed control of that area. Thus at the present time there are two Palestinian governments—one in Gaza controlled by Hamas and the other in the West Bank controlled by the PA—although both are represented by the same color on the map as if they were the same political entities.[33]

The Communities of the Bad, the Good, and the Unenlightened

While Spade and his allies claimed victory despite "a lot of painful backlash," he and his small cadre actually lost this and subsequent battles with the Seattle city government. The Seattle Public Safety, Civil Rights and Technology Commission not only reversed the decision of the LGBT Commission but also chastised its members for failing to make a sound decision informed by facts and evidence. The Israeli LGBTQ visit later proceeded without further incident. The Commission eventually understood the illogic of BDS, acquiring more knowledge of the situation through the testimonies of those who supported the Israeli LGBTQ delegation to Seattle, and discovering that the former were not propagandistic puppets of the Israeli government. However Spade, who identifies Zionists automatically as belonging to the community of the bad, has persisted with similar anti-Zionist propaganda and antisemitic conspiracy theories in his op-ed, "The Right Wing Leverages Trans Issues to Promote Militarism" (2017).

The opening of the op-ed features a large color photograph of approximately twenty BDS activists with rainbow balloons seated in a semi-circle on the steps of Seattle City Hall on Nakba Day.[34] Displaying in front of them large letters spelling "BOYCOTT APARTHEID," the protestors demanded that Seattle mayor Ed Murray—a gay man who had been instrumental in securing marriage equality in Washington state—cancel his trip to Israel; they claimed that the A Wider Bridge conference he planned to attend there would be a pinkwashing event. In fact, Murray did not think support for Israeli LGBTQ rights and Palestinian rights were mutually exclusive, and he planned to meet with both Israeli Jewish and Arab leaders on his trip, which he undertook despite these protests.[35]

But Spade ignores Mayor Murray. Instead he proceeds to note right-wing backlash against trans rights over bathroom facilities, as well as other forms of anti-transgender activism in Israel. Most important for his purposes, though, what he construes as the same right-wing attempts to leverage "transgender issues as a tool for promoting right-wing security and military agendas."[36] Spade describes Israeli lieutenant Shachar Erez as the "trans darling of the right" not because of Erez's politics, which are progressive, but simply because he happens to be an Israeli transgender man who serves in a leadership role in the IDF. Further, Spade once again returns to his disproven claim that StandWithUs, which he characterizes as a "right-wing Israel advocacy organization," has "coordinated" events with Erez across the United States.[37] He continuously, inaccurately, asserts that StandWithUs and other Israeli advocacy groups fund international "tours of LGBTQ activists from Israel aimed at painting an image of Israel as progressive, diverse and inclusive."[38] This same nefarious and amorphous "right-wing" uses accusations of antisemitism to silence critics of Israel, while "right-wing leaders and organizations that cultivate anti-Semitism unflinchingly support Israel, including illegal settlement expansion."[39] So, for Spade, antisemitic prejudice exists only on the right, whereas in fact both right- and left-wing versions of antisemitic prejudice exist.[40] As the links to this op-ed reveal, however, by the term "right-wing" Spade means everything from the Trump administration, Milo Yiannopoulos, and the antitrans organization CitizenGO[41] to the pro-LGBTQ Israeli organization StandWith Us, Lieutenant Erez, and the famous left-wing Israeli television performer Assi Azar. Spade includes Azar on this "list of shame" only because the Israeli does popular university and college tours in the United States. Indeed, Spade groups together Yiannopoulos, Azar, and Erez in one sentence, claiming that they all "signal the danger of a far-right queer and trans politics that embraces racist, anti-Muslim, Zionist ideologies."[42] The purpose of this paratactic clustering centers on discrediting Azar and Erez by placing them in the company of Yiannopoulos, an antitransgender and antifeminist gay agitator with extremist pro-Trump views who worked as an editor of the far-right syndicated news site *Breitbart*, and whose appearances on campuses have generated large protests from progressives and their allies.

Throughout his work, Spade shows that he has an absolutist belief in three distinct groupings of people—the community of the good, the community of the bad, and the community of the unenlightened—and that he has the educational obligation to repeat untruths until they are, through exhaustion or indifference in his audience, accepted as public beliefs. The "good" include the queer transgender movement that wants economic and racial justice, and that opposes militarism, prisons, same-sex marriage, and all things Israeli. The "bad" encompass the presumably predominantly white and corporate-funded gay and lesbian organizations that support military inclusion, hate crime legislation and antidiscrimination laws, same-sex marriage, and, of course, Israel and Zionism. And last, the "unenlightened" are the groups who, like the Seattle LGBTQ Commission, become the unwitting dupes of Israeli "pinkwashing campaigns." The most recent mistake of the unenlightened occurred on April 5, 2017, when they sponsored an event with Lieutenant Erez.[43] While Spade claims that StandWithUs was behind Erez's appearance, A Wider Bridge and Congregation Beth Shalom of Seattle actually hosted the event. For Spade, the Israeli propagandists are particularly dangerous—yet alluringly challenging—because they look and even act like ordinary, decent people with many of the social justice concerns Spade shares. Hence their masquerade of virtue and humanity convinces many unaware people. Spade sees his project as undertaking direct and, at times, assaultive action through anti-Israel protests that reveal Israel's use of LGBTQ rights to disguise its many alleged crimes—including militarism, police and prison brutality, apartheid, genocide, and settler colonialism.

Because Spade holds these convictions, he makes no distinctions between people, on the one hand, and the organizations in which they might belong or with which they might be involved, on the other. As Jessica M. Choplin and Debra Pogrund Stark observe, generalizations about the relations between people and organizations are justified only when an organization has a mission statement that advocates specific goals—such as the Hamas charter's pledge to annihilate all Jews worldwide. They note that making generalizations about the LGBTQ community in Israel demeans and insults:

> People—even those living under right-wing governments (Israelis, Poles, Hungarians, Americans)—have legitimate concerns of their own. They deserve the freedom to discuss those concerns. Sadly, when Israelis talk about their concerns their discussions are filtered through ancient prejudices of scheming, plotting Jews. The result is an anti-Semitic double standard. Poles, Hungarians, and Americans can discuss their concerns without the conversation being interpreted as somehow legitimizing the policies of their right-wing governments. Polish, Hungarian, and American LGBTQ groups are not immediately barraged with questions about the right-wing policies of their governments, nor are they immediately asked to disavow their governments. By contrast, when Israelis discuss their concerns their conversations are interpreted as part of a conspiracy to legitimize the policies of their right-wing government. Israeli LGBTQ groups are immediately barraged with questions about the right-wing policies of their government and they are immediately asked to disavow their government.[44]

Conclusion: The BDS Conspiratorial Style of Thinking

Like Puar, Davis, and Schulman, Spade believes in and staunchly supports conspiracy theories. He has an intensely inflected, oppositional, and divisive mode of thinking about the world, which also characterizes his book, *Normal Life: Administrative Violence, Critical Trans Politics, and the Limits of Law*. Just as Puar had moved from received definitions of pinkwashing into characterizations of how Israeli Jewish gays and lesbians reproduce the state (and Palestinian oppression) by becoming parents and having Jewish children, so too does Spade shift from Israel to the United States under then-president Barack Obama. Spade contends that the analyses developed to uncover pinkwashing in an Israeli context also apply to an American one:

> The United States under the Obama administration has also increasingly promoted a "progay" and to some extent "pro-LGBT" image of itself to cover up and distract from the ongoing expansions of brutal racist violence. . . . Outrage has been growing about Obama's drone wars, his record-breaking deportations, his administration's use of widespread surveillance technologies, his targeting of whistleblowers, the growing wealth divide and his scandalous upward transfer of wealth in the 2008 bailout, and police violence and the crisis-level expansion of imprisonment, including for-profit imprisonment, in the United States under his watch. The relentless revelations about the administration's actions and agenda threaten the national fantasy that the election of a Black president heralded increasing equality, justice, and progressivism. Gay rights, as a symbol of left politics associated with freedom and liberation, has provided a false marker of progressivism for the administration as it works to maintain this fantasy.[45]

Barack Obama would be the first person not only to aver that his presidency could not possibly end racism in the United States but also to contend, *contra* Spade, that he lacked the infinite powers that Spade ascribes to him either to prevent harm or accomplish good. So, too, does

Spade ascribe the limitless power to engage in conspiratorial pinkwashing and politically motivated evil to Israel, all the while denying that this country can act for the good. Rather than seeing either or both as contending with invidious limitations to their power to do well, Spade reduces them to abject moral failures. Denying the dignity of inevitably flawed decent humanity to his opposition, Spade insists that neither Obama nor Israel can do right. As Alice Dreger notes, Spade, in his work, reveals how "in activism as in war, truth is the first casualty."[46]

5

JUDITH BUTLER'S ONE-STATE SOLUTION TROUBLE

Speaking as a Jew as a Performative Trope

In 2013 Judith Butler, the Maxine Elliot Professor of Comparative Literature at UC Berkeley, gave a talk at Brooklyn College with Omar Barghouti on academic freedom and BDS. The lecture generated considerable controversy among those who oppose the pro-BDS and anti-Zionist views of Butler and Barghouti and wanted the talk canceled.[1] But the event went forward as scheduled, as the college's administration wisely remained neutral and refused to be drawn into partisan political controversies. An internationally famous philosopher, a lesbian Jewish American queer theorist, and the most influential BDS advocate in the United States, Butler holds considerable sway in the humanities. Since few have the temperamental fortitude, personal investments, skepticism, or knowledge of the subject matter required to challenge her authority, the dictates of the BDS movement dominate these and related fields of academic inquiry.

Butler took the occasion to outline for the audience her perspective on the values of academic freedom that, for those conversant with the tenets of the BDS movement, bear an uncomfortably fraught and, indeed, contradictory relationship with academic freedom. Butler, who seemed at pains both to elide and transcend these difficulties, said:

> I presume that you came to hear what there is to be said, and so to test your preconceptions against what some people have to say, to see

whether your objections can be met and your questions answered. In other words, you come here to exercise critical judgment, and if the arguments you hear are not convincing, you will be able to cite them, to develop your opposing view and to communicate that as you wish. In this way, your being here this evening confirms your right to form and communicate an autonomous judgment, to demonstrate why you think something is true or not, and you should be free to do this without coercion and fear. These are your rights of free expression, but they are, perhaps even more importantly, your rights to education, which involves the freedom to hear, to read and to consider any number of viewpoints as part of an ongoing public deliberation on this issue. Your presence here, even your support for the event, does not assume agreement among us. There is no unanimity of opinion here; indeed, achieving unanimity is not the goal.[2]

Her claims about the value of dispassionate inquiry, free expression, and rights to education notwithstanding, Butler and Barghouti came to Brooklyn College on a mission to persuade their audience to support BDS and anti-Zionism. They appeared to succeed beautifully with the enthusiastic audience, although there were dissenting voices.[3]

For his part, Barghouti provided litanies of crimes in his impassioned anti-Israel screed. As he insisted, the conflict, for which Israel, in his opinion, bore exclusive blame, had lasted too long and caused too much suffering, with no end in sight. He insisted that Israel had thus far refused to abandon the Zionist nightmare—the seedbed of violence, division, and hatred—dissolve itself as an ethnocentric Jewish and therefore racist nation in which Arab Israelis and Palestinians suffered apartheid, terminate the exclusive Jewish right of return, demolish the apartheid wall, and embrace a single democratic polity with a binational character in which Palestinian refugees could reclaim their former homes and all citizens, Jewish, Christian, and Arab, finally live together harmoniously in justice and equality.

Butler seconded Barghouti in laying out a vision of peace through a one-state solution, leaning implicitly on her stature as an academic to make her arguments seem less far-fetched or to occasion pause. She insisted that the BDS movement did not infringe on academic freedom, and that it represented a nonviolent means for ending the intolerable situation of perpetual warfare, and even the antisemitic passions that Zionism had exacerbated in the Levant and Middle East. The tragic and ill-considered Zionist movement for Jewish national self-determination had arisen in late nineteenth-century Europe in response to manifestations of antisemitic animus—including persecution, social exclusions, drummed-up legal prosecutions, and violent pogroms occasioned by the exclusions of the nation-state, which was then in its heyday. Some Jews had wished to emulate nationalism in a misguided effort to save themselves from the aggressions caused by the very entity responsible for Jewish oppression. The nation-state (under which Butler herself lives) had drummed up antisemitic passions. However, according to Butler, Zionism—founded on what she characterized as racist, Eurocentric, settler colonialist practices—had inflicted grave harms on the stateless and oppressed Palestinian people and, most important, had not lessened (as it had promised to do) but rather exacerbated antisemitic passions.[4] Zionism represented an historical mistake that needed to be amended through turning back the hands of time and dissolving the Jewish state. Butler propounded that, whereas Zionism had caused strife, removing this ideological cancer, which imperiled foundational Jewish ethics by making Jewish people complicit in the state violence committed in their name, could be accomplished through the amicable means of the BDS movement.

However, Butler's claim that BDS constitutes an ethically nonviolent route for resolution of the conflict that does not imperil academic freedom contains contradictions and evasions which she failed to address. For instance, the antinormalization dictates of the BDS movement, which forbid dialogue or any other action that might be interpreted as peaceful or collaborative with pro-Israel parties, can have deadly consequences in Palestine that go far beyond Western student or faculty rejection of dialogue with parties on the other side of the debate. Far from the eyes and ears of the civilized audience assembled at Brooklyn

College, Palestinian terrorist and paramilitary groups regularly punish what they construe as cooperative or peace-focused Israeli-Palestinian dialogue with death, violence, or threats, even as Israeli security forces, for their part, induce poor, desperate, or sick Palestinians into collaboration to receive cash, favorable treatment, or much-needed medical care.[5] As an example of retribution, Mohammed Dajani Daoudi, a Palestinian professor and peace activist, took a group of Al-Quds University students to Auschwitz, and suffered so many attempts on his life when he returned that he finally moved to the United States.[6] This tragic episode shows how much BDS can curtail the academic freedom of Palestinian professors and even students, who themselves experienced threats, intimidation, violence, and shunning.[7] And earlier, in 2006, Butler made comments supportive of terrorist organizations that hardly showed that she valued concepts such as democratic rule of law, academic freedom, or due process. She referred to Hamas and Hezbollah as "progressive" and "anti-imperialistic" leftist movements,[8] despite their systematic support for authoritarian violence, their trenchant abuse of women, and, perhaps most surprising for Butler as a lesbian critic, their often-harsh persecution of LGBTQ Palestinians.[9]

As Alan Johnson points out, the French philosopher Louis Althusser claimed that "every 'problematic'" contains potential as well as actual thoughts and "silences as well as presences, questions that cannot be posed as well as those that can." Anti-Zionists' "potential" thoughts can translate what appear to be classic antisemitic tropes into progressive language, such as opposition to Western imperialism and settler colonialism—all the while maintaining silence around Palestinian violence against Israeli Jews and the long traditions of Arab and Islamic antisemitism that oppose Jewish sovereignty in Israel.[10] As with disguising anti-Jewish sentiments in progressive language, BDS sustains an assurance of moral rightness by erecting a series of prohibitions against speaking about Palestinian violence against Israelis, Arab fantasies of destruction, and Middle Eastern ideological animus against Israel. Throughout her talk, Butler let the pressure behind these unspoken/unspeakable thoughts build up, but never addressed the proverbial elephant in the room: namely, antisemitism not caused by the nation-state, BDS's assaults on academic freedom, and the anti-Jew animus that is rife in the Middle East.

Narrative Reconstructions of Antisemitism and Nationhood

In a foray into historicized analysis in *Parting Ways: Jewishness and the Critique of Zionism* (2012), a collection of eight lectures written for diverse occasions—and in whose premises she appears to sincerely believe—Butler notes that throughout the nineteenth and earlier twentieth centuries, numerous Jewish thinkers objected to the establishment of the State of Israel. No one, she remarks, regarded such opposition as constituting self-loathing or antisemitic behavior. Indeed, she claims, anti-Israel arguments belonged to the long tradition of Jewish ethics that, in this case, opposed state-sponsored violence: "Jewish opposition to Zionism accompanied the founding proposals made by Herzl at the International Zionist Congress in 1897 in Basel, and it has never ceased since that time. It is not anti-Semitic or, indeed, self-hating to criticize the state violence *exemplified by* Zionism. If it were, then Jewishness would be defined, in part, by its failure to generate a critique of state violence" (emphasis mine).[11]

The use of the word *exemplify* reveals more than she had possibly intended to convey, for while Butler astutely notes that, historically speaking, Zionism, Jewishness, and Judaism are not the same things, she resorts to Jewish exceptionalism in making Zionist state violence somehow *exemplary*, and therefore especially worthy—as other and, indeed, far more egregious forms of state violence are not—of her particular critique. Rather, as Max Weber argues, the state maintains a monopoly on the legitimate use of force, primarily as a means of preventing violence within and beyond states.[12] Cary Nelson contends that "one of the key cultural and historical traditions that makes it possible to isolate Israel conceptually and politically from all other nations is anti-Semitism."[13] For, Johnson notes, every antiracist knows that "statements and actions can have *effects* without *intentions*."[14] However, Nelson's comments do not unequivocally establish that Butler has antisemitic intentions, for she claims that her critique stems from her conviction that Israeli state violence, rooted in a history of settler colonialism, stands in opposition to traditional Jewish ethics practiced in the *galut* or diaspora, where Jews had no state, but rather suffered discrimination and persecution because they lived under nation-states. While existence in states—whether viable or failing—represents the norm for modern human existence, in which there are comparatively few city-states, traditional empires, monarchies, or theoretical post-states, not having one would, Butler might believe, enable Jews to undertake their traditional ethical work of *tikkun olam*[15] by aspiring toward their eventual dissolution rather than committing injustices against the Palestinians to maintain their own state. In brief, in a formulation that reduces *all* states to the same problematic—not to mention the same abuse of state-sponsored violence—Butler implicitly argues that Jews were better off suffering rather than perpetrating state-sponsored persecution.

Two possible lessons or conclusions can be drawn from the fact that Jews experienced considerable state-sponsored violence, persecution, and discrimination in the *galut*, culminating not only in the Holocaust but also the forced removal of nearly one million Mizrachi Jews from their ancestral homes in the Middle East before or during the establishment of Israel as a Jewish state in 1948. One, supported by Butler and other BDS advocates, states that precisely *because* Jews suffered extreme state-sponsored violence, they should endeavor to avoid state-building, although this formulation leaves unanswered precisely under what political system Jews should (peacefully?) reside. The other, supported by Zionists, argues that the only plausible means for Jews to realistically address and avoid becoming victims of state-sponsored violence, not to mention preserve themselves and develop their culture, requires having a state of their own. Experience, observation, reasoned analysis, and, above all, history show that both positions have their strengths and weaknesses, and their avowals and disavowals. However, the former takes considerable risks on unknowable disaster, while the latter takes into account the extreme religious-based enmities and the likelihood of trading limited and known violence for the kind of Islamism and sectarian violence that has enveloped semi-failed Middle Eastern states such as Yemen, Iraq, Lebanon, Syria, and Afghanistan. Butler does not explain how or why things should fare better in Israel/Palestine despite the volatile neighborhood in which it exists.

Hence, strategic silences surrounding intractable contradictions partially structure *Parting Ways*. Further, Butler, in an act of not inconsiderable hubris, reduces the lives of millions of real human beings into an abstract thought problem with which to experiment by way of pressing home her arguments for the dissolution of Israel as a sovereign Jewish democratic state. In the messianic Erewhon Butler envisions, contemporary Israeli Jews would—as she claims they have in the diaspora—incorporate the non-Jew into their reconfigured so-called cohabitational identities, and reside in a polity whose citizens have binational personality-identities.[16] As Chaim Gans observes, the normative ethical desideratum that people treat others with consideration while maintaining their own discrete identities does not suffice. Rather, Jews must go beyond such ordinary moral demands and "integrate the other's group identity into their own personality-identity."[17]

What Butler means by this hybrid integration of group with individual personality-identity remains tantalizingly and perhaps intentionally obscure, for it is not clear how this scheme would work in an actual social or political landscape. Clarity would force the rubber of implicitly personal and familial or tribal and relational ethics to meet the public road of social ontology—or how people form viable modes of institutional, economic, social, and political exchange. One might almost speculate that Butler wishes those intending to found this diasporic Jewish-Palestinian post-state to convene as small groups of to-be-hybridized Israeli-Jewish-Palestinians to study *Parting Ways* in ideological *ulpans* for the purpose of undergoing identity makeovers. According to Butler, however, the injustice done to Palestinians before and during the Nakba through dispossession and statelessness cannot be remedied through the two-state solution of Israelis and Palestinians living side-by-side and pursuing their independent futures, because what she regards as that false solution leaves intact—and likely even more powerful and legitimized—Zionism, the crime of the Nakba, and the grievous offense against Jewish ethics of Israeli Jews possessing and controlling their own state, invariably to the continued detriment of Palestinians. Rather, Israel must do nothing less than to dismantle itself as a Jewish state and voluntarily[18] institute this dual exilic identity. In the diaspora, Butler notes, "Jews lived lives of irreversible heterogeneity as *cohabitees* and as such they developed a rich ethical tradition based on the relation to the non-Jew and the non-Jewish that foregrounded justice and respect for the Other; values that were experienced as an ethical obligation and demand for Jewishness."[19]

But here, alongside the paean to Jewish ethical respect for the Other, the evasive silences persist, for Butler does not mention diasporic Jewish suffering in the ghetto, the *shtetl* in the Pale of Settlement, or *dhimmitude* in Islamic lands—never mind the unspeakable horrors of the Holocaust or the dispossession of the Mizrachi Jews. She elides or blames on the nation-state the problem of horrendous experiences with egregious antisemitism in the diaspora—which the nation-state regularly coupled with importunate demands to assimilate or convert. But she conceivably sees these wrongs not only as the price to pay for abandoning the idea of statehood but also Jews' parts in working toward universal statelessness or postnationalistic socialism. In pursuing this teleological idea, she also not surprisingly ignores the articulations of projects for social justice in contemporary Israel, and the disavowing of antisemitism that can blossom and grow in the soil of such projects.[20]

Rather, Butler premises *Parting Ways* on four major contentions: (1) Palestinians' suffering and dispossession under Jewish Israeli settler colonialism necessitates the total repudiation of Zionism, despite the facts that Jews, like Palestinians, have legitimate claims to the land and that the settler colonialism argument remains a contentious dispute rather than a settled fact; (2) regardless of traditional definitions of Jewishness as constituting a people, a nation, and a religion, Jews must reject Zionism because it inflicts an erroneous nationalist interpretation of Judaism on Jews; (3) Zionism must be renounced for destroying the ethical character of Jewishness and thereby undermining Jews' capacities to cohabit with the Other; and, finally, (4) opposing Israel constitutes the proper ethical business of all Jews, since this nation undermines and seeks to destroy Jewish moral ideals of cohabitation and *tikkun olam*, or world repair.

The One-State Construct

Butler can profitably be considered as a kind of inverse Theodor Herzl. The founder of Zionism, Herzl propounded ideas regarded by most as fantasy fiction during his lifetime. However, as it turns out, he was more realistic about the establishment of a Jewish state than he was about the future of antisemitism. Hence, just as Herzl was wrong to conclude, in *The Jewish State* (1896), that creating a Jewish nation would end antisemitism,[21] so too does Butler err in contending that eliminating Zionism will also end hatred of Jews and, indeed, politically motivated violence, in her conception of Greater Palestine. Due to enmity and the confrontational history in Israel/Palestine and in the region, her scheme would result in the destruction or, at best, the severe marginalization of Palestinian Jews, and, even more likely, since Israeli Jews would not go down without a fight, the outbreak of a fierce civil war and the destruction of the nation-state and civil institutions.

As a case in point, in his rejoinder to Tony Judt's article "Israel: The Alternative,"[22] Leon Wieseltier argues against what he calls the "binational fantasy,"[23] or the cohabitation of Jewish Israelis and Palestinians in a two-part state. He notes that as an idea binationalism has a long pedigree that predates Butler by many decades. The American Jewish philosopher Noam Chomsky, who has advocated an anarcho-socialist version of binationalism for decades, and the Palestinian literary theorist Edward Said, whom Butler does discuss, support the idea that Butler advances with an innovative twist. Clearly, she experiences herself as tarnished by and implicitly identified with the actions of Israel; *Parting Ways* and her work to position herself as an anti-Israel and anti-Zionist Jew set her apart from the vast majority of Jews. What Wieseltier alleges of Judt, who opposes the existence of Israel, holds true of Butler as well:

> For the notion that all Jews are responsible for whatever any Jews do, that every deed that a Jew does is a Jewish deed, is not a Zionist notion. It is an anti-Semitic notion. But Judt prefers to regard it as an onerous corollary of Zionism. . . . He refuses to place the blame for this unwarranted judgment of himself on those who make it. . . . It is the essence of anti-Semitism, as it is the essence of all prejudice, to call its object its cause.[24]

As an American Jew, Butler has the good fortune to live in relative safety and with acceptance in a powerful and imperialistic democratic state, relatively free from antisemitic animus, although this situation has gradually changed for the worse more recently.[25] She still has what might plausibly be called the luxury to denounce Zionism rather than to regard Israel as a blessed refuge from persecution, violence, death, or dispossession. Convincing herself that her historical recipes for antistatist social revolution will produce peace, Butler joins a long tradition of Jews who flee their heritage out of fear and a desire for acceptance. The same cannot these days be claimed by some European or, certainly, Middle Eastern, Eastern European, or African Jews.[26] She nonetheless proffers what she calls her "impossible task,"[27] and takes it on herself to legislate the future for all Jews, Israeli or not. Butler comes to rescue contemporary Jews not from resurgent antisemitism but rather from the errors of Zionism that founded Israel and that have implicated the Jews, as empowered subjects rather than dispossessed objects of history, in state-sanctioned violence. As Chaim Gans notes, this proposal becomes radical on two levels: First, it requires that Jews make the Other a part of Jewish identities while, at least to some degree, "annulling our previous selves"; and second, it requires individuals living in the binational postnation to "acquire binational identities."[28] Butler desires that Greater Palestine become an entity inhabited by Jews and Palestinians who have "deconstructed their particular mono-national identities and then reconstructed themselves with binational identities."[29] What Butler means by the terms "postnation" and "binational identities" remains profoundly unclear, particularly since such arrangements have no concrete examples to which to refer.

An Alleged Anti-Zionist Jewish Tradition

Falling into the genres of political theory, philosophical meditation, and even speculative fiction, Butler sets out in *Parting Ways* to develop a Jewish ethics of "cohabitation" that enables a critique of Israel and offers a non-Zionist Jewish left as a "partner for peace."[30] She does not regard current Israeli Jews negotiating for a two-state solution as such authentic partners because they leave the nation-state intact. Alternate routes to peace have hitherto been made problematic, Butler claims, by ill-advised *prima facie* equating of critiques of Israel and Zionism with antisemitism. As made evident in her statements in the Bruce Robbins film *Some of My Best Friends Are Zionists* (2013), moreover, Butler had an arduous and even anguished journey toward embracing BDS and disentangling her identity from self-accusations of antisemitism and self-loathing.[31] Her personal historical struggle appears to inform her initial move to establish an authentically Jewish grounds for resisting this equation, but her testimony really involves using her Jewish identity performatively as a kind of weapon, mainly in front of non-Jews, against the vast majority of Jews, who happen to support the State of Israel. Just as she had done in her joint speech with Barghouti at Brooklyn College, so too elsewhere does Butler, as David Hirsh analyzes, perform herself as the ideal anti-Zionist minority Jew:

> This minority often mobilizes its Jewish identity, speaking loudly "as a Jew." In doing so, it seeks to erode and undermine the influence of the large majority of actual Jews in the name of an aesthetic, radical, diasporic and ethical, but largely self-constructed Judaism. . . . It tempts non-Jews to suspend their own political judgment as to what is, and what is not, antisemitic. The force of the "as a Jew" preface is to bear witness against the other Jews. It is based on the assumption that being Jewish gives you some kind of privileged insight into what is antisemitic and what is not—the claim to authority through identity substitutes for civil, rational debate. Antizionist Jews do not simply make their arguments and adduce evidence; they mobilize their

Jewishness to give themselves influence. They pose as courageous dissidents who stand up against the fearsome threat of mainstream Zionist power.[32]

Allied with this performance of herself as a model Jew who speaks "as a Jew" against most Jews, she conflates ideas with identities[33] and uses an eclectic mélange of modern Jewish thinkers whom she configures as resting outside the boundaries of pro-Zionist Jewish philosophy. At the center of her project, Butler marshals what she defines as a Jewish tradition of anti-Zionist diasporic voices: the messianic Marxist cultural critic Walter Benjamin, the Aristotelean[34] political thinker Hannah Arendt, the ethical philosopher Emmanuel Levinas, and the Holocaust writer Primo Levi. Apart from the bare fact that they are Jewish, these writers do not even remotely constitute an actual Jewish tradition inasmuch as they are not concerned with the normative issues, principles, or historical preoccupations that inform this Jewish tradition. In addition, she does not include thinkers from the rabbinical tradition. Further, as Russell Berman notes, "This provide[s] her own anti-Zionism with a false genealogy"—one that endeavors to misleadingly convince her audience that such rejection of a Jewish state constitutes a fundamental Jewish tradition. But this alternate "Jewish tradition" provides Butler and like-minded contemporary Jews ethically uncomfortable with Israeli state violence, and looking for a specifically Jewish basis for a parting of the waters (to paraphrase the title of her book ironically) between Jewishness and Zionism that thus obviates accusations of internalized antisemitism. This formulation, which exercises Butler so much that it almost appears to act as a disavowal, rests on the dubious and indeed fallacious premises that Jews cannot harbor anti-Jewish prejudice or, conversely, that Jewish opposition to the existence of Israel necessarily denotes antisemitism.

Alongside the so-called Jewish tradition she assembles, Butler positions the cultural critic Edward Said and the poet Mahmoud Darwish—who together symbolize the Palestinian Other with whom the newly minted Israeli Palestinian Jew must cohabit. Said and Darwish have already acknowledged their need, as members of the Palestinian diaspora, to cohabitate with Israeli Jews, whom they acknowledge as having the right to live in Israel/Palestine. For Butler, Said and Darwish serve to allegorize the hybrid identities and, presumably, the post-state existence that Palestinians and Jews will need to assemble and create together. At first glance it seems quixotic, ill-advised, and unfortunate that Butler does not include any of the major Jewish voices engaged in debating Zionism in the earlier twentieth century, but doing so would have forced her to engage with the multifaceted complexities of the Zionist idea rather than reduce it to a one-dimensional exemplar of the intrinsic evil of settler colonialism, an idea whose truth she treats as a given rather than a still very much open question that requires further investigation and deliberative debate.

Butler performs what she quite aptly calls this "impossible, necessary task," in chapter 1, where she analyzes Said analyzing Sigmund Freud analyzing Moses. Said, interpreting Freud's *Moses and Monotheism* (1939), expands on Freud's once-controversial claim that Moses was born an Egyptian who identified in a religious sense with the Hebrew people, rather than having been raised as an Egyptian but born a Hebrew who subsequently reclaimed his heritage. Said repositions Moses as an Arab Jewish prophet who founded Judaism and who, significantly, remained exilic and never entered the Promised Land. Moses therefore becomes the Arab-Egyptian-Jew who exemplifies this diasporic ethic of cohabitation under one postnational polity. But this formulation conveniently forgets that, according to Freud, the frustrated Israelites, angered by their separation from their beloved pantheon of Canaanite and Moabite gods, murdered Moses but then, feeling guilty for their sin against their father, revived and idealized his memory as their leader.[35] As Butler comments, Said calls on "the Jewish people to be mindful of their own experience of having been dispossessed of land and rights to forge an alliance with those who have been dispossessed by Israel."[36] This actually sounds like an anti-Zionist makeover of the Passover Haggadah—the latter of which traditionally (if inconveniently for Butler and other anti-Zionists) enjoins Jews to remember and to return to Jerusalem.[37] Like Butler, Said posits an idealistic vision of Israeli Jews and Palestinians as diasporic peoples whose "parallel histories" can generate peace and a sense of common purpose. However aspirational and noble, neither Middle Eastern politics nor Jewish or Palestinian Arab history can sustain this well-intentioned, if quixotic, construct. Rather, Butler and Said abandon complexity and nuance, and proffer to their audiences an ideal grounded in a division between good and evil, and a vision of transcendent justice that justifies the victory of the former over the latter.

Having assembled her requisite ideas and people—her Jewish tradition, her Palestinian Other, and her diasporic Moses as the prophetic Arab Jew who founds the binational ethos—Butler proceeds to outline her more specific propositions. Significantly, however, she makes no reference to historical anti-Zionists (with the exception of Martin Buber) or even to actual contemporary post-Zionist Israeli thinkers. One would have thought that the latter would have comprised an essential part of this mosaic, since Butler intends to banish other Israeli Jews from what they regard as the advantages of sovereign Jewish statehood.

But, through Butler, post-Zionist *Israeli* thinkers do execute a kind of backdoor Freudian return of the repressed. They end up literally relegated to footnotes, despite their extensive influence on her thinking throughout this book. Post-Zionist Israeli Jewish intellectuals are not canonical European thinkers, like the Jewish tradition she assembles, and not the exemplary Palestinian Other. Rather, they are Jewish and Israeli—and therefore, it would appear, inconvenient, embarrassing, or perhaps *necessarily* minor in her scheme of things. In brief, since Amnon Raz-Krakotzkin and Yehouda Shenhav are Israeli Jewish intellectuals who are products of the Zionist state, they must be sidelined and reduced to marginalia, and their influence on Butler suppressed. They are not polite or convenient intellectual company. As Gans notes, Raz-Krakotzkin's essay "Exile within Sovereignty" argues for an exilic interpretation of Israeli Jewish existence, while the sociologist Shenhav stresses the importance of Jewish-Arab hybridity in the Jewish identities of Mizrachi Jews, as well as the need, as Gans remarks, to critique the "Zionist movement for its Eurocentric marginalization of the non-Ashkenazi Jew."[38] This demotion—and the disavowed influence of these writers—symbolizes the *galut* status occupied by the Israeli Jew in the diasporic schema of *Parting Ways*, not to mention her reluctance to acknowledge unspeakable influences on her work. In brief, Butler shows that she conceives of herself as respectfully addressing American and, in addition, European audiences, but not the Israeli Jewish one that would be most impacted were her proposals ever to be realized in fact. They apparently do not signify except as pawns to be moved around this theoretical chess board, and she seems to regard their consent to the plans she formulates around them as beneath or beside consideration.

The Eternal Zion

Because of her political and ideological ambitions in *Parting Ways*, Butler ends up advancing static views of Jewishness that sound like the visions of Jewish diasporic identity held dear by late nineteenth-century Reform Judaism, where Jews, in order to assimilate and achieve acceptance, abandoned many Jewish rituals and focused rather on the universal ethical laws of the prophets.[39] Contradicting her admirable normative praxis of avoiding binary oppositional thinking, which characterizes her other writings about gender, sexuality, ethics, and power, she constructs a cartoon villain version of Zionism that has nothing to do with the variegated historical embodiments of Zionist ideas that might have complicated her unitary visions. She reduces Zionism to an ahistorical, one-dimensional cipher to bludgeon so that she can advance her argument. What the anti-Zionist and pro-BDS advocate Zachary Braiterman calls her "curious inattention to the Hegelian master-slave dialectic"[40] also seems unfortunate, since the book therefore flattens out dynamic historical contours and comes across as a one-dimensional utopian or—depending on one's perspective—dystopian project.

In brief, Butler writes a book about Zionism that erases Zionism—except as an entity that is coterminous with the state-sponsored violence of settler colonialism which, in a flourish of Jewish exceptionalism, Israel embodies. In addition, Braiterman comments that Butler attempts "to save Judaism by severing it from Zionism"—a move which "stands in mirror image to the form of political Zionism" that sought to rescue Jews by divorcing them from diasporic Judaism.[41] In *Song of Myself* Walt Whitman famously exclaimed: "Do I contradict myself? / Very well then, I contradict myself. / (I am large, I contain multitudes)."[42] This quotation applies as well to the long, capacious, multidimensional traditions of Jewish civilization. Zionist ethnonationalist identity believes in the Jewish right to national self-determination, while the post-Zionist Jewishness for which Butler advocates envisions a diasporic identity. But both are reasonable interpretations of Jewish experience, history, and identity that can and probably should exist side-by-side in mutual tolerance, instead of, as Butler does, attempting to eliminate the other as an exclusive strategy for Jewish existence.

But Butler cannot accept compromise or coexistence with political Zionism, not only because of what appears to be guilt by association but also because of its historical sins, which cannot be adequately redressed through living alongside the Palestinian Other in a two-state solution. The only route out of the legacies of the settler colonialism she attributes to Zionism involves correcting historical sins not only to the 1967 Six-Day War but also to the 1948 Arab-Israeli War, as this alone can put "an end to political Zionism" and to Israel as a sovereign Jewish state.[43] Butler otherwise does not fill in between the practical lines of her coloring book, and provides no detailed picture of what her "cohabitational" binationalistic polity would actually look like or how it would work in practice. As Seyla Benhabib notes, Butler's "ethics remain without normativity and her politics without historicity."[44]

Levinas and Arendt as Anti-Zionists

At the heart of *Parting Ways* lies not only Butler's morally problematic if passionately engaged treatment of the Holocaust and the lessons Jews have not but should draw from that cataclysmic disaster but also her extended encounter with Hannah Arendt and her arduous struggles with the pro-Zionist Jewish ethical philosopher Emmanuel Levinas. Levinas famously claims that what he calls the face—unlike the physical body—cannot be killed because, as Butler comments, "the face carries an interdiction against killing that cannot but bind the one who encounters that face and becomes subject to the interdiction the face conveys."[45] Beholding the face does not signify the actions or dispositions of a sovereign self toward the Other but rather a relational practice that, as Benhabib notes, "responds to an obligation that originates outside the subject,"[46] such as when a person responds tenderly to the distress of another human being or soothes a crying baby. But while such relational actions might ground primary ethics, they cannot produce the kind of normative ethical tradition in which Levinas, who distrusted state politics, evinces scant interest.

Normative ethics emerge from learning how to balance abstract moral rules against the complicated concrete situations and obligations that human beings confront under actual circumstances. While primary or relational ethics might be grounded in Levinas's encounter with the face, a comprehensive account of ethics must be able to do justice to the concrete as well as the universal or abstract Other. But Butler does not explain how her diasporic Jews are to reconcile primary ethical claims with abstract moral dicta without losing coherent ethical agency bound up in norms and abstract rules. As Benhabib perceptively and suggestively inquires, why does Butler resort to Levinas's foundational or primary ideas of the ethical to think critically about Jewishness and Zionism, since the latter exist in the domain of normative political ethics?[47]

As against Butler, Levinas admits that there are inescapable contradictions between relational ethics on the one hand and politics on the other. For example, he defended Israel in the wake of the Sabra and Shatila massacres in the Palestinian refugee camps in Lebanon under the protection of the IDF because of the conditions of war. Further, when asked whether Palestinians constituted the Other for Israelis, Levinas retorted sharply that

> my definition of the other is completely different. The other is the neighbor, who is not necessarily kin but who can be. . . . But if your neighbor attacks another neighbor or treats him unjustly, what

can you do? Then alterity takes on another character, in alterity we can find an enemy, or at least then we are faced with the problem of knowing who is right and who is wrong, who is just and who is unjust. There are people who are wrong.[48]

Of course Butler does not accept Levinas on this point, because doing so would mean giving credence to his Zionism as well as to acts of state-sponsored violence against those perceived as enemies. However, because she depends so heavily on his primary ethical notion of the face, she intertwines his concept of the infinite responsibility entailed in primary relational ethics with her idea of neighborliness (or encounter with the face) that, in her account, appears to place human beings in an uncertain, precarious, and unenviable predicament that hovers constantly on the verge of violence, bondage, or persecution:

> I am always possessed by an elsewhere, held hostage, persecuted, impinged upon against my will, and yet there is still this "I," or rather "me," who is being persecuted. To say that my "place" is already the place of another is to say that place itself is never singularly possessed and this question of cohabitation in the same place is unavoidable. It is in the light of this question of cohabitation that the question of violence emerges. Indeed, if I am persecuted, that is the sign that I am bound to the other. If I were not persecuted by this claim upon me, then I would not know responsibility at all.[49]

Butler appears to find herself persecuted by but bound to an inevitably sadomasochistic relation with the face to which she must retain allegiance to "know responsibility at all." But is this true? Does this constitute the only means to know responsibility, and what does this entail for the responsibilities of normative political or civic ethics? Beyond the personal relational ethics of the face, one has also the normative ethics of the public political sphere—and with it the ethical obligations to fight back, resist, and organize socially to battle against the Other as an enemy who is not a neighbor. Levinas argues for a responsible, judicious, even talmudic-like mediation between politics and ethics. But Butler, in contrast, ends up using Levinas's primary ethics against his politics.

If Butler casts aside normative ethics to read the theoretical anti-Zionist Levinas against the actual pro-Zionist Levinas, then she uses Arendt as the occasion to develop her own ideas of cohabitation. This happens specifically within her interpretation of Arendt's *Eichmann in Jerusalem: A Report on the Banality of Evil* (1963), where Butler gives cohabitation meanings that Arendt neither conveys nor intends to communicate in her work. Arendt had harshly condemned Adolf Eichmann as representing the kind of person who assumes the genocidal prerogative to determine who should or should not live in the world. Butler turns this observation, as well as Arendt's comments about the irreducible necessity for plurality—which she defines as the differences and sameness that make political life possible—into the idea of "cohabitation."[50] For Arendt, plurality denotes the speech and actions that human beings use to narrate and explain themselves as actors in social worlds, as such stories convey not only their humanity but also their generalizable specificity. Curiously but significantly, in contrast, Butler scrupulously avoids the social dimensions of speech and action in her account of cohabitation. The "dispersing of self that follows from that encounter" with the Other is silent and, indeed, presocial.[51] In brief, neither with Levinas nor with Arendt does Butler offer a political vision of how Palestinian Jews and Palestinian Arabs are actually going to cohabit as self-narrating and self-explaining social and political subjects. This absence means that Butler does not or cannot address how they could do so and produce stories that would manage peaceful cohabitation rather than endemic chaos, enmity, and violence.

Primo Levi and Holocaust Commemoration in Israel

In "Primo Levi for the Present," her chapter on what she construes as the abuses of Holocaust memory in contemporary Israel, Butler makes the self-evident claim that one should not "call upon the Shoah as a way of legitimating arbitrary and lethal Israeli violence against civilian populations."⁵² But apart from such verities, Butler does not use this occasion to interpret Levi—the author of the seminal works *Survival in Auschwitz* (1947) and *The Drowned and the Saved* (1986). Rather, she employs his moral qualms about the abuse of Holocaust discourse to invalidate Israel and its practices around the Shoah. Yet, just as Butler distorted Arendt's notion of cohabitation and Levinas's primary ethics of the face, so too here does she misconstrue Levi. While he defended the Palestinians against injustices perpetrated against them, Butler transforms him into a voice claiming that the founding rationale and ongoing existence of Israel are mired in moral and historical fraudulence and criminality—a militaristic state masquerading as a democracy. But in truth, as Butler herself admits, Levi "clearly valued the founding of Israel as a refuge for Jews from the Nazi destruction" and took a stand not against Israel itself but rather "against some Israeli military actions."⁵³

She cites Idith Zertal's *Israel's Holocaust and the Politics of Nationhood* (2005), which argues that Holocaust remembrances marked moments of collective dispossession or violence for Israeli Jews: when Jewish European refugees arrived after World War II, during the 1948 War, when the nation felt imperiled in subsequent wars, and at the present, when Israel faces the existential threat that Iran will acquire nuclear weapons.⁵⁴ But while an anti-Israel discourse persists that regards the Holocaust as unfinished business, and while, in contrast, former prime minister Benjamin Netanyahu and others regularly abuse Holocaust remembrance for political advantage, Israel does not (nor should it) use the Holocaust to justify every policy or military action against the Palestinians. Indeed, Israel downplayed Holocaust remembrance until the Eichmann trial in 1961, which underscored personal testimonies of victims, but it was not until 1980 that the national curriculum placed emphasis on the Shoah. At that point, school trips to Auschwitz became common. Nothing supports Butler's claim that Israelis and the political culture of Israel are currently consumed by the Holocaust, even though existential anxieties about the nuclear ambitions of Iran specifically and eliminationist rhetoric more generally run high.

Notwithstanding these facts, Butler contends that Israel, founded on the traumatic wounds of the Shoah, licenses defensive actions and censors speech in the name of those traumas. In other words, speech that declares that negative responses to Israel are not about antisemitism but rather about Israeli state violence are silenced under the sign of the Holocaust, which provides a kind of perpetual shield against justified criticism of Israel and of Zionism as the founding discourse of the state. Butler argues that anti-Zionist voices must be heard to confront Israeli state-sponsored violence on its own terms. In addition, she contends that Israel has, as a national project, learned precisely the wrong lesson from the Shoah. For instance, self-defense of the nation-state constitutes the traumatic reinjury necessitated by the founding problematic of creating the nation-state in the first place, particularly since doing so caused, through settler colonialism, the dispossession and statelessness of the Palestinians.

For Butler the solution does not reside in Israeli Jewish acknowledgment of the trauma inflicted by the Nakba, or in compensation around that disaster. Rather, the only remedy involves the drastic action of dissolving the nation-state and living in a stateless present. As Butler asserts, "Paradoxically, only by allowing the Shoah to become past can we begin to derive those principles of justice and equality and respect for life and land on the basis of that experience."[55] Butler becomes exercised about the traumatic wounds involved in the displacement of hundreds of thousands of Palestinians from their ancestral homes because these injuries are unfolding into the indefinite present. The trauma inflicted by the Nakba has not been addressed, resolved or, certainly, commemorated as part of public memory in the fashion of the Shoah. However, if Butler appears to show little concern for the Mizrachi Jews displaced from their ancient homelands or for refugees from the Shoah, that is because their traumas have become historical and historicized. For Butler, it is necessary to "rethink and rewrite the history of the founding of the Israel state" in order to "unlink the way in which the Nazi genocide continues to act as a permanent justification for this state."[56]

Conclusion

As against Butler's all-encompassing allegiances to an ahistorical anti-imperialism, Seyla Benhabib insightfully observes that "the age of innocence for the Palestinian resistance movement has ended, just as it has ended for the idealist visions of early Zionism."[57] Realism must now take center stage, and decisions based on rational calculations of cause and effect, and historical and political facts, must enter into serious discussions of the Israel/Palestine conflict. The BDS movement that informs *Parting Ways* has a coercive character based on the unaccountable fantasies that Jews should accept a return to the diaspora (and, with it, the ghetto) and that Palestinians, who should be the numerical majority, will somehow not choose to politically, ethnically, religiously, and culturally subjugate Palestinian Jews. The mythical journey Butler takes toward an idiosyncratic diasporic inwardness should occasion a serious examination of the relationship between abstract theoretical speculation on the one hand and the responsibility entailed in making policy recommendations on the other. Forwarding claims of nonviolence that bear no relation to facts, Butler, like other BDS advocates, does not provide a roadmap to the hard choices involved in peace but rather, ironically, promulgates an insidious recipe for endemic, catastrophic warfare and the destruction of value and social structure for all concerned.

CONCLUSION

QUEERING THE FUTURE OF THE ISRAEL/PALESTINE CONFLICT

Postmodernism and Queer BDS Academic Activists

This book has explored the work of five influential pro-BDS queer academic activists—Sarah Schulman, Jasbir Puar, Angela Davis, Dean Spade, and Judith Butler—each of whom exemplify different ideological and critical practices around anti-Zionism.

In her rambling journey to Israel, Europe, and New York, Schulman has recourse to a deceptively facile prose that distorts, elides contradictions, and flattens out complex social-historical realities, as when she implicitly claims the homophobia faced by her and her Palestinian comrades is essentially the same; presents Tel Aviv as a grotesque caricature; and seriously suggests that the irksome Jewish "problem" of Israel's existence be solved by having 6.9 million Israeli Jews move to New York City, where they will remain ethical by never again wielding state power. For her part, Puar boldly disregards fact, cause and effect, and logic in pursuit of her assemblagelike conviction that, through stunting and maiming, not to mention harvesting Palestinians' organs and giving Israeli Jewish lesbians and gays rights so that they can produce children to fight Palestinians, Israel stands as the most pernicious nation on earth. And in her particular iteration of Israel demonization, Davis instrumentalizes intersectionality theory to argue that Black Americans and Palestinians face the same struggle against racist oppression, and that differences of history, religion, ethnicity, and demography do not matter, even if Hamas steals Black Africans' organs to help finance their interminable wars against Israel. For Spade, shameless lies, mischaracterizations, and the assaultive tactics of public disruption and intimidation serve the greater good of reducing Israel to a hateful public disgrace. Finally, Butler wants, in the unique case of Israel, to unwind the spool of history, discard the two-state solution as countenancing the Original Sin of Israeli settler colonialism, and have Jewish Palestinians live under majoritarian rule by Palestinian Arabs, where peace and amity rather than war and violence will somehow materialize.

In the meantime, all these intellectuals otherwise claim to fly under the banner of postmodernism: They evince ironic skepticism about grand narratives and ideologies, repudiate binary oppositions, and describe knowledge claims and value systems not as absolutes, but rather as contingent and socially conditioned products of historical, political, economic, or cultural discourses. They assail universalist ideas of objective reality, morality, truth, human nature, reason, science, language, and social progress. They espouse a field of post-knowledge that relishes the pluralistic, the irreverent, and the performative, as well as the self-conscious and the self-referential. They perceive moral and epistemological relativism as an article of faith.

As *Queering Anti-Zionism* has made clear, these postmodern tenets inform their work with one singular exception: Israel.

These critics desert postmodernism with the particular form of Israeli so-called homonationalism they call pinkwashing. They view the Jewish state as a one-dimensional master narrative that represents nothing but the dystopian, negative, and absolute. In their work Israel is an irredeemable black hole—an empty cipher that lacks value, positive meaning, complex historical truths, or real people living in the multivalent situatedness of ordinary human existence. This absolutism seems all the more puzzling given the complexities inherent in the Israel/Palestine situation. Yet Amos Oz notes, in *Dear Zealots: Letters from a Divided Land* (2018), that as "the questions grow harder and more complicated, people yearn for simpler answers, one-sentence answers, answers that point unhesitatingly to a culprit who can be blamed for all our suffering, answers that promise that if we only eradicate the villains, all our troubles will vanish."[1]

This anti-postmodern refusal to complicate, or qualify, their critical narratives around Israel stems in part from their view of the Jewish state as an intellectual object of complete evil. But it also emerges from the BDS credo of not debating or, more important, engaging with plural perspectives on Israel/Palestine that reside outside the domain of their belief system, which allows only quasireligious conversion to BDS, not persuasion, compromise, or encounters with contrasting viewpoints that might generate new knowledge. Thus the BDS movement reproduces not only a master narrative but also the elisions that censor inconvenient truths and mute multivalent voices. While Palestinians, Israelis, and, in particular, Palestinian LGBTQ individuals, suffer in their discrete fashions from the failure to resolve the conflict, the BDS narrative keeps the conflict not only alive but also frozen in time and space as an interminable, remorseless, and demoralizing war of attrition.

Disorienting the Israel/Palestine Opposition in *Oriented*

In contrast to this frozen and exhausting ideological warfare, the 2015 documentary film *Oriented*, directed by British director Jake Witzenfeld in collaboration with the Israeli Palestinian group Qambuta, assumes a genuinely postmodernist perspective on the conflict from an Israeli Palestinian point of view that engenders complex and humane knowledge. As an ironic consequence, the film creates a more convincing critique of Israeli policies and politics than that generated in the works of BDS activist academics, who produce disquieting reservations in an impartial reader through their totalizing interpretations, strategies of denunciation, contempt for people and facts on the ground, disavowals, and exclusions and distortions of critical information in their discourses.

Oriented follows the adventures of three Palestinian Israeli gay friends—Khader, Fadi, and Naeem who live in Tel Aviv. Khader, from a prominent and on the whole accepting Muslim family, lives with his Israeli Jewish boyfriend, David. Fadi, a committed Palestinian nationalist, finds himself falling in love with an Israeli Zionist against his better judgment. Naeem, fearful of violence and rejection, nonetheless successfully confronts his family with the truth about his sexuality. They are determined to "change their reality." The documentary revolves around their conversations and travels in different environments, tracking how they gain inspiration to create a nonviolent resistance movement called Qambuta, through which they fight for gender, sexuality, and nationalist equality.[2]

This film creates dramatic tension by interrogating the oppositions that animate the Israeli landscape—the discrete and mutually exclusive spaces, Israel and Palestine/the Occupied Territories—juxtaposed against the Palestinian citizens of Israel, whose existence becomes an explicit problematic around the assumed complete separation of the two societies. As such, the documentary questions tenets of Israeli nationalism, and the symbols, narratives, and territorial and historical conflicts that separate the two peoples.

Palestinian/Queer/Israeli

Through exploring the lives of gay Palestinian citizens of Israel, *Oriented* undoes the logic underpinning Israeli sexual utopianism. The documentary focuses on the tensions occasioned for those who are gay, Palestinian, and citizens of Israel, representing their lives as animated by contrastive opportunities, exigencies, and desires. Significantly, however, through the postmodern lens of this documentary, the lives of the men depicted are more ambiguous and multifaceted than any series of dualities can encompass.

For instance, near the beginning of the documentary, Khader, one of the three principal protagonists, delivers a talk at the Tel Aviv Municipal LGBTQ Center, which has invited him to discuss what it means to be gay and Palestinian in Israel. In ironic recognition of the rhetoric implicit in this topic, Khader relates an amusing story about a BBC journalist who contacted him and wanted to write about Palestinian gay men and the presumed tragedy of their lives. Humor results from the disjunction between the way Khader distances himself from the tropes of the oppressed gay Palestinian and the reporter's search for a putatively authentic expression of gay Palestinian tragedy. Khader has a familial experience of what he claims as unconditional love and acceptance, in addition to his romantic relationship with an Israeli Jewish immigrant. Both serve to problematize discourses that simply portray Israel as modern and LGBTQ-friendly in contrast to a more homophobic and repressive Palestinian culture.

While distancing himself from the discourses of the Palestinian victim from a homophobic familial background, Khader defines himself as the representative of the new Palestinian he intends to present in his talk. At the moment he aligns his gay sexuality with the ethnic/national category of Palestinian; however, a Jewish Israeli member of the audience quizzes Khader about the official status he enjoys in Israel, asking him why he identifies himself as Palestinian rather than as Israeli. Palestinian citizens of Israel possess blue identity cards and thus can travel throughout Israel/Palestine, with the exception of Gaza. Residents of the West Bank, in contrast, possess orange identity cards that deny them Israeli citizenship and freedom of movement or other sociopolitical benefits. They must have passes and go through the checkpoints that control the border between Israel and the West Bank, as well as the towns within the West Bank. The audience member questions his identification as Palestinian in an Israeli space, given that Khader enjoys the advantages of Israeli citizenship. In brief, Khader entered the welcoming space of the LGBTQ Center speaking as a gay subject but was challenged the moment he brought his Palestinian identity to the fore.

Critically, the disjunction between Palestinian/Israeli does not represent an idiosyncratic feature of this particular moment but rather colors the entire documentary. Gay and lesbian Palestinians are acceptable and visible to the extent that they quiet their Palestinian identities. In an Israeli Jewish context, they speak only to rearticulate the rhetoric of the tragic queer Palestinian subject within an oppressive Arab culture. And yet despite these tropes, Khadar lays claim to belonging in this Israeli space and, like Fadi and Naeem, feels the genuine appeal of Western-style gay liberation. By responding that he has a blue identity card, he reaffirms his status as a citizen of Israel and his right to speak of his gay Palestinian identity through the power structures that had endeavored to question him. More important, he underscores the historical ties between his family and the city of Jaffa before the establishment of the State of Israel, when Palestinian/Arab was an unchallenged identity category. Thus Khadar performs the meaning of his embodiment as a new Palestinian/Israeli subject that makes "gay" and "Palestinian" mutually exclusive in an Israeli Jewish space. This discursive push and pull culminates at the end of the exchange when he uses the metaphor of Israeli Jews and Palestinians being "stuck in one another's asses"[3] to convey the tense, intermeshed, and intrusive character of Israeli Palestinian/Jewish cohabitation.

Throughout the documentary, travel to diverse spaces—including the village homes of their families, Berlin, Tel Aviv cafes, apartments, and Amman, Jordan—illustrates how context informs what they express about the significance and meaning of their lives. For instance, Khadar performs acts of belonging to Israel and coming from an accepting family within the Israeli Jewish space of the LGBTQ Center. However, a very different picture emerges when he, along with Fadi and Naeem, go to an underground concert in Amman, Jordan. There Khadar and his friends speak Arabic mixed with English, which suggests transcendence of local differences, as the film does not elsewhere use English except for a scene in which a female Palestinian Israeli friend counsels Fadi to embrace personal happiness over his politicized objections to falling in love with a gay Zionist.

Khadar, who seems otherwise mostly affirmative about Israel, appears comfortable speaking in Hebrew. Yet in Amman he makes a significant statement about the use of Arabic in achieving a positive sense of Palestinian selfhood. He uses the English verb "should" in the demotic clause "you're living how you should be living"[4] This usage marks the use of Arabic in the context of Amman, Jordan, as the principal language that communicates an authentic Palestinian life. In turn it conveys an explicit critique of linguistic discourse in Israel where, when the film was made, Arabic was a de jure language on par with Hebrew, but a de facto minority language with lower status in Jewish Israeli society. Along with exclusion from national symbols and narratives, this linguistic imbalance alienates Arabic-speaking experiences and renders Tel Aviv, the presumed "Gay Capital of the World," an ambivalent space—a dystopian utopia that both repels and attracts Israeli/Palestinians.

Khader avers that "there are a lot of exceptions" to the stereotypes and "a lot of freedoms" in Tel Aviv, thus reproducing gay utopian views of Tel Aviv; but his use of qualifiers introduces the sense of constriction and limitation, as seen in his ironic imitation of an Israeli Jewish voice saying, "You must be one of us."[5] Tel Aviv and Israel loom as problematic spaces that, however progressive regarding LGBTQ rights, constrict Palestinians by demanding they adopt an Israeli gay script. In contrast, Amman represents an alternative space, which becomes a counter-site to Tel Aviv for Khader, where gay Palestinian subjects can challenge Israeli tropes of gay liberation. In Amman, LGBTQ Palestinians can dream about personal happiness, living in sync with an imagined community of other queer Arabic speakers, where they can escape before returning to Israel.

The characters further elaborate on the alienating qualities of Israel during a discussion in David and Khader's Tel Aviv apartment in 2014. They are in the midst of an IDF reprisal attack on Hamas, which had fired Grad rockets into southern Israel. More than two thousand Palestinian casualties resulted from that war.[6] Khader provides a gloomy account about the power imbalance that causes the impasse between Palestinians and Israelis. Khader voices his disillusionment over the possibilities of future change. But Fadi expresses hope that Israel can transform into a civic nation-state, where distinctions on the basis of ethnic identity are irrelevant. Fadi references the United States, which he naively represents as an ideal melting pot. Applied to Israel, Fadi says, a civic polity would be possible only through refusing to define Israel as a Jewish state. Through reconstructing Israeli nationalism, a more equal dialogue and cohabitation would be possible. Fadi not only lays claim to belonging to

Israel but also rests his hopes on the prospect of change. As he repeatedly insists, "Never, never give up."[7]

While Fadi expresses hope about future political transformation, Khader remains skeptical. For Khader, a one-state nonethnic polity is an illusion that will never materialize because Israel won't allow a non-Jewish majority to emerge. Fadi optimistically represents his determination as something that can make a real difference in the political future of Israel, but Khader feels Fadi is making an empty gesture that substitutes words for actions. While other Palestinians are killed in Gaza, they are sitting around discussing politics instead of taking action. Earlier, Khader had imagined Palestinian/Jewish cohabitation through the metaphor of being "stuck in one another's asses." Here, the image conveys suffocating intimacy between silent partners who might be glued to one another but can neither enjoy nor disentangle themselves from this scenario. There is no one to speak to—no genuine partner for peace from either side: not from Hamas, which instigated the rocket attacks in Gaza, and not from the Israeli government, which responded in kind, albeit in defense. Hamas and the IDF, speaking the language of rocket fire, silence the human voices of everyone else.

The sitting room in David and Khader's Tel Aviv apartment functions as a microcosm for the incompatible multiple spaces that constitute Israel. Fadi asserts that he belongs to Israel through his political act of hope, where Palestinian agency will contribute to a more meaningful and beautiful future, while Khader experiences disenchanted frustration that articulates his sense of inertness and capture. The concert in Amman represented the transient, precarious, but joyous place of possibilities and futurity; whereas for Khader Israel represents the grave: the place of ghostly death for the thousands of Palestinians killed in Gaza, and also the place that checks or arrests Palestinians and keeps Israeli/Palestinians from achieving more inclusive social and political futures. The attachment to Israel becomes an alienated belonging to a home that cannot ever serve as a true home.

Khader and his Israeli Jewish boyfriend, David, attempt to break with this conflicted and confining space during their three-month holiday stay in Berlin. However, when the option arises for Khader to move permanently to Berlin with David, he ultimately decides to remain in Israel. The main reason is the waning of Khader and David's erotic passion, which turns their romantic attachment into an intimate friendship of mutual regard and respect. Increasingly aware that beneath the utopian landscape of Berlin lies entrenched European Islamophobia, Khader is also cognizant of his longing for his sense of home, however baffled and incomplete. Khader says of Israel that "it looks like I'll stay here for a little—for another go at living in this hell."[8] This is perhaps the strongest manifestation of how Israeli gay discourses both entice and constrain queer Palestinians like Khader; they are bound up in a state of alienated belonging to an arrested space of stasis where they cannot attain a sense of complete belonging and ease. Khader, noticing that there are no flags from Islamic nations at the Berlin Gay Pride parade, says that to give meaning to their lives they must work toward contributing toward a reality where Islamic countries fly their flags at Gay Pride parades and Israel transforms into an interethnic democratic polity where all enjoy equality and peaceful coexistence.

Coda

Queering Anti-Zionism has critiqued the anti-postmodernism of BDS activist academics around Israel. We have seen how this movement jeopardizes academic freedom and how it rejects dialogue that aims at creative resolution and resilient adaptation to constrained circumstances. Like *Oriented*, this text has endeavored to respect the uncertain, the multifaceted, the complicated, and the ambiguous. Khader, Fadi, and Naeem express an affective attachment to Israel and its heady atmosphere of gay liberation, even as the film simultaneously represents an alienated bond that is tenuous, complicated, and, at particular times, a source of distress and dis-identification. But this admixture of stances models the complexities of these gay Palestinian lives and refuses to reject or reduce them to something politically or ideologically unacceptable and, therefore, beneath analytical consideration. This one-sided reductionism characterizes the stance of BDS critics on homonationalism, Israel, and pinkwashing. For the Palestinian/Israeli gay men in the film, Israel constitutes an imagined space of juxtapositions where they feel intimate and unmoored, liberated and constrained, and enabled and disempowered. They live within identities marked by incongruities and tensions in which personal experience is always more nuanced and complicated than the political ideologies that attempt to articulate and constrain it. Analysis that classifies social practice as compelled to fall on one or another side of an unbridgeable divide risks reproducing silences, master narratives, and exclusions, while ignoring the numerous realities that construct multiple identities, including those informing the lives of LGBTQ Israeli Palestinians working for a more capacious future not only in Israel/Palestine but also throughout the Middle East.

NOTES

Prologue: My Education in Homophobia, Anti-Zionism, and Extremism

1 The FBI defines a hate crime as a "criminal offense against a person or property motivated in whole or in part by an offender's bias against a race, religion, disability, sexual orientation, ethnicity, gender, or gender identity." https://www.fbi.gov/investigate/civil-rights/hate-crimes. Accessed June 6, 2020. I have subsequently considered that the component of the hate crime that focused on anti-Zionism was omitted because it is not included in categories recognized within hate crime legislation.
2 See Janet L. Freedman, "For the Women's Studies Association, the BDS Vote Was Over Before It Began." https://forward.com/sisterhood/325637/for-the-womens-studies-association-the-bds-vote-was-over-before-it-began/. November 30, 2015. Accessed June 9, 2020. As Freedman describes from her own perspective in this article, the attack on academic freedom embodied by the NWSA's BDS resolution left me robbed of a community that had long nourished me.
3 Geoffrey R. Stone, "Aims of Education 2016 Address." https://college.uchicago.edu/student-life/aims-education-address-2016-geoffrey-r-stone. Accessed June 9, 2020.
4 Kenneth S. Stern, *The Conflict Over the Conflict: The Israel/Palestine Campus Debate* (Toronto: University of Toronto Press, 2020), 18. I am indebted to Stern for many ideas concerning pedagogical methods for teaching the conflict.
5 James E. Waller, "Our Ancestral Shadow: Hate and Human Nature in Evolutionary Psychology." Paper presented at the Conference to Establish the Field of Hate Studies. Spokane, WA. March 19, 2004.

6 See Michael A. Hogg, Janice R. Adelman, and Robert D. Blagg, "Religion in the Face of Uncertainty: An Uncertainty-Identity Theory Account of Religiousness," *Personality and Social Psychology Review* 14, no. 1 (2010): 72–83.
7 Ibid., 75.
8 See, for example, USACBI (US Campaign for the Academic and Cultural Boycott of Israel; usacbi.org), PACBI (Palestinian Campaign for the Academic and Cultural Boycott of Israel; bdsmovement.net), and Canary Mission (canarymission.org).
9 Stern, *Conflict Over the Conflict*, 184.
10 See American Association of University Professors (AAUP), September 2007 Statement, "Freedom in the Classroom." https://www.aaup.org/report/freedom-classroom. Accessed June 11, 2020.

Introduction: Pinkwashing, Israel/Palestine Campus Activism, and Academic Freedom

1 This op-ed subsequently went by the title "Israel and Pinkwashing."
2 See Sarah Schulman. "A Documentary Guide to Pinkwashing," *Huffpost*, December 6, 2011; updated February 2, 2016. According to Schulman, in "April 2010 the Bay-Area organization QUIT (Queers Undermining Israeli Terrorism) used the word 'pinkwashing' as a twist on 'greenwashing,' when companies claim to be eco-friendly in order to make profit." Dunya Alwan attributes the term to Ali Abunimah, editor of *The Electronic Intifada*, who said at a meeting in 2010, "We won't put up with Israel whitewashing, greenwashing or pinkwashing." https://www.huffingtonpost.com/sarah-schulman/israel-pinkwashing_b_1132369.html. Accessed June 26, 2020.
3 See R. Amy Elman, "BDS & the Queer Appropriation of Pinkwashing." AEN Pamphlet Series, No. 6, April 2019.
4 Neil MacFarquhar, "Gay Muslims Find Freedom, of a Sort, in the U.S.," *New York Times*, November 7, 2007. https://www.nytimes.com/2007/11/07/us/07gaymuslim.html?.?mc=aud_dev&ad-keywords=auddevgate&gclid=Cj0KCQjwnJaKBhDgARIsAHmvz6e3Q0CFq4hqYsOzJZ2zdU63vWXaM7lCf5WB2MxVcV2_y7z8s1m2Kl0aAjOZEALw_wcB&gclsrc=aw.ds. Accessed September 18, 2021.
5 Sarah Schulman, "Israel and 'Pinkwashing,'" *New York Times*, November 22, 2011. https://www.nytimes.com/2011/11/23/opinion/

pinkwashing-and-israels-use-of-gays-as-a-messaging-tool.html. Accessed December 31, 2021.
6. The list of countries that, as of 2020, have legalized marriage equality or same-sex civil unions/domestic partnership benefits is impressive and suggests that the globe is increasingly divided between pro-West, gay-friendly "modern" states and "non-modern" states that define themselves in part through their often-harsh discrimination against LGBTQ people. "Countries Where Gay Marriage Is Legal," *World Population Review*. https://worldpopulationreview.com/country-rankings/countries-where-gay-marriage-is-legal.
7. Katherine Franke, "Dating the State: The Moral Hazards of Winning Gay Rights," *Columbia Human Rights Law Review* 44, no. 1 (2012).
8. Stern, *Conflict Over the Conflict*. 184.
9. See Johann Neem, "The Subtle Erosion of Academic Freedom," *Inside Higher Ed*, April 16, 2019. https://www.insidehighered.com/views/2019/04/16/three-subtle-forces-weakening-academic-freedom-opinion. Accessed June 26, 2020.
10. See, for one example, "China's Global Threat to Human Rights." *Human Rights Watch*, World Report, 2020. In Xinjiang Uyghur Autonomous Region, authorities subject predominantly Muslim ethnic groups to intrusive surveillance, arbitrary detention, and forced indoctrination. From early 2017, after the Xinjiang government had enacted a regulation enforcing so-called de-extremification, an estimated one million Uyghurs, Kazakhs, and other ethnic minority people were sent to internment camps. Also see "The Uyghar American Association: Democracy, Human Rights, and Self-Determination for the Uighar People of East Turkestan." https://www.uyghuraa.org. Accessed June 19, 2020. The website registers a not-uncommon frustration among groups of people across the world who are subject to gross human rights abuses that the Israel/Palestine conflict receives the lion's share of attention. It notes that, "rather than arguing over the rights and wrongs of Palestine, responsible journalists should question its importance by exploring the other, much more destructive, conflicts around the world. We should do more than satisfy lazy narratives and reinforce divisions, and the best way to do that is to stop exaggerating a few conflicts and ignoring the inconvenient rest." Also see Jane Perlez, "China Wants the World to Stay Silent on Muslim Camps. It's Succeeding," *New York Times*, September 25, 2019. The article notes that, "backed by its diplomatic and economic might, China has largely

succeeded in quashing criticism. Chinese officials have convinced countries to support Beijing publicly on the issue, most notably Muslim ones in Africa, Asia and the Middle East." https://www.nytimes.com/2019/09/25/world/asia/china-xinjiang-muslim-camps.html. Accessed June 22, 2020.

11 I am indebted to Amy Elman for these insights into what amounts to the sadomasochistic pleasures associated with perpetuating this conflict. In this connection, see R. Amy Elman, "Pinkwashing Antisemitism: The Origins of Queer Anti-Israel Discourse," in *Poisoning the Wells: Antisemitism in Contemporary America*, ed. Corinne E. Blackmer and Andrew Pessin (New York: ISGAP, 2021).

12 See Scholars at Risk Network, https://www.scholarsatrisk.org. Accessed June 27, 2020.

13 Cary Nelson, *Israel Denial: Anti-Zionism, Anti-Semitism, & the Faculty Campaign Against the Jewish State* (Washington, DC/ Bloomington, IN: Academic Engagement Network/Indiana University Press, 2019), 25–26. By "micro-boycotts," Nelson refers to those manifold incidents of subtly punishing pro-Israel professors, such as denying them grants, tenure, promotion, other professional advancements, and, for their students, refusing to write letters of recommendation pertaining to study in Israel or Israel-related topics.

14 Olivia B. Waxman, "How the Nazi Regime's Pink Triangle Was Repurposed for LGBTQ Pride," *Time*, May 31, 2018. https://time.com/5295476/gay-pride-pink-triangle-history/. Accessed January 3, 2022.

15 Karuna Jaggar, "Think Before You Pink: Stop the Distraction," *Huffington Post*, October 1, 2014; updated December 6, 2017. Accessed January 3, 2022. This article provides a detailed analysis of the fraud, concealment, and condescending gender stereotypes used in breast cancer cause marketing.

16 Cary Nelson, "Pinkwashing," in *Dreams Deferred: A Concise Guide to the Israeli-Palestinian Conflict & the Movement to Boycott Israel* (Bloomington: Indiana University Press, 2016), 267.

17 Schulman, "A Documentary Guide."

18 "Full Text of Netanyahu's Speech at the 2016 UN General Assembly," *Times of Israel*, September 22, 2016. https://www.timesofisrael.com/netanyahus-full-remarks-at-un-general-assembly/. Accessed June 13, 2020.

19 Corinne E. Blackmer, "The Real Pinkwashers," *Algemeiner*, April 22, 2016. This article analyzes the difference between those who champion LGBTQ Israeli rights, often to the chagrin and outrage of left-wing

Israeli queers who are pro-Palestinian, and those who use them cynically, opportunistically, and in bad faith to make invidious comparisons for their own political advantage.

20 Quoted in Michael Luango, "Pinkwashing Issues," Columbia Law School Review. https://nanopdf.com/download/pinkwashing-issues-columbia-law-school_pdf. Accessed November 16, 2018.

21 Matti Friedman, "Amir Ohana Is Gay and Right-Wing. How Far Can He Go in Israel?" *New York Times*, June 6, 2019. https://www.nytimes.com/2019/06/06/opinion/amir-ohana-israel-gay.html. Accessed June 18, 2020.

22 Lisa Duggan, "The New Homonormativity: The Sexual Politics of Neoliberalism," in *Materializing Democracy: Toward a Revitalized Cultural Politics*, ed. Russ Castronovo and Dana D. Nelson (Durham, NC: Duke University Press, 2002), 175–96. Duggan defines this term as the privileging of white, cis-gendered, masculine, gay men at the expense of people of color, butch lesbians, transgender people, and rural, fat-positive, or disabled gays. She also critiques the emphasis on marriage equality as privatizing, domesticating, and depoliticizing queers through putative imitation of a heteronormative monogamous ideal.

23 Ironically, the vast majority of Islamic religious scholars follow the homophobic interpretation of the story of Sodom and Gomorrah first formulated by the Jewish Neoplatonist philosopher Philo of Alexandria, who lived around the same time as Jesus of Nazareth. Unlike Jesus, who followed the traditional view that inhospitality and insular arrogance constituted the sin of Sodom, Philo adopted a sexualized view of this and other stories and laws in the Hebrew Bible. As the Church Fathers read his work, Philo's hatred of same-sex relations spread throughout the Roman Empire and, eventually, to Islamic lands.

24 See *alQaws for Sexuality & Gender Diversity in Palestinian Society*. http://alqaws.org/. Accessed June 19, 2020. Their mission statement reads: "At individual, community, and societal levels, alQaws disrupts sexual and gender-based oppression, and challenges regulation of our sexualities and bodies, whether patriarchal, capitalist, or colonial. We work collaboratively to transform Palestinian society's perspectives on gender and sexual diversity, homosexuality and LGBTQ issues, and to struggle for broader social justice. Our locally-based programs support and advocate for diverse LGBTQ individuals and their families, create opportunities that inspire youth to become community leaders, open spaces for diverse communities at local and national levels, develop engaging and relevant

educational materials to train civil society organizations, movements, and counseling professionals, and challenge social norms and common misperceptions with far-reaching innovative media initiatives."

25 See Muslims for Progressive Values, https://www.mpvusa.org/sexual-diversity. Accessed June 19, 2020. Also see "Audacity in Adversity: LGBTQ Activism in the Middle East and North Africa." *Human Rights Watch*, 2018. https://www.hrw.org/report/2018/04/16/audacity-adversity/lgbt-activism-middle-east-and-north-africa. Accessed June 19, 2020.

26 See Brian Whitaker, *Unspeakable Love: Gay and Lesbian Life in the Middle East* (Oakland: University of California Press, 2006) and Alina Dain Sharon, "Israel and Arab Countries Are Miles Apart on LGBTQ Rights," *Outward Magazine*. http://www.outwordmagazine.com/inside-outword/glbt-news/1239-israel-and-arab-countries-are-miles-apart-on-lgbt-rights. Accessed June 27, 2018. Both provide informed, in-depth discussions of the situation for gay Arabs and Israelis.

27 The relation between acceptance of gay people and democratic institutions might be correlative rather than causal. The most important of these attributes are a strong civil society, freedom of speech and association, an independent judicial system, the rule of law, and collaboration among different human rights social movements.

28 See "LGBT Rights in Palestine." https://en.wikipedia.org/wiki/LGBT_rights_in_the_State_of_Palestine. Accessed September 17, 2021.

29 Toi Staff, "High Court Extends Surrogacy Rights to Gay Couples, Single Men." *Times of Israel*, February 27, 2020. https://www.timesofisrael.com/high-court-extends-surrogacy-rights-to-gay-couples/. Accessed June 13, 2020. Prior to this ruling, which the Knesset had to ratify within one year, gay male couples had to go to the considerable expense and trouble of obtaining overseas surrogacy services.

30 Ilan Lior, "In Unprecedented Ruling, Israeli Court Prohibits Discrimination of Transgender Employees." *Haaretz*. June 9, 2015. Accessed December 31, 2021.

31 For a further explanation of Israeli annexation, with maps, see Oliver Holmes, "What Would Israeli Annexing the West Bank Mean?" *Guardian*, June 9, 2020. https://www.theguardian.com/world/2020/jun/09/what-would-israel-annexing-the-west-bank-mean. Accessed June 20, 2020.

32 Quoted in Corinne E. Blackmer, "Why I Am a Proud, Queer, Jewish 'Pinkwasher,'" *Algemeiner*, April 7, 2016.

33 Agence France-Presse, "Three Shot Dead at Gay Center in Tel Aviv," *New York Times*, August 1, 2009. https://www.nytimes.com/2009/08/02/world/middleeast/02israel.html. Accessed June 16, 2020.
34 Robert Swift, "Israeli Society & Culture: LGBTQ Rights in Israel," *Jewish Journal*, August 4, 2015. Swift comments that, after Banki's death and the wounds suffered by six others, there was an extended debate in Israel as to whether the killer was a deranged lone wolf or whether the homophobia in Israeli society contributed to the murders.
35 Miriam Elman, "Reverse Pinkwashing: Exploiting Isolated Israeli Anti-Gay Violence to Excuse Widespread Palestinian LGBTQ Persecution," *Legal Insurrection*, August 6, 2016. https://legalinsurrection.com/2015/08/reverse-pinkwashing-exploiting-isolated-israeli-anti-gay-violence-to-excuse-widespread-palestinian-lgbt-persecution/. Accessed June 13, 2020.
36 Schulman, "Documentary Guide."
37 James Kirchick, "Pink Eye," *Tablet Magazine*, November 29, 2011. https://www.tabletmag.com/jewish-news-and-politics/84216/pink-eye. Accessed June 15, 2020.
38 Ibid.
39 "China's Global Threat," *Human Rights Watch*, 2020.
40 The pinkwashing campaign does not appear to have had much success, as in 2019 Israel hosted the largest gay pride parade in the Middle East, with more than 250,000 attendees from Israel and other nations. See Sydney Dennen, "Tel Aviv Pride Parade Held with 250,000 Attendants Celebrating LGBTQ," *Jerusalem Post*, August 20, 2019. https://www.jpost.com/israel-news/tel-aviv-pride-parade-kicks-off-for-21st-time-with-theme-the-struggle-continues-592539. Accessed June 15, 2020.
41 Jasbir Puar, "Citation and Censorship: The Politics of Talking about the Sexual Politics of Israel," *Feminist Legal Studies* 19, no. 2 (2011): 133.
42 Benjamin Weinthal, "Only 5% of Palestinians and 6% of Lebanese Accept Gay Relationships," *Jerusalem Post*, July 1, 2019. https://www.jpost.com/middle-east/only-5-percent-of-palestinians-and-6-percent-of-lebanese-accept-gay-relationships-594179. Accessed June 15, 2020.
43 See "Israel Adds $5 Million in Funding to Serve the LGBTQ Community's Needs," *JTA*, October 6, 2016. Notably, Israeli gay activists denied an initial governmental plan to fund gay tourism in Israel, even though this would have benefited gay-owned businesses, because this move would have played into the pinkwashing narrative rather than taking care of the local needs of Israeli LGBTQ people.

44 "Pinkwatching Israel." http://www.pinkwatchingisrael.com/about-us/. Accessed June 19, 2020.
45 "In Limbo—Palestinian Gays," *Radio Netherlands: Archives*, August 8, 2004. https://www.radionetherlandsarchives.org/in-limbo-palestinian-gays/. Accessed June 17, 2020.
46 See "LGBTQ Rights in the State of Palestine." https://en.wikipedia.org/wiki/LGBT_rights_in_the_State_of_Palestine. Accessed June 21, 2020.
47 See "A Selective Sanctuary: 'Pinkwashing' and Gay Palestinian Asylum-Seekers in Israel," *Yale Review of International Studies* (October 2014). http://yris.yira.org/comments/1435. Accessed June 20, 2020.
48 Palestinians seeking asylum in Israel also include religious minorities and women fleeing domestic abuse.
49 Yariv Mozer (dir.), *The Invisible Men* (2012). http://nfct.org.il/en/movies/the-invisible-men/. Accessed June 16, 2020. The ironies of labeling this documentary pinkwashing propaganda include that the director not only indicts the murderous homophobia of Palestinian society but also—even more so—the anti-Palestinian policies of the Israeli government, which rounds up these men and returns them home to their almost certain deaths.
50 Dean Spade, *Pinkwashing Exposed: Seattle Fights Back*, 2015. http://www.deanspade.net/projects/pinkwashing-exposed/. Accessed June 16, 2020.
51 Israel has taken major steps toward the right to seek asylum, including those based on sexual orientation, which are becoming ever more routine in international refugee law. The United Nations has sometimes intervened to help resettle gay Palestinians to third countries, but the UN refugee office in Jerusalem also cooperates with Israel in excluding Palestinians from the asylum system. The continued refusal of Israel to consider asylum claims from gay Palestinians violates the rule of international law—recognized by Israel's high court—against returning a foreigner to a territory where his or her life or freedom may be in danger. Under international law, no state may discriminate by nationality with regard to asylum-seekers.
52 Franke, "Dating the State," 18.
53 See Jerusalem Open House. https://joh.org.il. Accessed June 21, 2020.
54 See Aswat: Palestinian Center for Gender and Sexual Freedoms. https://www.aswatgroup.org/mission-vision. Accessed June 21, 2020.
55 Quoted in Adam Rasgon, "PA Police Ban Palestinian LGBTQ Group from Holding Activities in West Bank," *Times of Israel*, August 19, 2019.

https://www.timesofisrael.com/pa-police-ban-palestinian-lgbt-group-from-holding-activities-in-west-bank/. Accessed June 21, 2020. A sixteen-year-old Palestinian boy, standing outside an LGBTQ shelter in Tel Aviv, was stabbed by an assailant suspected of being his brother. alQaws responded by organizing a protest in Haifa at the start of August to demand an end to the kind of homophobia in the Palestinian community that had led the boy to seek refuge in the first place. alQaws began receiving very frequent threatening and hateful messages following this protest, and the PA ban came following their announcement of a queer camp, organized for the end of August 2019, where LGBTQ Palestinians could share their experiences.

56 Quoted in Jaclynn Ashly, "PA Rescinds Ban on LGBTQ Group After Protests," *Electronic Intifada*, August 27, 2019. https://electronicintifada.net/content/pa-rescinds-ban-LGBTQ-group-after-protests/28201. Accessed June 21, 2020.

57 Melissa Thiel, "The Israeli-Palestinian Conflict: A Historiographic Essay." https://www.studocu.com/en-gb/document/the-chancellor-masters-and-scholars-of-the-university-of-cambridge/law/the-israeli-palestinian-conflict/21549252. Accessed September 14, 2020.

58 Shmuel Ettinger, "Jewish Immigration in the 19th Century," *My Jewish Learning*. https://www.myjewishlearning.com/article/jewish-emigration-in-the-19th-century/. Accessed September 20, 2020.

59 "Israel & Palestine: A Common Historical Narrative," *The Israel Palestine Project*. https://www.israelpalestineproject.org/narrative_chapter_3. Accessed September 14, 2020.

60 "Refugees," *United States Holocaust Memorial Museum*. https://encyclopedia.ushmm.org/content/en/article/refugees. Accessed September 14, 2020.

61 "Hajj Amin Al-Husayni: Arab Nationalist and Muslim Leader," *United States Holocaust Memorial Museum*. https://encyclopedia.ushmm.org/content/en/article/hajj-amin-al-husayni-arab-nationalist-and-muslim-leader. Accessed September 14, 2020.

62 Amy Telbel, "Two-State Solution," *Washington Post*, January 28, 2020. https://www.washingtonpost.com/business/two-state-solution/2020/01/27/e6bc438e-4135-11ea-99c7-1dfd4241a2fe_story.html. Accessed September 14, 2020.

63 "Immigration to Israel: British Restrictions on Jewish Immigration to Palestine," *Jewish Virtual Library*. https://www.jewishvirtuallibrary.org/british-restrictions-on-jewish-immigration-to-palestine. Accessed September 14, 2020.

64 Alan Jay Gerber, "Hitler's Mufti and the Rise of Radical Islam," *Jewish Star*, July 24, 2019. https://www.thejewishstar.com/stories/hitlers-mufti-and-the-rise-of-radical-islam,18141. Accessed September 14, 2020.

65 Tel Becker, "The Claim for Recognition of Israel as a Jewish State: A Reassessment," *Washington Institute* (February 2011). https://www.washingtoninstitute.org/policy-analysis/claim-recognition-israel-jewish-state-reassessment. Accessed September 14, 2020.

66 "Proclamation of Independence," *Knesset*, May 5, 1949. https://www.knesset.gov.il/docs/eng/megilat_eng.htm. Accessed September 14, 2020.

67 Mitchell Bard, "The Palestinian Refugees: History & Overview," *Jewish Virtual Library*. https://www.jewishvirtuallibrary.org/history-and-overview-of-the-palestinian-refugees. Accessed September 14, 2020.

68 "Palestinian Refugees," *Anti-Defamation League*. https://www.adl.org/resources/glossary-terms/palestinian-refugees. Accessed September 11, 2020.

69 Shaul M. Gabbay, "The Status of Palestinians in Jordan and the Anomaly of Holding a Jordanian Passport," *Journal of Political Sciences & Public Affairs* 2, no. 1 (2014). https://www.longdom.org/open-access/the-status-of-palestinians-in-jordan-and-the-anomaly-of-holding-a-jordanian-passport-2332-0761.1000113.pdf. Accessed September 11, 2020.

70 Tanya Kramer, "The Controversy of a Palestinian 'Right of Return' to Israel," *Arizona Journal* (2002). http://arizonajournal.org/wp-content/uploads/2015/11/Kramernote.pdf. Accessed September 11, 2020.

71 "List of Towns and Villages Depopulated During the 1948 Palestinian Exodus," *Wikipedia*. https://en.wikipedia.org/wiki/List_of_towns_and_villages_depopulated_during_the_1948_Palestinian_exodus. Accessed September 11, 2020.

72 "Jews in Islamic Lands: The Treatment of Jews," *Jewish Virtual Library* (September 2011). https://www.jewishvirtuallibrary.org/the-treatment-of-jews-in-arab-islamic-countries. Accessed September 12, 2020. According to this entry, "Peoples subjected to Muslim rule usually had a choice between death and conversion, but Jews and Christians, who adhered to the Scriptures, were allowed as dhimmis (protected persons) to practice their faith. This 'protection' did little, however, to ensure that Jews and Christians were treated well by the Muslims. On the contrary, an integral aspect of the dhimma was that, being an infidel, he had to openly acknowledge the superiority of the true believer—the Muslim. . . . Dhimmis were excluded from public office and armed

service, and were forbidden to bear arms. They were not allowed to ride horses or camels, to build synagogues or churches taller than mosques, to construct houses higher than those of Muslims or to drink wine in public. They were not allowed to pray or mourn in loud voices—as that might offend the Muslims. The dhimmi had to show public deference toward Muslims—always yielding them the center of the road. The dhimmi was not allowed to give evidence in court against a Muslim, and his oath was unacceptable in an Islamic court. To defend himself, the dhimmi would have to purchase Muslim witnesses at great expense. This left the dhimmi with little legal recourse when harmed by a Muslim. Dhimmis were also forced to wear distinctive clothing. In the ninth century, for example, Baghdad's Caliph al-Mutawakkil designated a yellow badge for Jews, setting a precedent that would be followed centuries later in Nazi Germany."

73 Joshua Washington, "Hitler Knew of the Mizrachi Jews. Why Don't We?" *Times of Israel*, April 3, 2019. https://blogs.timesofisrael.com/hitler-knew-of-the-mizrahi-jews-why-dont-we/?fbclid=IwAR0hiAB_ROplTwZXKUaMPYxZItdbZQjtE8eosslJo_z673tbd_UxDH1qF10. Accessed September 11, 2020.

74 "Refugees," *United States Holocaust Memorial Museum*. https://encyclopedia.ushmm.org/content/en/article/refugees. Accessed September 11, 2020.

75 "The Impact of Academic Boycotts of Israel on US Campuses," *AMCHA Initiative: Protecting Jewish Students* (October 2017). https://amchainitiative.org/wp-content/uploads/2017/10/Faculty-Report.pdf. Accessed June 22, 2020. Indeed, less-politicized sectors of the university, including the sciences and the social sciences, do not have active BDS campaigns and, in contrast, have active collaborations with Israeli universities in technology, medicine, physical sciences, business, and environmentalism/water reclamation.

76 See Graham Wright et al., "The Limits of Hostility: Students Report on Antisemitism and Anti-Israel Sentiment at Four US Universities," *Brandeis University: Steinhardt Social Research Institute* (2007). https://www.brandeis.edu/ssri/pdfs/campusstudies/LimitsofHostility.pdf. Accessed June 18, 2020.

77 Omar Barghouti, *Boycott, Divestment, Sanctions: The Global Struggle for Palestinian Rights* (Chicago: Haymarket Books, 2011), 100.

78 See Cary Nelson, *Israel Denial*, for an extensive discussion of these and other abusive practices.

79. See Corinne E. Blackmer and Andrew Pessin, "Introduction," in *Poisoning the Wells: Antisemitism in Contemporary America* (New York: ISGAP, 2021), for an extensive review of the antisemitic events of May 2021.
80. Martin Kramer, "The Unspoken Purpose of the Academic Boycott," *Israel Affairs* 27, no. 1 (2021): 27–33.
81. See Cary Nelson, "Defining Academic Freedom," *Inside Higher Ed*, December 21, 2010. https://www.insidehighered.com/views/2010/12/21/defining-academic-freedom. Accessed June 23, 2020.
82. See Scott Jaschik, "Chicago Professors Fire Back," *Inside Higher Ed*, September 14, 2016. https://www.insidehighered.com/news/2016/09/14/u-chicago-professors-issue-letter-safe-spaces-and-trigger-warnings. Accessed June 25, 2020.
83. See "Adopting the Chicago Statement," *Fire*, June 22, 2017. https://d28htnjz2elwuj.cloudfront.net/wp-content/uploads/2017/06/22101147/adopting-the-chicago-statement.pdf. Accessed June 27, 2020.
84. https://news.uchicago.edu/sites/default/files/attachments/Dear_Class_of_2020_Students.pdf. Accessed June 24, 2020.
85. See Martin A. Weiss, "Arab League Boycott of Israel," *Congressional Research Services: Informing the Legislative Debate* (August 2017). Due in part to internal inertia and US resistance, the boycott has at best been sporadically and unevenly enforced. https://fas.org/sgp/crs/mideast/RL33961.pdf. Accessed June 18, 2020.
86. The UN delegates voted to reject the language that accused Israel of racism, and the published report contained no such allegations. Colin Powell denounced the wording that "singles out only one country in the world, Israel, for censure and abuse" in the draft text, and Tom Lantos, US delegate to the conference against racism, stated that the conference had been "wrecked by Arab and Islamic extremists." However, some saw the withdrawal of the US delegation as related not entirely to the language on Israel but rather, in part, to a reluctance of the United States to address the issue of slavery—principally if not exclusively through reparations. The potential repercussions of the conference were annulled by the attacks of September 11, 2001. See "World Conference Against Racism 2001." https://en.wikipedia.org/wiki/World_Conference_against_Racism_2001. Accessed January 3, 2022.
87. The NGO platform at the Durban UN conference also attempted to reinstate UN General Assembly Resolution 3379, which declared that Zionism was a form of racism and racial discrimination, and which had been overturned in 1991.

88 Mitchell Bard, "Anti-Semitism: History of the Boycott, Divestment and Sanctions (BDS) Movement." https://www.jewishvirtuallibrary.org/bds-movement. Accessed January 3, 2022. Bard explains that BDS advocates portray the call as a response to Israel's refusal to submit to a ruling of the International Court of Justice condemning Israel's security barrier, although that ruling was an advisory opinion that Israel had no obligation to accept.

89 Amos Harel, "Israel's Walls: Do They Work?" *Foreign Affairs*, February 17, 2017. https://www.foreignaffairs.com/articles/israel/2017-02-17/israels-walls. Accessed January 3, 2022.

90 Omar Barghouti, "Relative Humanity: The Essential Obstacle to a Just Peace in Palestine," December 13–14, 2003. https://www.counterpunch.org/2003/12/12/relative-humanity-the-essential-obstacle-to-a-just-peace-in-palestine/. Accessed January 3, 2022.

91 See Chaim Gans, "A Review of Parting Ways: Jewishness and a Critique of Zionism." *Notre Dame Philosophical Reviews*, December 13, 2012. https://ndpr.nd.edu/reviews/parting-ways-jewishness-and-the-critique-of-zionism/. Accessed September 17, 2021.

92 Until Palestinians gain a state of their own as part of an equitable two-state solution, Israel will remain vulnerable to the settler-colonialist accusation, especially when no model exists for future political and national arrangements in the West Bank. Further, Palestinian Arabs suffered multiple losses from the incursion of Zionists into the Levant. During the first stage, in the initial waves of the Aliyah, they went from making up the majority the population to becoming a minority; along with antisemitism exacerbated anti-Zionist sentiment. During the Nakba, or catastrophe, which Israeli Jews refer to as the 1948 War of Independence, between 700,000 and 800,000 Arab Palestinians were ejected from their ancestral homes, leaving them stateless. This created a refugee crisis that persists into the present, stoking Palestinian rage and accounting for most of the violence between Israelis and Palestinians today. Until Israeli Jews come to grips with the political and cultural legacies of the Nakba, calm, stability, and peace will continue to elude the area. The BDS movement gained momentum following the international condemnation of what many perceived as Israel's use of excessive force, especially against civilians, in the 2008 Gaza War. Having been barraged with rockets from Hamas, which had won election in 2007 shortly after the IDF withdrew from Gaza, the war resulted in the deaths of more than one thousand civilians, and the destruction of thousands of buildings

and civilian structures. Subsequent firing of rockets, sometimes in the thousands, as well as construction of elaborate tunnels from Gaza into southern Israel, led to further military actions on Israel's side and, with them, further condemnations. These internationally broadcast images of Israel, in addition to the right-wing policies of Netanyahu's Likud government, have led the international community to distance itself further from Israel. Netanyahu has apparently concluded that he cannot risk a repeat of the events of 2007, when Hamas came into power, stopped all elections, and used international aid to perpetuate war against Israel. Finally, in addition to the escalating military clashes between Israel and Hamas since 2007, queer intellectuals responded to the War on Terror, as well as the burgeoning of neoliberalism, globalization, and Islamophobia, all of which elicited distress and a sense of outraged injustice on behalf of the Palestinians.

93 In refusing to engage in public debate, BDS supporters often compare pro-Israel parties to Holocaust deniers or Nazis, and on these grounds refuse to debate them.

94 See "Cultural Boycott," https://bdsmovement.net/cultural-boycott. Accessed June 22, 2020.

95 See Stern, *Conflict Over the Conflict*, 90–91. For the full statement, see https://bdsmovement.net/pacbi/cultural-boycott-guidelines. Accessed June 19, 2020.

96 Kenneth Roth, "China's Global Threat to Human Rights," *Human Rights Watch*, 2019. https://www.hrw.org/world-report/2020/country-chapters/global#. Accessed June 28, 2020.

97 For an extensive examination of the effects of the BDS Movement on Arab Israeli students and Palestinian universities, see Cary Nelson, *Not in Kansas Anymore: Academic Freedom in Palestinian Universities* (New York: Academic Engagement Network, 2021).

98 Menachem Magidor and Sari Nusseibeh, "Counter Boycott by British Association of University Teachers: Joint Hebrew University–Al-Quds University Statement on Academic Cooperation Signed in London." May 19, 2005. Accessed June 22, 2020.

99 See "Mission Statement." *Alliance for Academic Freedom—The Third Narrative*. https://thirdnarrative.org/uncategorized/alliance-for-academic-freedom/. Accessed June 28, 2020.

Chapter 1. Sarah Schulman's Queer Adventures in Israel/Palestine

1 Sarah Schulman, *Israel/Palestine and the Queer International* (Durham, NC: Duke University Press, 2012), 3.
2 See Rachael Rojanski, *Yiddish in Israel: A History* (Bloomington: Indiana University Press, 2020). Rojanski argues that while the leaders of Israel pushed for Hebrew as the main language of Israel, they never adopted an official position regarding Yiddish; the language, which many Israeli Ashkenazi leaders knew and loved deeply, has enjoyed an abiding presence in Israel, and has recently also been revived by the descendants of Holocaust survivors.
3 Schulman, *Ties That Bind: Familial Homophobia and Its Consequences* (New York: New Press, 2009).
4 Schulman's left-wing Christian girlfriend incorrectly attributed the massacres at the camps of Shatila and Sabra, which occurred during the Lebanese Civil War, to the IDF. In fact, the Lebanese Christian Phalangist militia was responsible for the mass deaths that took place at the two Beirut-area refugee camps in September 1982. Israeli troops allowed the Phalangists to enter Sabra and Shatila because the IDF was told they intended to destroy terrorist cells believed to be located there. It had been estimated that there may have been up to 200 armed men in the camps, working out of the countless bunkers built by the Palestinian Liberation Organization (PLO) over the years. After Israeli soldiers ordered the Phalangists out, they found many hundreds dead. The killings came on top of an estimated 95,000 deaths that had occurred during the civil war in Lebanon from 1975 to 1982.
5 Schulman, *Israel/Palestine*, 7.
6 See *ADL Global 100: Index of Anti-Semitism.* http://global100.adl.org/?_ga=2.118417993.1300342366.1532874127-1439491303.1529083815. Accessed July 29, 2018. The ADL surveyed people in 102 nations and found that 74 percent of the people living in the Middle East held antisemitic beliefs, as opposed to 34 percent of Eastern Europeans.
7 Schulman, *Israel/Palestine*, 10.
8 See "The Resurgence of Anti-Semitism in Europe," *Council on Foreign Relations*, April 16, 2015. https://www.cfr.org/conference-calls/resurgence-anti-semitism-europe. Accessed July 25, 2018. Also see Amy Elman, *The European Union, Antisemitism, and the Politics of Denial* (Lincoln: University of Nebraska Press, 2014).

9. See Bernard Lewis's *Semites and Anti-Semites* (New York: Norton, 1999), where Lewis notes that antisemitism in Arab countries has risen, but Jew-hating in Christian countries has plummeted. For example, even with anti-Semitism still extant within the Catholic Church, most Westerners consider the Second Vatican Council's 1964 decision to repudiate the charge of deicide as a landmark moment. In Islam, however, traditional teaching that the Jews did not kill Christ has reversed. In some measure Islam and Christianity have switched places on antisemitism, which is now virulent and normative in Islamic countries.
10. See "Postwar Refugee Crisis and the Establishment of the State of Israel," *US Holocaust Memorial Museum*. https://encyclopedia.ushmm.org/content/en/article/postwar-refugee-crisis-and-the-establishment-of-the-state-of-israel. Accessed July 3, 2020.
11. Steven Mintz, "Immigration Polciy in World War II." The Gilder Lehrman Institute of American History. https://www.gilderlehrman.org/history-resources/teaching-resource/immigration-policy-world-war-ii. Accessed January 4, 2022.
12. Schulman, *Israel/Palestine*, 12.
13. Ibid., 13.
14. Ibid., 14.
15. Sharon Nazarian and Aykan Erdemir, "The Middle East's Religious Minorities Are Facing Extermination. The World Must Act," *Washington Post*, March 8, 2021. https://www.washingtonpost.com/opinions/2021/03/08/middle-easts-religious-minorities-are-facing-extinction-world-must-act/. Accessed September 17, 2021.
16. Klaus-Michael Mallmann and Martin Cüppers, *Nazi Palestine: The Plans for the Extermination of the Jews of Palestine*. (New York: Emigma Books, 2010). According to the authors, "The Mufti visited Axis capitals and met Adolf Hitler and Heinrich Himmler. Not only did Nazi Germany promise to end the European 'colonial presence' that had replaced the Ottoman Empire after 1918, it also pledged to wipe out the Jews who had been living in Palestine since time immemorial as well as the new arrivals from the beginning of the modern Zionist movement in the nineteenth century and following the Balfour Declaration in 1917."
17. Schulman, *Israel/Palestine*, 14.
18. Ibid., 14.
19. See "Are Palestinians Indigenous?" *Postil Magazine*, April 1, 2018. https://www.thepostil.com/are-palestinians-indigenous/#.W1sUgq2ZOU1. Accessed January 4, 2021.

20 See "Jewish Refugees from Arab Countries," *Jewish Virtual Library*. https://www.jewishvirtuallibrary.org/jewish-refugees-from-arab-countries. Accessed July 4, 2020. These refugees were largely forgotten because they were assimilated into their new homes, most in Israel, and neither the UN nor any other international agency took up their cause or demanded restitution for the property and money taken from them.

21 See Michael Eisenstadt and David Pollock, "Friends with Benefits: Why the U.S.-Israeli Alliance Is Good for America," *Foreign Affairs*, November 7, 2012. https://www.washingtoninstitute.org/policy-analysis/view/friends-with-benefits-why-the-u.s.-israeli-alliance-is-good-for-america. Accessed January 4, 2022. In addition to security and shared political values, "U.S. companies' substantial cooperation with Israel on information technology has been crucial to Silicon Valley's success. . . . Israeli innovators have also come up with novel solutions to the water and food security challenges posed by population growth, climate change, and economic development. By necessity, given the geography of the Middle East, Israel is a world leader in water conservation and management and high-tech agriculture. Israel recycles more than eighty percent of its wastewater—the highest level in the world—and has pioneered widely used techniques of conserving or purifying water, including drip irrigation and reverse osmosis desalination. And a number of Israeli companies are leaders in the development of renewable energy sources; BrightSource Industries, for example, is building a solar power plant in California using Israeli technology that will double the amount of solar thermal electricity produced in America. These innovations, bolstered by the substantial American investment in Israel, contribute to long-term U.S. domestic and foreign policy objectives relating to sustainable development."

22 Schulman, *Israel/Palestine*, 15.

23 See Aryeh Tepper, "Mizrachi History Finds Its Place in Israeli Education," *Tower Magazine* 43 (2016). http://www.thetower.org/article/mizrahi-history-finds-its-place-in-israeli-education/. Accessed July 28, 2018.

24 "The Reparations Agreement of 1952 and Its Response in Israel." https://web.nli.org.il/sites/nli/english/collections/personalsites/israel-germany/division-of-germany/pages/reparations-agreement.aspx. Accessed July 4, 2020.

25 Schulman, *Israel/Palestine*, 17.

26 Ken Blady, *Jewish Communities in Exotic Lands* (New York: Jason Aronson, 2000). Blady presents the history of Jews from Asia, Africa, and the

Far East whose stories of persecution and displacement in the modern era have often not been told, since they have not been translated from the Hebrew. Their history counters the stereotyped and monolithic image of Jews as Western people.

27 Schulman, *Israel/Palestine*, 17.
28 Gaza War (2008–9). https://en.wikipedia.org/wiki/Gaza_War_(2008%E2%80%932009). Accessed September 18, 2021.
29 Ruth Sherlock, "Parents in Gaza and Israel Are Doing Their Best to Shield Kids from the Trauma of War," *NPR*, May 25, 2021. https://www.npr.org/2021/05/25/999811879/parents-in-gaza-and-israel-are-doing-their-best-to-shield-kids-from-the-trauma-of-war. Accessed September 17, 2021.
30 Schulman, *Israel/Palestine*, 18.
31 See the Hamas Covenant 1988: The Covenant of the Islamic Resistance Movement. http://www.acpr.org.il/resources/hamascharter.html. Accessed July 26, 2018. Hamas represents itself as leading the struggle against "World Zionism," since "Zionist scheming has no end, and after Palestine, they will covet expansion from the Nile to the Euphrates River." The covenant also repeats homicidal tropes against Jews: "The Day of Judgment will not come until Muslims fight Jews and kill them. Then the Jews will hide behind rocks and trees, and the rocks and trees will cry out, 'O Muslim, there is a Jew hiding behind me, come and kill him.'"
32 See Khaled Abu Toameh, "Palestinians: No Place for Gays," *Gatestone Institute*, June 12, 2018. https://www.gatestoneinstitute.org/12496/palestinians-gays. Accessed July 26, 2018. Toameh notes that "in 2016, Hamas executed one of its top military commanders, Mahmoud Ishtiwi, 34, after he was found guilty of 'moral turpitude'—a thinly veiled reference to homosexuality."
33 Schulman, *Israel/Palestine*, 19.
34 Ibid., 22.
35 See https://bdsmovement.net.
36 Schulman, *Ties That Bind*, 26.
37 Schulman, *Israel/Palestine*, 46.
38 "Warsaw Ghetto Uprising." https://en.wikipedia.org/wiki/Warsaw_Ghetto_Uprising. Accessed September 18, 2021.
39 Schulman, *Israel/Palestine*, 49.
40 Ibid., 50.
41 Ibid., 58.
42 Ibid.

43 Ibid., 60.
44 Ibid.
45 In her nonfiction work, *Stagestruck: Theater, AIDS, and the Marketing of Gay America* (Durham, NC: Duke University Press, 1998), Schulman claims that Jonathan Larson, the straight white man who created *Rent* (1996), the hit Broadway show about AIDS and gay life in New York City, plagiarized her novel, *People in Trouble* (1991), which also concerned AIDS, romance, and gay life in New York City. *Rent* has the kitschy, derivative, antiseptic qualities of its genre. Both works are similar at the levels of basic plot, character, and setting. But they are distinct along every other parameter, including the language, visions, aesthetics, and the politics of the authors.
46 See "Jewish Voice for Peace," *ADL*. https://www.adl.org/resources/backgrounders/jewish-voice-for-peace#introduction. Accessed July 28, 2018. The website notes that "JVP's rhetorical drumbeat promoting the view that Zionism and supporting Israel is of a piece with white supremacy, racism, ethnic cleansing and genocide, has the effect of demonizing this constituency of U.S. Jews." It also accuses Jews of Islamophobia.
47 Schulman, *Israel/Palestine*, 62.
48 Ibid., 63
49 Ibid., 65.
50 Ibid., 66.
51 See James Kirchick, "Queer Theory," *New Republic*, October 8, 2007. https://newrepublic.com/article/62069/queer-theory. Accessed January 4, 2022. Mahmoud Ahmadinejad, the former president of Iran, claimed that the country had no homosexuals, even though "homosexuals" have been executed there regularly. According to Kirchick, the "Queen Boat" incident of May 11, 2001, occurred when a horde of truncheon-wielding Egyptian police officers boarded a Nile River cruise known as the Queen Boat, a floating disco for gay men. Fifty-two men were arrested, and many of them were tortured and sexually humiliated in prison. In a sensational, months-long ordeal, they were paraded in public, and images of them shielding their faces were blared on state television and printed in government newspapers. Most of the men were eventually acquitted, but twenty-three received convictions for either "habitual debauchery," "contempt for religion," or both.
52 Schulman, *Israel/Palestine*, 66.
53 John E. Helliwell, Richard Layard, and Jeffrey D. Sachs, "United Nations World Happiness Report 2018." http://worldhappiness.report/ed/2018/.

Accessed July 28, 2018. The report notes that "all the top countries tend to have high values for all six of the key variables that have been found to support well-being: income, healthy life expectancy, social support, freedom, trust and generosity."

54 Schulman, *Israel/Palestine*, 96.
55 See Jasbir Puar, "Rethinking Homonationalism," *International Journal of Middle East Studies* 45 (2013). https://genderandsecurity.org/projects-resources/research/rethinking-homonationalism. Accessed July 5, 2020. Since the publication of her book, *Terrorist Assemblages*, which argued against the then-common view that gays and lesbians were marginalized within the nation-state, Puar has rethought homonationalism, and now defines it not as a "bad identity" but rather as "an analytic category deployed to understand and historicize how and why a nation's status as 'gay-friendly' has become desirable in the first place. Like modernity, homonationalism can be resisted and re-signified, but not opted out of: we are all conditioned by it and through it."
56 Schulman, *Israel/Palestine*, 123.
57 Ibid.
58 See Palestinian Media Watch, https://www.palwatch.org. Accessed July 5, 2020.
59 Schulman, *Israel/Palestine*, 124.
60 Ibid., 130.
61 Liel Leibovitz, "IDF Introduces New Microdevices Designed to Break into Terrorist Structures Without Causing Collateral Damage," *Tablet Magazine*, July 30, 2018. https://www.tabletmag.com/scroll/267357/idf-introduces-new-micro-devices-designed-to-break-into-terrorist-structures-without-collateral-damage. Accessed January 4, 2021. As Leibovitz explains, "Because the terrorist group frequently operates from residential homes, schools, hospitals, and other civilian structures, using women and children as human shields, the IDF now possesses the capacity to enter these structures and surgically target the terrorists alone."
62 Schulman, *Israel/Palestine*, 134.
63 Peter Hessler, "Egypt's Failed Revolution," *New Yorker*, January 2, 2017. https://www.newyorker.com/magazine/2017/01/02/egypts-failed-revolution. Accessed January 4, 2022.
64 See Neela Ghostali, "More Arrests in Egypt's LGBTQ Crackdown, But No International Outcry. Human Rights Watch," January 2, 2018. https://www.hrw.org/news/2018/01/22/more-arrests-egypts-lgbt-crackdown-no-international-outcry. Accessed January 4, 2022.

65 See Joseph A. Massad, *Desiring Arabs* (Chicago: University of Chicago Press, 2007).
66 Schulman, *Israel/Palestine*, 134.
67 Josh Mitten, "Gay and Trans Syrians Routinely Mutilated, Raped and Anally Violated by ISIS Militants and Government Officials Alike," *Pink News*, July 29, 2020. https://www.pinknews.co.uk/2020/07/29/gay-trans-syria-conflict-rape-mutilation-torture-anal-isis-islamic-state-human-rights-watch/. Accessed September 18, 2021.
68 Schulman, *Israel/Palestine*, 163.
69 Ibid., 159.
70 Ibid., 162.
71 Ibid.
72 Ibid.
73 Ibid., 165.
74 Ibid., 166–67.
75 Schulman, *Ties That Bind*.
76 Bruce Bawer, "Cuny's Despicable Anti-Pinkwashing Conference," *Frontpage Magazine*, April 13, 2013. https://www.frontpagemag.com/fpm/185730/cunys-despicable-anti-pinkwashing-conference-bruce-bawer. Accessed January 3, 2022.

Chapter 2. Jasbir Puar, or, Zionophobia in Homonationalist Times

1 See US Campaign for the Academic and Cultural Boycott of Israel (USACBI), "Letter in Support of Professor Jasbir Puar Regarding Right-Wing Attacks on Her Recent Speech at Vassar College." http://usacbi.org/2016/02/letter-in-support-of-professor-jasbir-puar-regarding-right-wing-attacks-on-her-recent-talk-at-vassar-college/. Accessed July 9, 2018.
2 See Mark G. Yudof and Ken Waltzer, "Majoring in Anti-Semitism at Vassar," *Wall Street Journal*, February 17, 2016. https://www.wsj.com/articles/majoring-in-anti-semitism-at-vassar-1455751940. Accessed January 2, 2022. According to Yudof and Waltzer, Puar repeated "vicious lies that Israel had 'mined for organs for scientific research' from dead Palestinians—updating the medieval blood libel against Jews—and accused Israelis of attempting to give Palestinians the 'bare minimum for survival' as part of a medical 'experiment.'" In addition, see Jonathan Marks, "Blood Libeling at Vassar," *Campus Watch*, February 9, 2016, for

an analysis of how Puar claims that the Jewish Israelis have appropriated the Holocaust. https://www.meforum.org/campus-watch/articles/2016/blood-libeling-at-vassar-on-jasbir-puar. Accessed January 2, 2022. According to Marks, "Puar also renews a charge she has made elsewhere, that the Jews are hogging the privilege of being victims of genocidal violence. 'The Jewish Israeli population cannot afford to hand over genocide to another population. They need the Palestinians alive in order to keep the kind of rationalization for their victimhood and their militarized economy.' This is a remarkable move. Evidently realizing that it is hard to sustain the charge of genocide against the Israelis in light of the increasing Palestinian population, Puar adds the failure to commit genocide to the list of Israel's crimes.'"

3 Jasbir Puar, "Speaking of Palestine: Solidarity and Its Censors," *Jadaliyya*, March 16, 2016. https://www.jadaliyya.com/Details/33095. Accessed August 16, 2020.

4 Petra Marquardt-Bigman, "Anti-Israel Lecturer Threatens to Sue Anyone Who Publishes Her Talk," *Tower*, March 10, 2016. http://www.thetower.org/2072-scholar-who-gave-anti-israel-lecture-threatens-to-sue-anyone-who-publishes-transcript/. Accessed January 2, 2022. Marquardt-Bigman notes that, "given that even her supporters have implicitly acknowledged that Puar's 'views are controversial,' Puar's conduct means in effect that the controversy she generated by exercising her academic freedom and her right to free speech cannot lead to a serious debate that reflects academic norms and contributes to a deeper understanding of the complex discussions about contemporary anti-Semitism. Puar is obviously intent on forcing her critics to rely on unpublished documentation that was shared with a very limited number of people under the strictest fair use conditions, while her supporters passionately denounce the criticism of her Vassar talk as 'heinous and misinformed attacks' against a well-respected academic."

5 See Cinnamon Stillwell, "In New Low, Scholars Defend Medieval Blood Libel Charges Against Israel," *Daily Caller*. March 7, 2016. http://dailycaller.com/2016/03/07/in-new-low-scholars-defend-medieval-blood-libel-charges-against-israel/. Accessed January 2, 2022. According to Stillwell, letters in support of Puar had alluded "to the specter of death threats—whether real or imagined—a time-honored tradition among academics unaccustomed to the twin horrors of criticism and accountability."

6 Jasbir K. Puar, *The Right to Maim: Debility, Capacity, Disability* (Durham, NC: Duke University Press, 2017), 136.

7 Quoted in Cary Nelson, *Israel Denial: Anti-Zionism, Anti-Semitism, & the Faculty Campaign Against the Jewish State* (Washington, DC/ Bloomington, IN: Academic Engagement Network/ Indiana University Press, 2019), 254.
8 Ibid., 210.
9 Ibid., 251.
10 "Critique of Jasbir Puar Feb. 3 Lecture at Vassar." http://fairnesstoisraelatvassar.blogspot.com/p/critique-of-jasbir-puar-feb-3-lecture.html. Accessed July 9, 2018.
11 Nelson, *Israel Denial*, 208.
12 See ibid.
13 Aron Moss, "Organ Donation in Judaism." https://www.chabad.org/library/article_cdo/aid/635401/jewish/Organ-Donation-in-Judaism.htm. Accessed August 17, 2020. While organ donations during life are regarded as manifestations of lovingkindness, it is forbidden to tamper with a corpse in any way unless it is in order to directly save a life. But when you sign a consent form to have your organs removed, not all of those organs will necessarily be used for an immediate transplant. They may be used for research, or stored away, or even discarded if not needed. Jewish law allows organ donation only if it can be ensured that the organs will indeed be used to save lives. But there is a much more serious concern. To be usable in a transplant, most organs have to be removed while the heart is still beating. But many authorities of Jewish law maintain that if the heart is still beating, the person is still alive. They define the moment of death as when the heart stops. So to remove organs from a brain-dead patient while the heart is still beating would be tantamount to murder.
14 Nelson, *Israel Denial*, 209.
15 Puar, "Speaking of Palestine."
16 See ADL, "Blood Libel: A False, Incendiary Claim Against Jews." https://www.adl.org/education/resources/glossary-terms/blood-libel. Accessed August 17, 2020. The blood libel is particularly appalling in light of the fact that Jews follow the Hebrew Bible's law, found in the book of Leviticus, to not consume any blood. For an animal to be considered kosher, all its blood must have been drained and discarded.
17 Harriet Salem, "Discreet Funeral and No Autopsy: Israel Places Strict Conditions on Return of Palestinian Attackers' Bodies," *Vice*, February 19, 2016. https://www.vice.com/en_us/article/8x3kbk/discreet-funeral-and-no-autopsy-israel-places-strict-conditions-on-return-of-palestinian-attackers-bodies. Accessed August 23, 2020. Israel's public

security ministry, which handles the return of remains to families living in Jerusalem, has refused to hand back most of the bodies it is responsible for, citing concerns that large funerals and protests often held after burials were offensive and would incite more attacks against Israelis.

18 Quoted in Nelson, *Israel Denial*, 216.
19 Consanguineous marriage, which is also linked to poverty and is found in numerous parts of the world, is a union between two people who are related as second or first cousins.
20 See "Cousin Marriage in the Middle East," *Wikipedia*. https://en.wikipedia.org/wiki/Cousin_marriage_in_the_Middle_East#cite_ref-1. Accessed August 17, 2020. Ladislav Holý explains that in the Middle East marriage to a father's brother's daughter is particularly significant, and many Middle Eastern peoples express a preference for this form of marriage. Holý explains that it is not an independent phenomenon but merely one expression of a wider preference for so-called agnatic solidarity, or solidarity with one's father's lineage. With emphasis placed on the male line, the daughter of the father's brother is seen as the closest marriageable relation. According to Holý, the reason for cousin marriage in keeping property in the family is, in the Middle Eastern case, just one specific manifestation of keeping intact a family's whole symbolic capital. In fact, cousin marriage in general can be seen as trading off one socially valuable outcome—namely marital alliances with outsiders and the resulting integration of society—with the alternative outcome of greater in-group solidarity. The notion of honor is another social characteristic Holý identifies as being related to Middle Eastern cousin marriage. In many societies the honor of the males surrounding a woman is sullied when she misbehaves or when she is attacked. In societies like Europe that place greater value on affinal, or non-consanguineous relations, responsibility for a married woman rests with both her husband's family and her own. In the Middle East the situation is different, in that primary responsibility continues to rest with the woman's own family even after she is married. Her male relatives therefore cannot release her from control upon marriage due to the risk to their honor. They, and not the husband, may be responsible for killing her, or sometimes her lover, if she commits adultery.
21 Ghazi O. Tadmouri et al., "Consanguinity and Reproductive Health Among Arabs." *Reproductive Health*, October 8, 2009. https://www.ncbi.nlm.nih.gov/pmc/articles/PMC2765422/. Accessed September 18, 2021.
22 See Nelson, *Israel Denial*, 218.

23 Luke Baker, "Gaza Unlivable Ten Years After Hamas Seized Power: U.N," *Reuters*, July 11, 2017. https://www.reuters.com/article/us-palestinians-gaza-un/gaza-unliveable-ten-years-after-hamas-seized-power-u-n-idUSKBN19W17T. Accessed August 17, 2020.

24 See "Palestinian Socioeconomic Crisis Now at the Breaking Point," *UNCTAD*, September 10, 2019, for a detailed overview of the dire situation now confronting not only Gaza but also the West Bank. https://unctad.org/news/palestinian-socioeconomic-crisis-now-breaking-point. Accessed September 18, 2021.

25 Nelson, *Israel Denial*, 226.

26 Puar, *Right to Maim*, 108.

27 See Equal Rights for People with Disabilities Law, 5758/1998. https://www.jewishvirtuallibrary.org/jsource/Health/TheEqualRightsforPeoplewithDisabilitiesLaw575819.pdf. Accessed July 20, 2018.

28 Bassam Yousef Ibrahim Banat, "Palestinian Suicide Martyrs (Istishhadiyin): Facts and Figures," February 25, 2010. https://papers.ssrn.com/sol3/papers.cfm?abstract_id=1557041. Accessed August 21, 2020. Martyrdom is not suicide; rather it "involves using one's death in a defense of one's holies, homeland, money and children by inflicting losses on an enemy, not on suicide which is the self-inflicted intentional act designed to end one's own life. This kind of Martyrdom is called for by the collective Palestinian mentality, and it is reinforced by the Palestinian societal culture; this is a social, respected and acceptable behavior since it is the title of sacrifice for the sake of others, lifting of injustice and regaining of Palestinian lands and rights."

29 David Brooks, "The Cult of Martyrdom," *Atlantic*, June 2002. https://www.theatlantic.com/magazine/archive/2002/06/the-culture-of-martyrdom/302506/. Accessed January 2, 2022. According to the excerpts Brooks cites, "The crucial factor informing the behavior of suicide bombers is loyalty to the group. Suicide bombers go through indoctrination processes similar to the ones that were used by the leaders of the Jim Jones and Solar Temple cults. The bombers are organized into small cells and given countless hours of intense and intimate spiritual training. They are instructed in the details of *jihad*, reminded of the need for revenge, and reassured about the rewards they can expect in the afterlife. They are told that their families will be guaranteed a place with God, and that there are also considerable rewards for their families in this life, including cash bonuses of several thousand dollars donated by

the government of Iraq, some individual Saudis, and various groups sympathetic to the cause. Finally, the bombers are told that paradise lies just on the other side of the detonator, that death will feel like nothing more than a pinch." While Brooks's observations are useful, the main motivations of the suicide bombers remain rational and *political*, and their bodies become, like other bodies in warfare, instruments for the gaining of political objectives through violence.

30 Puar, *Right to Maim*, 95–96.
31 Ibid, 96.
32 Jasbir Puar, *Terrorist Assemblages: Homonationalism in Queer Times* (Durham, NC: Duke University Press, 2007).
33 Ibid., 97.
34 Jasbir Puar, "Rethinking Homonationalism," *International Journal of Middle East Studies* 43 (2013). According to Puar, "Instead of thinking of homonationalism as an accusation, an identity, a bad politics, I have been thinking about it as an analytic to apprehend state formation and a structure of modernity: as an assemblage of geopolitical and historical forces, neoliberal interests in capitalist accumulation both cultural and material, biopolitical state practices of population control, and affective investments in discourses of freedom, liberation, and rights. Homonationalism, thus, is not simply a synonym for gay racism, or another way to mark how gay and lesbian identities became available to conservative political imaginaries; it is not another identity politics, not another way of distinguishing good queers from bad queers, not an accusation, and not a position. It is rather a facet of modernity and a historical shift marked by the entrance of (some) homosexual bodies as worthy of protection by nation-states, a constitutive and fundamental reorientation of the relationship between the state, capitalism, and sexuality."
35 Puar, *Right to Maim*, 97.
36 See Israeli AIDS Task Force, https://www.aidsisrael.org.il/. Accessed June 27, 2018.
37 Puar, *Right to Maim*, 99.
38 See "Out Right Action International: Human Rights for LGBTQ People Everywhere." https://outrightinternational.org/. Accessed July 20, 2018.
39 Tom Rosentiel, "Trends in Attitudes Towards Religion and Social Issues: 1987–2007." *Pew Research Center*, October 18, 2007. https://www.pewresearch.org/2007/10/15/trends-in-attitudes-toward-religion-and-social-issues-19872007/. Accessed September 18, 2021.

40 See E. J. Graff, "How the Gay-Rights Movement Won," *American Prospect*, June 7, 2012. https://prospect.org/culture/books/gay-rights-movement-won/. Accessed September 18, 2021.
41 Puar, *Right to Maim*, 108.
42 Ibid., 109.
43 See Matt Gurney, "Hamas Fires Rockets, Israel Delivers Food and Medicine," *National Post*, November 21, 2012. https://nationalpost.com/opinion/matt-gurney-while-hamas-fires-rockets-israel-delivers-food-and-medicine. Accessed January 2, 2022.
44 See Jeremy Sharon and Jonathan Weber Rosen, "Gay Couples Denied Right to Surrogacy in New Law," *Jerusalem Post*, July 18, 2018. https://www.jpost.com/Israel-News/Surrogacy-bill-passes-Netanyahu-flip-flops-on-homosexual-surrogacy-562810. Accessed January 2, 2022.
45 Toi Staff, "High Court Extends Surrogacy Rights to Gay Couples, Straight Men," *Times of Israel*, February 27, 2020. https://www.timesofisrael.com/high-court-extends-surrogacy-rights-to-gay-couples/. Accessed August 21, 2020.
46 Puar, *Right to Maim*, 117.
47 Ibid., 118.
48 Palko Karasz, "85,000 Children in Yemen May Have Died of Starvation," *New York Times*, November 21, 2018. https://www.nytimes.com/2018/11/21/world/middleeast/yemen-famine-children.html. Accessed August 28, 2020.
49 Simon Tisdall, "Don't Call Them Syria's Child Casualties. This Is the Slaughter of the Innocents," *Guardian*. https://www.theguardian.com/world/2019/aug/03/syria-idlib-child-deaths-airstrikes-assad-putin-russia. Accessed August 28, 2020.
50 Jack Moore, "ISIS Torture Methods Revealed: Sitting with Severed Heads, Fuel Dousing and the 'Flying Carpet,'" *Newsweek*, August 15, 2017. https://www.newsweek.com/torture-methods-isis-revealed-sitting-severed-heads-fuel-dousing-and-flying-650828. Accessed August 28, 2020.
51 Kara Anderson, "'Cubs of the Caliphate': The Systematic Recruitment, Training, and Use of Children in the Islamic State." https://www.drake.edu/media/departmentsoffices/international/nelson/2016%20paper,%20Children%20in%20ISIS,%20K.%20Anderson.pdf. Accessed August 28, 2020.
52 Patricia Gossman, "Afghan War's Terrible Toll on Children," *Human Rights Watch*, July 1, 2019. https://www.hrw.org/news/2019/07/01/afghanistan-wars-terrible-toll-children. Accessed August 28, 2020.

53 See Save the Children, https://www.savethechildren.org/us/charity-stories/worst-conflict-affected-countries-to-be-a-child. Accessed September 18, 2021.

54 See "Children in the Israeli-Palestinian Conflict," *Wikipedia*. https://en.wikipedia.org/wiki/Children_in_the_Israeli%E2%80%93Palestinian_conflict. Accessed September 4, 2020.

55 Max Fisher, "This Chart Shows Every Person Killed in the Israeli-Palestinian Conflict Since 2000," *Vox*, July 14, 2014. https://www.vox.com/2014/7/14/5898581/chart-israel-palestine-conflict-deaths. Accessed September 4, 2020.

56 Laurel Holliday, *Children of Israel, Children of Palestine* (New York: Simon & Schuster, 1999), xv. https://www.christianbook.com/children-israel-palestine-own-true-stories/laurel-holliday/9780671008048/pd/08048.

57 "UN: Ensure Integrity of Children's 'List of Shame,'" *Human Rights Watch*, June 4, 2015. https://www.hrw.org/news/2015/06/04/un-ensure-integrity-childrens-list-shame. Accessed August 28, 2020.

58 Puar, *Right to Maim*, 128.

59 NWSA Letter in Support of Jasbir K. Puar, September 26, 2018. https://www.nwsa.org/news/483403/NWSA-Letter-in-Support-of-Jasbir-K.-Puar.htm. Accessed January 2, 2022.

Chapter 3. Angela Davis: Israel as the Queer Intersectional Outsider

1 Lally Weymouth, "East Germany's Dirty Secret," *Washington Post*, October 14, 1990. https://www.washingtonpost.com/archive/opinions/1990/10/14/east-germanys-dirty-secret/09375b6f-2ae1-4173-a0dc-77a9c276aa4b/?utm_term=.57513a74a678. Accessed August 8, 2018. As Weymouth explains, East Germany was not only a sponsor but also a haven for terrorists. She notes that, "'Carlos' (Illich Ramirez Sanchez), an international terror chieftain, was welcomed to East Berlin, as were George Habash, head of the Popular Front for the Liberation of Palestine; Abu Nidal, the ultra-radical Palestinian, and Abu Daoud, who organized the massacre of the Israeli Olympic team at Munich in 1972. Yasser Arafat, the PLO leader, was a frequent visitor. In East German training camps, terrorists and would-be terrorists were taught sabotage and related arts—some of the 'students' were Sandinistas, others were Chilean 'dissidents.'"

2 Dissidents, who included the religious, pro-democracy advocates, nationalists, would-be emigrants, and homosexuals, were subjected to torturous psychiatric abuses in what Soviets called the *psikhushka*, or mental hospital.
3 Quoted in Alan Johnson, "What Does Angela Davis Know About Freedom?" *Telegraph*, October 5, 2013.
4 Eric Heinze, "Angela Davis's Racism: A Glance at Morality and History," *Critical Legal Thinking*, November 25, 2013.
5 See Michael Johns, "Seventy Years of Evil: Soviet Crimes from Lenin to Gorbachev," *Policy Review* (Fall 1987), 10–23.
6 Frederick C. Barghoorn and Thomas F. Remington, *Politics in the USSR*, 3d ed. (Boston: Little Brown, 1986), 71–72.
7 Nikita Khrushchev, quoted in "Political Abuse of Psychiatry in the Soviet Union," *Wikipedia*. https://en.wikipedia.org/wiki/Political_abuse_of_psychiatry_in_the_Soviet_Union. Accessed August 4, 2018. "A crime is a deviation from generally recognized standards of behavior frequently caused by mental disorder. Can there be diseases, nervous disorders among certain people in a Communist society? Evidently, yes. If that is so, then there will also be offences, which are characteristic of people with abnormal minds. Of those who might start calling for opposition to Communism on this basis, we can say that clearly their mental state is not normal."
8 Heinze, "Angela Davis's Racism."
9 Aleksandr Solzhenitsyn, *Detente, Democracy and Dictatorship* (New York: Taylor & Francis, 2018), 89.
10 Ibid.
11 While antisemitism has declined in the former Soviet Union, particularly since the 2000s, and while Russian Federation president Vladimir Putin has crafted cordial relations with Israel, there are always fears of a resurgence of popular antisemitism.
12 Heinze, "Angela Davis's Racism."
13 See Harold Sachar, *A History of the Jews in the Modern World* (New York: Knopf, 2005), 722. Sachar remarks that, "in late July 1967, Moscow launched an unprecedented propaganda campaign against Zionism as a 'world threat.' . . . In its flagrant vulgarity, the new propaganda assault soon achieved Nazi-era characteristics. The Soviet public was saturated with racist canards. . . . Yuri Ivanov's *Beware: Zionism*, a book that essentially replicated *The Protocols of the Elders of Zion*, was given nationwide coverage."

14 UN General Assembly Resolutions: Resolution 3379, November 10, 1975. https://www.jewishvirtuallibrary.org/un-general-assembly-resolution-3379-november-1975. Accessed August 3, 2018. Also see "Fighting the 'Zionism is Racism' Lie: Moynihan's Historic U. N. Speech," *UN Watch*, November 10, 1975. In his speech before the UN, Daniel Patrick Moynihan noted that "the United Nations is about to make anti-Semitism international law," and said during his speech that the United States "does not acknowledge, it will not abide by, it will never acquiesce in this infamous act. . . . A great evil has been loosed upon the world." https://unwatch.org/moynihans-moment-the-historic-1975-u-n-speech-in-response-to-zionism-is-racism/.

15 Christopher Gacek, "Removing the Stain of the United Nations' 'Zionism is Racism' Resolution," *Heritage Foundation*, September 12, 1991. https://www.heritage.org/node/21312/. Accessed September 19, 2021.

16 "When I See Them, I See Us: Intersectional Struggle & Transnational Solidarity with Palestine," October 14, 2015. http://www.blackforpalestine.com/read-the-statement.html. Accessed January 2, 2021. In one section, this group makes the following statement: "Black-Palestinian solidarity is neither a guarantee nor a requirement—it is a choice. We choose to build with one another in a shoulder to shoulder struggle against state-sanctioned violence. A violence that is manifest in the speed of bullets and batons and tear gas that pierce our bodies. One that is latent in the edifice of law and concrete that work together to, physically and figuratively, cage us. We choose to join one another in resistance not because our struggles are the same but because we each struggle against the formidable forces of structural racism and the carceral and lethal technologies deployed to maintain them. This video intends to interrupt that process—to assert our humanity—and to stand together in an affirmation of life and a commitment to resistance. From Ferguson to Gaza, from Baltimore to Jerusalem, from Charleston to Bethlehem, we will be free."

17 A black disabled lesbian might live in a segregated neighborhood deficient in public wheelchair access, and cannot receive help purchasing groceries from her parents who have disowned her for her lesbianism.

18 Kimberlé Crenshaw, "Demarginalizing the Intersection of Race and Sex: A Black Feminist Critique of Antidiscrimination Doctrine, Feminist Theory and Antiracist Policies," *University of Chicago Legal Forum* 8, no. 1 (1989): 140

19 Ibid., 152.

20 Although Davis did not come out as a lesbian until 1997, when she was 53, which makes her characterization of Soviet dissidents as "common criminals" all the more troubling, as homosexuals were considered mentally ill and subjected to psychiatric prisons or hard labor. See http://outhistory.org/exhibits/show/aa-history-month-bios/angela-davis. Accessed January 2, 2022.

21 Sohrab Ahmari, "Why Postmodern Intersectionality Imperils Israel and Jews," *Commentary*, March 20, 2018. https://www.commentarymagazine.com/sohrab-ahmari/why-postmodern-intersectionality-imperils-israel-and-jews/. Accessed July 17, 2020.

22 While I am not suggesting that intersectional analyses of exteriorized phenomena—which differ along the axes of politics, religion, nation, culture, language, and history—are impossible, they are very difficult to do with accuracy and insight.

23 Angela Y. Davis, *Women, Race and Class* (New York: Vintage, 1983), 172–73.

24 Mazin Sidahmad, "Critics Denounce Black Lives Matter Platform Accusing Israel of 'Genocide,'" *Guardian*, August 11, 2016. https://www.theguardian.com/us-news/2016/aug/11/black-lives-matters-movement-palestine-platform-israel-critics. January 2, 2022. To be completely accurate, the policy platform, A Vision for Black Lives, which was drafted by more than sixty organizations known as the Movement for Black Lives, contained the accusation that the Israelis were guilty of genocide, in addition to apartheid.

25 Anna Isaacs, "How the Black Lives Matter and Palestinian Movements Converged," *Moment*, March–April 2016. https://momentmag.com/how-the-black-lives-matter-and-palestinian-movements-converged/. Accessed September 19, 2021.

26 Benjamin Gladstone, "It's Time for Intersectionality to Include the Jews," *Tablet Magazine*, March 20, 2017. https://www.tabletmag.com/scroll/227837/its-time-for-intersectionality-to-include-the-jews. Accessed January 2, 2022.

27 See Jewish Virtual Library, "Black-Jewish Relations in the United States." https://www.jewishvirtuallibrary.org/black-jewish-relations-in-the-united-states. Accessed August 8, 2018.

28 Shiryn Ghermezian, "Activists Say Historical Black Struggle 'Hijacked' After 'Black Lives Matter' Leaders Endorse BDS," *Algemeiner*, August 9, 2015. https://www.algemeiner.com/2015/08/19/activist-says-historical-black-struggle-hijacked-after-blacks-lives-matter-activists-endorse-bds/. Accessed January 2, 2022.

29 Larry Buchanan, Ford Fessenden, K. K. Rebecca Lai, Haeyoun Park, Alicia Parlapiano, Archie Tse, Tim Wallace, Derek Watkins, and Karen Yourish, "What Happened in Ferguson?" *New York Times*, updated August 10, 2015. https://www.nytimes.com/interactive/2014/08/13/us/ferguson-missouri-town-under-siege-after-police-shooting.html. Accessed August 4, 2018.

30 Nedra Pickler, "Obama: Ferguson Police Discrimination 'Oppressive and Abusive,'" *PBS News Hour*, March 7, 2015. "A Justice Department investigation found patterns of racial profiling, bigotry and profit-driven law enforcement and court practices within the Ferguson Police Department. Ferguson city leaders are to meet with Justice Department officials in about two weeks to put forth an improvement plan." https://www.pbs.org/newshour/politics/obama-calls-ferguson-police-discrimination-oppressive-abusive-citing-doj-report. Accessed January 2, 2022.

31 For a complete accounting of the 2014 Gaza War, see https://en.wikipedia.org/wiki/2014_Gaza_War. Accessed September 19, 2021.

32 Dominic Green, "The Intersectionality of Fools," *New Criterion* 35, no. 5 (2017). https://www.newcriterion.com/issues/2017/1/the-intersectionality-of-fools. Accessed January 2, 2022.

33 See *When I See Them*.

34 Yoav Fromer, "How Israel Is Being Framed: Why Palestine Is No Ferguson," *Tablet Magazine*, December 3, 2015. https://www.tabletmag.com/jewish-news-and-politics/195487/how-israel-is-being-framed. Accessed January 2, 2022.

35 Maxime Rodinson, *Israel: A Colonial-Settler State?* (New York: Pathfinder Press, 1973), 94.

36 Communist Party of Great Britain, *Communist Party to Meet the Crisis: Reports of the 21st National Congress of the Communist Party* (London: MW Books, 1949), 30.

37 Fromer, "How Israel Is Being Framed."

38 "Remembering Martin Luther King, Jr.," *American Zionist Movement*, January 12, 2021. https://azm.org/remembering-mlk. Accessed September 19, 2021.

39 "U.S.-Israel Strategic Cooperation and Joint Police and Law Enforcement Training," *Jewish Virtual Library*. https://www.jewishvirtuallibrary.org/joint-us-israel-police-and-law-enforcement-training. Accessed August 10, 2018.

40 Angela Y. Davis, *Freedom Is a Constant Struggle: Ferguson, Palestine, and the Foundations of a Movement* (Chicago: Haymarket Books, 2016), 16.

41 Ibid., 19.
42 Ibid., 21.
43 "Hamas Covenant 1988: The Covenant of the Islamic Resistance Movement," *Yale Law School*. https://avalon.law.yale.edu/20th_century/hamas.asp. Accessed September 19, 2021.
44 Chloe Valdary, "To Students for Justice in Palestine, a Letter from an Angry Black Woman," *Tablet Magazine*, July 28, 2014. https://www.tabletmag.com/sections/news/articles/students-justice-palestine. Accessed January 2, 2022.
45 Moshe Phillips and Benyamin Korn, "Conclusive Proof that Hamas Uses Palestinians as Human Shields," *Algemeiner*, August 7, 2014. https://www.algemeiner.com/2014/08/07/conclusive-proof-that-hamas-uses-palestinians-as-human-shields/. Accessed January 2, 2022. According to the authors, on "August 5, the Israeli Army released copies of an official Hamas manual that it discovered in the Shuja'iya neighborhood of Gaza, where one of the fiercest battles of the war was fought. It's titled 'Urban Warfare.' . . . The manual includes detailed instructions on how to use the civilians of Gaza against Israel. It explains how because of Israel's concern about civilian casualties, Hamas can use the 'presence of civilians' to its military advantage. Having civilians nearby causes the Israelis '(1) Problems with opening fire; (2) Problems in controlling the civilian population during operations and afterward; (3) Assurance of supplying medical care to civilians who need it.'"
46 Fred Pleitgen, "Human Trafficking in the Sinai: To Fight It We Need to Know It," *CNN*, February 22, 2013. Pleitgen reports that "some of the major traffickers, including Abu Ahmed and Abu Khaled, have declared in interviews reported in the media, to be part of Hamas. In Sudan, through this massive fundraising activity focused on the abduction and sale of human beings, they are preparing the future stages of the war against the 'infidels,' Western culture and the State of Israel. This is after the nation has experienced a terrible racial genocide. Even in Egypt, the jihadist Rashaida control, along with other jihadist Bedouin groups (again linked to Hamas), organized crime, supplying this arsenal of terrorism. The rockets that are hitting Israel repeatedly, and the Kalashnikovs in possession of Hamas militants are bought with profits from the slave and human organs trade." See "Human Trafficking in the Sinai: To Fight It We Need to Know It," *The Global Muslim Brotherhood Daily Watch*, March 25, 2013. https://www.globalmbwatch.com/2013/03/25/recommended-reading-human-trafficking-in-the-sinai-to-fight-it-we-need-to-know-it/. Accessed January 2, 2022.

Chapter 4. Dean Spade's BDS Activist Malpractice

1 See A Wider Bridge. https://awiderbridge.org/about/. Accessed August 13, 2018. AWB characterizes its mission as building "*personal rather than political relationships* [emphasis mine] with Israel and LGBTQ Israelis, providing leaders, organizations and communities, both in Israel and North America, with opportunities for engagement, advocacy, and philanthropy. We believe two kinds of outcomes will result from this bridge building: equality *in* Israel, and equality *for* Israel. Equality *in* Israel: With the support of North American LGBTQ people and allies, Israel's LGBTQ community will be better positioned to advance social, political and cultural change. LGBTQ equality will strengthen Israel as a society where all people labeled 'the other' are welcomed and celebrated throughout the country. Equality *for* Israel: Israel should be included and treated with fairness in our LGBTQ communities, by our local and national institutions, and within the community of nations. We believe our communities are strengthened when people move from demonizing and delegitimizing Israel to a place of understanding, empathy, and engagement."
2 Hannah Elyse Simpson, "Chicago's Creating Change Conference Was a Mess," *Advocate*, February 5, 2016. https://www.advocate.com/commentary/2016/2/05/chicagos-creating-change-conference-was-mess. Accessed July 11, 2020.
3 Mark Joseph Stern, "The LGBTQ Left Has an Anti-Semitism Problem," *Slate*, January 25, 2016. http://www.slate.com/blogs/outward/2016/01/25/creating_change_protest_of_a_wider_bridge_was_anti_semitic.html. Accessed August 13, 2018.
4 Simpson, "Chicago's Creating Change."
5 Michael K. Lavers, "Protesters Disrupt Reception with Israeli Activists at LGBT Conference," *Washington Blade*, January 23, 2015. http://www.washingtonblade.com/2016/01/23/protesters-disrupt-reception-with-israeli-activists-at-lgbt-conference/. Accessed January 1, 2022.
6 Michael Lucas, "The Creating Change Protest Was Pure Anti-Semitism," *Out*, January 27, 2016. https://www.out.com/2016/1/27/op-ed-creating-change-protest-was-pure-anti-semitism. Accessed January 1, 2022.
7 "A Wider Bridge: Creating Change, Not Hate," https://www.youtube.com/watch?time_continue=13&v=Rz4KkvvjBB8. Accessed August 13, 2018.

8 See Jerusalem Open House for Pride and Tolerance, https://docs.wixstatic.com/ugd/df5bd8_7fa4881f1c484593ac35cc81bcef77e6.pdf. Accessed August 13, 2018.
9 Yaniv Kubovich, "16-Year-Old Stabbed in Jerusalem Pride Parade Succumbs to Wounds," *Haaretz*, August 2, 2015. https://www.haaretz.com/teen-stabbed-in-j-lem-pride-parade-dies-1.5382156. Accessed January 1, 2022. Another five people received nonfatal knife wounds. The assailant, Yishai Schlissel, had been convicted of stabbing three pride parade marchers in 2005, and had just been released from a ten-year prison sentence for those crimes when he again went on a stabbing rampage.
10 Jonathan Capehart, "This Show of Anti-Semitism at an LGBT Conference Should Bring Change," *Washington Post*, January 27, 2016. https://www.washingtonpost.com/blogs/post-partisan/wp/2016/01/27/this-show-of-anti-semitism-at-an-lgbt-conference-should-bring-change/. Accessed July 11, 2020.
11 Bret Stephens, "The Progressive Assault on Israel," *New York Times*, February 8, 2019. https://www.nytimes.com/2019/02/08/opinion/sunday/israel-progressive-anti-semitism.html. Accessed July 11, 2020.
12 John Becker, "Anti-Semitism Becoming More Brazen, Including in LGBTQ Spaces," *Advocate*, February 13, 2019. https://www.advocate.com/commentary/2019/2/11/anti-semitism-becoming-more-brazen-including-lgbtq-spaces. Accessed July 11, 2020.
13 Creating Change Conference Website, https://www.thetaskforce.org/creating-change. Accessed January 1, 2022.
14 Dean Spade, "A Synopsis of Pinkwashing Exposed." http://www.deanspade.net/projects/pinkwashing-exposed/. Accessed August 14, 2018.
15 Melanie Nathan and Scott Rose, "Seattle LGBT Commission's Boycott of Israeli LGBTI Guests Opens Wounds," *O-Blog-Dee Blog*, March 16, 2012. https://oblogdee.blog/2012/03/16/seattle-lgbt-commissions-boycott-of-israeli-lgbti-guests-opens-wounds/. Accessed August 14, 2018.
16 Arthur Slepian, "An Inconvenient Truth: The Myths of Pinkwashing," *Tikkun*, July 3, 2012. https://www.tikkun.org/nextgen/an-inconvenient-truth-the-myths-of-pinkwashing. Accessed September 20, 2021.
17 StandWithUs, https://www.standwithus.com/about. Accessed September 20, 2021.
18 Slepian, "An Inconvenient Truth."

19 According to the Anti-Defamation League, "Jewish Voice for Peace is a radical anti-Israel activist group that advocates for a complete economic, cultural and academic boycott of the state of Israel. JVP rejects the view that the Israeli-Palestinian conflict is a tragic dispute over land which has been perpetuated by a cycle of violence, fear, and distrust on both sides, in favor of the belief that Israeli policies and actions are motivated by deeply rooted Jewish racial chauvinism and religious supremacism." https://www.adl.org/resources/backgrounders/jewish-voice-for-peace. Accessed August 14, 2018.

20 Dean Spade (dir.) and Amy Mahardy (ed.), *Pinkwashing Exposed: Seattle Fights Back*, May 6, 2015. https://pinkwashingexposed.net/2015/05/06/watch-pinkwashing-exposed-seattle-fights-back/. Accessed August 14, 2018.

21 Spade, *Pinkwashing Exposed*.

22 Yariv Mozer (dir.). *The Invisible Men* (2015). http://nfct.org.il/en/movies/the-invisible-men/. Accessed August 15, 2018. The ironies of labeling this documentary pinkwashing propaganda include that the director not only indicts the murderous homophobia of Palestinian society but also—even more so—the anti-Palestinian policies of the Israeli government, which rounds up these men and returns them home to their almost certain deaths.

23 Spade, *Pinkwashing Exposed*.

24 Ibid.

25 Shany Mor, "The Mendacious Maps of Palestinian 'Loss,'" *Tower Magazine* 22 (January 2013). http://www.thetower.org/article/the-mendacious-maps-of-palestinian-loss/. Accessed January 1, 2022.

26 Arthur James Balfour, "The Balfour Declaration," November 2, 1917. http://avalon.law.yale.edu/20th_century/balfour.asp. Accessed August 15, 2018.

27 British White Paper of 1939. https://www.myjewishlearning.com/article/british-white-paper-of-1939/. Accessed August 15, 2018. On the eve of the Holocaust, the British, responding to Arab pressure, ended Jewish immigration to *Eretz Yisrael*.

28 See Klaus-Michael Mallman and Martin Cuppers, *Nazi Palestine: The Plans for the Extermination of the Jews of Palestine* (New York: Enigma Books, 2010). As the authors explain, Mohammed Amin al-Husayni, the Grand Mufti of Jerusalem, visited Axis capitals and met Adolf Hitler and Heinrich Himmler. Not only did Nazi Germany promise to end the European "colonial" (read: Jewish) presence that had replaced the Ottoman Empire after 1918, it also pledged to wipe out the Jews who

had been living in Palestine since time immemorial, as well as the new arrivals from the beginning of the modern Zionist movement in the nineteenth century and following the Balfour Declaration in 1917. The process of extermination was to be activated, and SS and SD officers were selected and assigned to the effort. They were to operate behind the lines with the help of those in the region who were eager to join the task force. When the Afrika Korps was defeated at El Alamein, the *Einsatzkommando* shifted its operations to Tunisia, where it implemented cruel anti-Jewish policies for many months.

29 See Alan Taylor, "The Signing of the Egypt-Israel Peace Treaty," *Atlantic*, March 26, 2015. https://www.theatlantic.com/photo/2015/03/on-this-day-36-years-ago-the-signing-of-the-egyptisrael-peace-treaty/388781/. Accessed January 1, 2022. As Taylor remarks, Sadat and Begin were both awarded the 1978 Nobel Peace Prize for their collaborative work. President Sadat was later assassinated by Egyptian Islamic extremists outraged by his rapprochement with Israel.

30 Mor, "Mendacious Maps."

31 Office of the Historian, "Oslo Accords and Arab-Israeli Peace Process." https://history.state.gov/milestones/1993-2000/oslo. Accessed August 16, 2018.

32 Michael C. Horowitz, "The Rise and Spread of Suicide Bombing," *Annual Review of Political Science* 18 (May 2015): 69–84. https://www.annualreviews.org/doi/full/10.1146/annurev-polisci-062813-051049. Accessed January 1, 2022. Horowitz notes that contemporary suicide bombing began in Lebanon during the 1980s, then spread to Israel, where it was used by Palestinians against Israeli civilian targets.

33 See Mor, "Mendacious Maps."

34 See "1948 Palestinian Exodus." https://en.wikipedia.org/wiki/1948_Palestinian_exodus. Accessed August 16, 2018. Nakba, or al-Nakbah, which is the Arabic word for catastrophe, refers to the expulsion of Arab Palestinians from their homes during the Israeli War of Independence, December 1947 to January 1949.

35 Jon Bridge and Hemda Arad, "Mayor Murray's Israel Trip Supports Human Rights," *Seattle Times*, May 20, 2015. https://www.seattletimes.com/opinion/mayor-murrays-israel-trip-supports-human-rights/. Accessed January 1, 2022.

36 Dean Spade, "The Right Wing Is Leveraging Trans Issues to Promote Militarism," *TRUTHOUT*, April 5, 2017. https://truthout.org/articles/the

-right-wing-is-leveraging-trans-issues-to-promote-militarism/. Accessed January 1, 2022.
37. Ibid.
38. Ibid.
39. Ibid.
40. See David Hirsh, *Contemporary Left Antisemitism* (New York: Routledge, 2017). This book homes in on the ways those who raise the issue of antisemitism are often accused of doing so in bad faith, in an attempt to smear or silence "legitimate" criticism of Israel. Opposition to Israel has become a signifier of identity, connected to opposition to imperialism, neoliberalism, and global capitalism.
41. See the CitizenGO website, which opposes policies that accommodate transgender people, supports "biological reality," and publicizes the violent, destructive, and disruptive protests against their provocative activism. https://www.citizengo.org/en. Accessed September 19, 2021.
42. Spade, "Right Wing."
43. Nada Elia, "Once Again, Seattle LGBTQ Commission Falls for Israeli 'Pinkwashing' Campaign, *Mondoweiss*," April 2, 2017. https://mondoweiss.net/2017/04/commission-pinkwashing-campaign/. Accessed September 19, 2021.
44. Jessica M. Choplin and Debra Pogrund Stark, "A Response to an Anti-Semitic View," *A Wider Bridge*, April 14, 2017. https://awiderbridge.org/a-response-to-an-anti-semitic-view/. Accessed January 1, 2022.
45. Dean Spade, *Administrative Violence, Critical Trans Politics, and the Limits of Law* (Durham, NC: Duke University Press, 2015), 141.
46. Alice Dreger, *Galileo's Middle Finger: Heretics, Activists, and One Scholar's Search for Justice* (New York: Penguin, 2016), 87.

Chapter 5. Judith Butler's One-State Solution Trouble

1. Stanley Fish, "Academic Freedom Vindicated at Brooklyn," *New York Times*, February 11, 2013. https://opinionator.blogs.nytimes.com/2013/02/11/academic-freedom-vindicated-in-brooklyn/. September 19, 2021. Fish explains that nine members of the Council of the City of New York found it "offensive" that the college was giving "official support and sponsorship to speakers who equate terrorists with progressives and the Israeli people with Nazis." But as Fish goes on to note, these "public efforts at intimidation drew a vigorous response from educational

experts and from officials at Brooklyn College and its parent, the City University of New York. President Gould hit the nail on the head ... when she explained in a statement that 'Brooklyn College does not endorse the views of the speakers visiting our campus next week, just as it has not endorsed those of previous visitors to our campus with opposing views.' ... Barbara Bowen, president of CUNY's Professional Staff Congress, in a letter to the hapless public officials, skewered the 'balance' argument: 'Academic freedom is "the free search for truth and its free exposition." Academic freedom is not "balance"; it is not the requirement that departments support only forums that advocate equally strongly for two "sides."'"

2 Judith Butler, "Judith Butler's Remarks to Brooklyn College on BDS." *Nation*, February 7, 2013. https://www.thenation.com/article/archive/judith-butlers-remarks-brooklyn-college-bds/. September 19, 2021.

3 See, for instance, A. Jay Adler, "Response to Judith Butler at Brooklyn College," *Algemeiner*, February 15, 2013. https://www.algemeiner.com/2013/02/15/response-to-judith-butler-at-brooklyn-college/. Accessed September 19, 2021. Among other things, Adler objected to Butler's frequent use of Yiddish phrases in a speech that was so fervently anti-Israel and anti-Zionist.

4 See Logan Lender, "The Case for Rational Zionism," *Metric*, November 23, 2017. https://themetric.org/articles/the-case-for-rational-zionism. Accessed August 29, 2020.

5 "Harm to Palestinians Suspected of Collaborating with Israelis," *B'Tselem: The Israeli Information Center for Human Rights in the Occupied Territories*, January 1, 2017. https://www.btselem.org/inter_palestinian_violations/copy%20of%20index. Accessed August 27, 2020. The website states that, "during the first intifada, hundreds of Palestinians were killed by their fellow Palestinians for allegedly collaborating with Israel. The definition of 'collaboration' was much broader then, and included, for example, directly assisting Israeli security forces by gathering information and trapping wanted persons, serving on Israel's behalf in political positions in local authorities, the Civil Administration, and the Israel Police Force, brokering and selling land to Israeli organizations, failing to participate in work strikes, marketing banned Israeli merchandise. Also, collaboration included actions defined as 'immoral,' even if not directly related to assisting the Israeli authorities. Prostitution and drug dealing came within this category. In the current intifada, individuals who maintain contacts with Israel's security services are deemed

collaborators. In many cases, the attacks against suspected collaborators were particularly brutal. Some suspects were abducted, tortured, killed and then had their bodies mutilated and placed on public display. These acts against collaborators, particularly the killing of suspects, are patently illegal and immoral. They constitute grave breaches of the Four Geneva Conventions, and the International Criminal Court Statute defines these acts as war crimes. Every state, organization and individual, even those that are not formal parties to these international agreements, are subject to its rules and principles. International law also provides that a person may be punished only after being charged and convicted of a recognized criminal offense. In addition, defendants are entitled to due process and the opportunity to properly defend themselves. Israeli security forces pressure Palestinians to collaborate. A usual method entails the security forces requiring Palestinians to collaborate as a condition to receiving the permits necessary to earn a livelihood, obtain medical treatment, and the like, in exchange for information. It is also common practice for Israel to pay for information, a practice that takes advantage of the poverty that prevails in the Occupied Territories."

6 Neta Alexander, "The Palestinian Professor Who Took Students on Auschwitz Trip and Paid a Heavy Price," *Haaretz*, October 4, 2018. https://www.haaretz.com/israel-news/.premium.MAGAZINE-the-palestinian-who-leads-tours-through-auschwitz-1.5435444. Accessed August 27, 2020.

7 See Cary Nelson, *Not in Kansas Anymore: Academic Freedom in Palestinian Universities* (New York: AEN, 2020), for an extended treatment of how so-called collaborators and peace-seekers are regularly targeted for abuse and violence.

8 See James Kirchick, "The Professor's Shoddy History," *Tablet Magazine*, October 5, 2012. https://www.tabletmag.com/sections/news/articles/the-professors-shoddy-history. Accessed September 21, 2021. After the *Jerusalem Post* published criticism of Butler for her qualified support for these terrorist organizations, Butler attempted, as Kirchick points out, to "paint her subjective description of the Islamic terrorist groups as a normative one." She replied, "Those political organizations define themselves as anti-imperialist, and anti-imperialism is one characteristic of the global left, so on that basis one could describe them as part of the global left." What Butler means by "the global left" remains unclear, and she has a naïve view of Third World anti-imperialist struggles, uninformed by post-colonialist history.

9 "Human Rights Watch Country Profiles: Sexual Orientation and Gender Identity," *Human Rights Watch*, June 23, 2017. https://www.hrw

.org/news/2017/06/23/human-rights-watch-country-profiles-sexual-orientation-and-gender-identity. Accessed August 30, 2020. In Gaza, "unnatural intercourse" of a sexual nature, understood to include same-sex relationships, is a crime punishable by up to ten years in prison. In February 2016 Hamas's armed wing executed one of its fighters ostensibly for "behavioral and moral violations," which Hamas officials acknowledged meant same-sex relations.
10 Alan Johnson, "Book Review: Parting Ways: Jewishness and the Critique of Zionism," *Fathom* (Spring 2013). http://fathomjournal.org/book-review-parting-ways-jewishness-and-the-critique-of-zionism/. Accessed September 1, 2020
11 Butler, *Parting Ways: Jewishness and the Critique of Zionism* (New York: Columbia University Press, 2013), 116.
12 See Max Weber, "Politics as a Vocation." Weber, in his introduction to this essay, defines the state as an entity that exercises a monopoly on the legitimate exercise of force within a territorial jurisdiction. http://fs2.american.edu/dfagel/www/Class%20Readings/Weber/PoliticsAsAVocation.pdf. Accessed January 1, 2022.
13 Cary Nelson, "The Problem with Judith Butler: The Political Philosophy of the Movement to Boycott Israel." *Los Angeles Review of Books.* March 16, 2014, 19.
14 Johnson, "Book Review."
15 *Tikkun olam*, the Hebrew phrase for "repair of the world," is the essential Jewish ethical obligation to restore the world and act beneficially and constructively for world betterment.
16 See Butler, *Parting Ways*.
17 Chaim Gans, "Review—*Parting Ways: Jewishness and the Critique of Zionism*," *Notre Dame Philosophical Reviews*, December 13, 2012. https://ndpr.nd.edu/news/parting-ways-jewishness-and-the-critique-of-zionism/. Accessed January 1, 2022.
18 As a proponent of BDS, Butler would see this embrace of diasporic identities less as "voluntary" and more as constrained or necessitated by the successful outcome of a BDS movement that would isolate, demonize, and economically cripple Israel.
19 Quoted in Johnson, "Book Review."
20 "Social Justice as a Gateway to the Israel Experience," *AMEINU*, April 29, 2019. https://www.ameinu.net/blog/israel/social-justice-as-a-gateway-to-the-israel-experience/. Accessed August 29, 2020.
21 See Natan Sharansky, "The Recurring Issue: On Hating the Jews," *World Zionist Organization.* http://www.wzo.org.il/index.php?dir=site&

page=articles&op=item&cs=3150&langpage=eng. Accessed August 23, 2018. Sharansky observes that, "Theodor Herzl, the founder of modern Zionism, became convinced that the primary cause of anti-Semitism was the anomalous condition of the Jews: a people without a polity of its own. In his seminal work, *The Jewish State* (1896), published two years after the trial, Herzl envisioned the creation of such a Jewish polity and predicted that a mass emigration to it of European Jews would spell the end of anti-Semitism. Although his seemingly utopian political treatise would turn out to be one of the 20th century's most prescient books, on this point history has not been kind to Herzl; no one would seriously argue today that anti-Semitism came to a halt with the founding of the state of Israel. To the contrary, this particular illusion has come full circle: while Herzl and most Zionists after him believed that the emergence of a Jewish state would end anti-Semitism, an increasing number of people today, including some Jews, are convinced that anti-Semitism will end only with the disappearance of the Jewish state."

22 Tony Just, "Israel: The Alternative," *New York Review of Books*, October 23, 2003. https://www.nybooks.com/articles/2003/10/23/israel-the-alternative/. Accessed January 1, 2022.

23 Leon Wieseltier, "What Is Not to Be Done," *New Republic*, October 27, 2003. https://newrepublic.com/article/62173/what-not-be-done. Accessed January 1, 2022.

24 Wieseltier, "What Is Not to Be Done."

25 To the best of my knowledge, Butler is not involved in efforts to return indigenous lands in the current United States to their original inhabitants.

26 See Melanie Phillips, "The Toxic Reality of Antisemitism in Europe," *Jerusalem Post*, April 18, 2018. https://www.jpost.com/Opinion/The-toxic-reality-of-antisemitism-in-Europe-549675. January 1, 2022.

27 Butler, *Parting Ways*, 1.

28 Gans, "Review—Parting Ways."

29 Ibid.

30 Butler, *Parting Ways*, 20.

31 Bruce Robbins (dir.), *Some of My Best Friends Are Zionists*, March 13, 2013. https://vimeo.com/67424923. Accessed January 1, 2022.

32 David Hirsh, *Contemporary Left Antisemitism* (New York: Routledge, 2018), 228.

33 See Irene Tucker, *A Brief Genealogy of Jewish Republicanism: Parting Ways with Judith Butler*. (New York: Creative Commons, 2016).
34 Russell Berman, "Representing the Trial: Judith Butler Reads Hannah Arendt Reading Adolf Eichmann," *Fathom*, April 18, 2016. https://fathomjournal.org/representing-the-trial-judith-butler-reads-hannah-arendt-reading-adolf-eichmann/. Accessed September 1, 2020.
35 Sigmund Freud, *Moses and Monotheism* (New York: Vintage, 1955).
36 Butler, *Parting Ways*, 29.
37 See Michele Alperin, "Next Year in Jerusalem," *My Jewish Learning*. https://www.myjewishlearning.com/article/next-year-in-jerusalem/. Accessed September 1, 2020.
38 Gans, "Review—Parting Ways."
39 See "Reform Judaism." *Encycolpedia.com*. https://www.encyclopedia.com/history/united-states-and-canada/us-history/reform-judaism. Updated May 14, 2018. Accessed September 19, 2021.
40 Zachary Braiterman, "Parting Ways: Jewishness and the Critique of Zionism," *Jewish Philosophy Place: Aesthetics and Critical Thought*, September 14, 2012. https://jewishphilosophyplace.com/2012/09/14/parting-ways-jewishness-and-the-critique-of-zionism-judith-butler/. Accessed January 1, 2022.
41 Braiterman, "Parting Ways."
42 Walt Whitman, *Song of Myself* (New York: 2013), no. 51, 67.
43 Butler, *Parting Ways*, 18.
44 Seyla Benhabib, "Ethics Without Normativity and Politics Without Historicity: On Judith Butler's *Parting Ways: Jewishness and the Critique of Zionism*," *Constellations* 20, no. 1 (2013). https://onlinelibrary.wiley.com/doi/abs/10.1111/cons.12028. Accessed January 1, 2022.
45 Butler, *Parting Ways*, 54.
46 Benhabib, "Ethics Without Normativity."
47 Ibid.
48 Quoted in Benhabib, "Ethics Without Normativity," 154.
49 Butler, *Parting Ways*, 62.
50 Ibid., 151.
51 Ibid., 26.
52 Ibid., 187.
53 Ibid., 186, 187.
54 See Idith Zertal, *Israel's Holocaust and the Politics of Nationhood* (New York: Cambridge University Press, 2005).
55 Ibid., 201.

56 Quoted in Nelson, *Israel Denial*, 112.
57 Benhabib, "Ethics Without Normativity," 157; Amos Oz, *Dear Zealots: Letters from a Divided Land*, trans. Jessica Cohen (New York: Houghton Mifflin Harcourt, 2018), 5.

Conclusion

1 Amos Oz, *Dear Zealots: Letters from a Divided Land*, trans. Jessica Cohen (New York: Houghton Mifflin Harcourt, 2018), 5.
2 *Oriented* (dir. Jake Witzenfeld, in collaboration with Qambuta, 2015). https://www.orientedfilm.com. Accessed September 11, 2020.
3 Ibid.
4 Ibid.
5 Ibid.
6 See "2014 Gaza War," https://en.wikipedia.org/wiki/2014_Gaza_War. Accessed September 18, 2021.
7 Ibid.
8 Ibid.

INDEX

Abu Ahmed, 175n46
Abu Daoud, 170n1
Abu Khaled, 175n46
Abu Nidal, 170n1
Abunimah, Ali, 144n2
academic freedom: anti-Zionism/
   antisemitism/homophobia and threats
   to, 3–5; BDS as infringement of, xiii,
   3, 15, 21–24, 114; Butler on BDS and,
   111–13; Puar on, 53–54, 164n4; university policies on, 23–24, 180–81n1
Adler, A. Jay, 181n3
Afghanistan War, 71, 117
African Jews, 32, 34, 36, 120
Ahmadinejad, Mahmoud, 161n51
Ahmari, Sohrab, 84
AIDS/HIV activism and ACT UP, xiii, 5,
   44, 66, 67, 100
alQaws, 8, 14, 17, 96, 147–48n24, 151n55
Althusser, Louis, 114
Alwan, Dunya, 144n2
Anti-Defamation League (ADL), 12,
   157n6, 178n19
antisemitism: blood libel, 53, 163–64n2,
   165n16; Butler and, 113–16, 122;
   critiques of Israel and, 4, 8, 22–23,
   26, 121, 180n40; deicide and,
   158n9; at Durban Conference, 24;
   of Hamas, 160n31; rise and patterns
   of, 18, 158n9; in Russia, 171n11;
Schulman and, 31, 34–37, 47, 50;
   Soviet, 78, 80; Zionism and, Butler
   on, 113–14. *See also* intersectionality
   of anti-Zionism, antisemitism, and
   homophobia
anti-Zionism. *See* Zionism
apartheid state, representation of Israel
   as: by Butler, 112; by Davis, 81, 82, 86,
   90, 173n24; in pinkwashing and BDS
   advocacy, 21, 22, 24–27; by Puar, 55,
   56; by Schulman, 43, 46, 49, 50; by
   Spade, 96, 97, 101, 106, 108
apartheid wall. *See* security barrier /
   apartheid wall
Arab-Israeli War / War of Independence /
   Nakba (1948), 19–20; Butler and,
   117–18, 126, 130, 131; Davis and,
   89–90; definition of Nakba, 179n34;
   ejection of Palestinians from their
   homes in, 155n92; Schulman and, 27,
   35, 37; Spade and, 104, 106
Arab League Council, 24
Arab Revolt (1936–39), 18
Arafat, Yasser, 25, 105, 170n1
Arendt, Hannah, 122, 126, 129, 130
al-Assad, Bashar, 71
assemblages, Puar on, 54–55, 59, 61,
   62–68, 70, 73, 133, 168n34
assisted reproductive technologies (ART),
   54, 70

Association of Israeli LGBT Educational Organizations, 99–100
A Wider Bridge (AWB), 96–97, 99–101, 106, 107, 176n1
Azar, Assi, 107

Balfour Declaration, 103, 179n28
Banka, Shiri, 11, 98, 149n34, 177n9
Bard, Mitchell, 155n88
Barghouti, Omar, 21, 25–27, 46, 49, 111–12, 121
barrier wall, 25, 46, 90, 155n88. *See also* security barrier / apartheid wall
Begin, Menachem, 179n29
Benhabib, Seyla, 126, 127, 132
Benjamin, Walter, 122
Berman, Russell, 122
binationalism, 112, 117, 119–20, 124, 126
Black Laundry (Kvisa Shchora), 6
blacklisting, xv, 4, 8, 22, 29
Black Lives Matter, 82, 86, 89, 93, 173n24
Blady, Ken, 159–60n26
blood libel, 53, 163–64n2, 165n16
Bowen, Barbara, 181n1
Boycott, Divestment, and Sanctions (BDS) advocacy, 20–30; academic freedom, as infringement of, xiii, 3, 15, 21–24, 114; aims of, 25–27; annexation of LGBTQs by, 1–5, 29–30; anti-BDS legislation and legal actions, 4; anti-normalization policies of, 15, 25, 27, 39; Butler and, 111–16, 121, 125, 132, 183n18; campus activism of, 20–25, 153n75; contemplating "euthanasia" of Israel, 25, 27; Davis and, 77, 81, 90, 91, 93; on Gaza War (2008), 38, 39; inability to engage with Israel or pro-Israelis, 7–8, 15; as infringement of academic freedom, xiii, 3, 15, 21–24; Israel, anti-BDS legislation proposed in, 48; Israeli military operations triggering, viii; NWSA resolution, xiii; origins of, 24–25; on Palestinian LGBTQs, 15–16; pinkwashing and, 1–5, 8, 11–14, 15; postmodernism and queer BDS academic activists, 133–35; pro-Israel forces versus, 22–23; Puar and, 53, 54, 56, 60, 61, 68–70, 72, 73; Schulman and, 31–34, 39–42, 46, 48, 50; settler colonialism and, 25, 26, 155–56n92; Spade and, 96, 97, 99, 102, 105, 106, 109–10; Third Narrative versus, 28–29
"Brand Israel" campaign, 2, 101
breast cancer cause marketing, 5–6, 7, 146n15
Brezhnev, Leonid, 79
Britain: BDS originating in, 21; Palestinian Mandate under, 18–19, 89, 102–3
Brown, Michael, 87, 88, 91
Buber, Martin, 124
Butler, Judith, 111–32; on academic freedom and BDS, 111–13; antisemitism and, 113–16, 122; as anti-Zionist, 111–13, 115–19, 122; on Arendt and Levinas, 122, 126–29, 130; Barghouti, joint lecture with, 111–15, 121, 180–81n1; BDS advocacy of, 111–16, 121, 125, 132, 183n18; on binationalism, 112, 117, 119–20, 124, 126; cohabitation, on Jewish ethics of, 111–32; Davis and, 81, 89; Islamic terrorist organizations, normalization of, 114, 182n8; on Jewish anti-Zionism, 115–19, 121–25; as lesbian Jewish American queer theorist, 113, 114; on Primo Levi, 122, 129–31; on nationalism and the nation-state, 113, 116–18; one-state solution proposed by, 25, 119–20; performative use of Jewish identity by, 121–22, 123; on pinkwashing, 2; postmodernism and, 133–35; Puar and, 55; reductionist view of Zionism, 125–26; Schulman and, 40, 41, 47, 50

Camp David peace talks, 25
Canary Mission, 4, 22
Canning, Tom, 95–96
Capehart, Jonathan, 98
Carey, Rea, 96–97
Catholic Church, 1, 158n9
Children of Israel/Palestine (Holliday), 73
China, human rights violations in, 13, 145–46n10
Chomsky, Noam, 119
Choplin, Jessica M., 108
Christian evangelicals supporting Israel, homophobia of, 35
CitizenGO, 107, 180n41
Civil Rights movement, 86, 89, 93
cohabitation, Butler's Jewish ethics of, 117–19, 121–23, 125, 128–29, 130
colonialism, classical, 89. *See also* settler colonialism
consanguineous marriage, Palestinian practice of, 59
Creating Change LGBTQ conference, Spade's disruption of, 95–99
Crenshaw, Kimberlé, 82–83
Czechoslovakia, Davis on, 77, 78–79

Daoudi, Mohammed Dajani, 114
Darwish, Mahmood, 122–23
Davis, Angela, 77–94; anti-Zionism and intersectionality theory of, 81–85; BDS advocacy and, 77, 81, 90, 91, 93; Butler and, 81, 89; Ferguson, Missouri, and Israel/Palestine, on intersectionality of, 82, 85–93; human trafficking of Africans in Sinai by Hamas, failure to acknowledge, 94; LGBTQ community and, 78, 79, 81, 173n20; misapplication of intersectionality theory by, 83–84; on pinkwashing, 2; postmodernism and, 133–35; pro-Soviet views and opposition to American racism, 77–81, 83,
91, 94, 173n20; Puar and, 55, 81, 89; on same-sex relations in Middle East, 7; Schulman and, 81, 89; Spade and, 81, 89, 109; suffragism and racism, on intersectionality of, 84–85
Dear Zealots (Oz), 134–35
Defense for Children International, 72
Defense of Marriage Act (DOMA), 96
DeGraffenreid v. General Motors, 83
deicide, 158n9
Deleuze, Gilles, 54
Desiring Arabs (Massad), 44
Détente, Democracy and Dictatorship (Solzhenitsyn), 79–80
dhimmi laws, 20, 35, 118, 152–53n72
Dreger, Alice, 110
Drowned and the Saved, The (Levi), 130
Duggan, Lisa, 7, 147n22
Durban Strategy, 24–25

East Germany, 77, 80, 170n1
Egypt: in Arab-Israeli War (1948), 19, 35, 104; Arab Spring movement in, 48; Freud on Moses and, 123; Gaza and, 59, 68, 72, 104; LGBTQ community in, 9, 48, 161n51; peace treaty with Israel, 104, 179n29; pre-Ottoman control of Palestine by, 102; Rashaida in, 175n46; Six-Day War (1967), 81, 90, 104
Eichmann, Adolf, 129, 130
Eichmann in Jerusalem (Arendt), 129
Ellenson, David, xx
Elman, Miriam, xx, 11
Elman, R. Amy, xx, 146n11
Erez, Shachar, 106, 107

Faderman, Lillian, xx
Fatah, 105
Felix Guattari, Felix, 54
Ferguson, Missouri, and Israel/Palestine, Davis on intersectionality of, 82, 85–93

First Intifada, 65, 66, 181n5
Fish, Rachel, xx
Fish, Stanley, 180–81n1
Flawless (film), xix
Franke, Katherine, 2, 16
Freedman, Janet L., 143n2
Freedom Is a Constant Struggle (Davis), 81, 85, 88, 91
Freud, Sigmund, 123, 124
Fromer, Yoav, 89

galut, 32, 37, 41, 116, 125
Gandhi, Mahatma, 90
Gans, Chaim, 117, 120, 124
Gay Days (film), xix
gays and gay pride. *See* LGBTQ community
Gaza War (2008), 37–39, 40–41, 72, 155n92
genocide: Butler on, 129, 131; in class on Israel/Palestine conflict, xiv, xv, xvii, xviii; Davis on, 78, 86, 90, 94, 173n24, 175n46; increasing Palestinian population and, 164n46; Jews accused of hogging claim of, 164n46; pinkwashing and BDS advocacy, 12, 22, 24; Puar on, 56, 164n2; Schulman on, 35, 36, 37, 38, 41, 42, 43, 161n46; Spade on, 95, 96, 97, 101, 102, 108
Germany: Butler on LGBTQ community in, 47; East Germany and Davis, 77, 80, 170n1; Schulman in, 40. *See also* Holocaust; Nazis
Green, Dominic, 88
greenwashing, 6, 144n2
Gregory, Tyler, 97
Gross, Aeyal, 6

Habash, George, 170n1
Hamas: African human trafficking and organ harvesting by, 94, 134, 175n46; BDS advocacy and, 22; Butler on, 114; control of Gaza by, 105; Davis on, 88, 90, 93, 94; Israel, military clashes with, vii, viii, 22, 37, 41, 155–56n92; in *Oriented* (documentary), 139, 140; Palestinians used as human shields by, 175n45; pinkwashing discourse and, 14; Puar on, 59, 68, 72, 73; same-sex sexual activity, treatment of, 139, 140, 182–83n9; Schulman on, 37–39, 41; Spade on, 101, 105, 108. *See also* Gaza War
Hamas Covenant 1988, 160n31
Harris, Rachel S., xx
hasbara, 28
Hasidic community, 38
hate crimes: defined, 143n1; intersectional anti-Zionist, antisemitic, and homophobic, vii–xii, xx
havruta, xvii
Hebrew language, 31–32, 157n2
Heinze, Eric, 78, 79
Herzl, Theodor, 119, 184n21
Hezbollah, 114
Himmler, Heinrich, 158n16, 178n28
Hirsh, David, 121–22, 180n40
Hiss, Yehuda, 56–57
Hitler, Adolf, 18, 158n16, 178n28
Hogg, Michael, xv
Holder, Eric, 87
Holliday, Laurel, 73
Holocaust: Al-Quds University students visiting Auschwitz, 114; Butler and, 116, 118, 122, 126, 129–31, 178n27; Davis and, 80, 86; emigration to Israel and, 103; hate crimes against author and, xi, xiv; Primo Levi and, 129–31; pinkwashing and BDS advocacy, 10, 18, 24, 156n93; Puar and, 67, 164n2; Schulman and, 31, 35–37, 40, 45, 157n2
Holocaust and the Politics of Nationhood (Zertal), 130

Holý, Ladislav, 166n20
homonationalism, Puar on, 7, 46, 54, 62–68, 73, 74, 147n22, 162n55, 168n34
homonormativity, Duggan on, 7, 147n22
homophobia. *See* intersectionality of anti-Zionism, antisemitism, and homophobia; LGBTQ community
Honecker, Erich, 77, 80
honor killings, 45, 166n20
Horowitz, Michael C., 179n32
Hoshen, 99
Human Rights Watch (HRW), 73
al-Husayni, Mohammed Amin, 18, 35, 178n28
Hutchins, Robert M., xiii

intersectionality of anti-Zionism, antisemitism, and homophobia, vii–xxi; academic freedom, threats to, 3–5; in class promoting critical thinking about Israel/Palestine conflict, xii–xix, xx; community supporting Palestinian, Israeli, and LGBTQ rights, xx–xxi; hate crimes involving, police, media, and colleagues interpretation of, vii–xii, xx; LGBTQ community, anti-Israeli animus in, xix–xx; Schulman's failure to recognize possibility of, 33, 40, 45
intersectionality theory: Davis on (*see* Davis, Angela); defined, 82–83; exteriorized phenomena and, 173n22
Invisible Men, The (film), 16, 101–2, 150n49, 178n22
Isha L'isha (Woman to Woman), 17, 46
Ishtiwi, Mahmoud, 160n32
ISIS, 49, 71
Islam and Muslims: asylum seekers, LGBTQ and feminist Muslims as, 2; *dhimmi* laws, 20, 35, 118, 152–53n72; homophobia and, 40, 43–47, 141, 160n32, 161n51; same-sex relations in Middle East and, 7–11; Schulman on, 33–35, 37, 40–42, 44, 46, 47
Islamic terrorist groups: Butler's normalization of, 114, 182n8. *See also specific organizations*
Islamism (Islamic fundamentalism): Sadat, assassination of, 179n29; semi-failed Middle Eastern states, development in, 117; threats to women, religious minorities, and LGBTQ people from, xxi, 33
Islamophobia: anti-Zionist student accusing author of, xviii; escalation of, since 9/11, 7; free speech / academic freedom and, 4, 8; pinkwashing and, 1 (*see also* pinkwashing); Puar on homonationalism and, 66; Schulman and, 33, 37
Israel: American and Israeli police compared by Davis, 91; anti-BDS legislation proposed in, 48; calls for dissolution of, 25, 27, 39, 50, 93, 97; cis-gendered masculinity in, Puar on, 67–68; Egypt, peace treaty with, 104, 179n29; establishment of, 19, 103–4; focus on wrongs of, versus other nations, 13, 24–25, 41–42, 71–73, 95, 96, 115, 117, 145–46n10, 185n25; Law of Return in, 20; military operations, anti-Zionist activity triggered by, vii, viii; as one-dimensional black hole in BDS critiques of, 134–35; Palestinian collaboration, coercing, 114, 181–82n5; Palestinian LGBTQs and, 16, 150n51; Puar's allegations against state of (*see* Puar, Jasbir); same-sex relations in, 7–11; in UN World Happiness Report, 45

Israeli Defense Force (IDF): Butler on, 127; campus protests and activities of, vii, 22; Davis on, 81, 86, 88; Gaza, withdrawal from (2008), 155n92; Haganah as prototype of, 18; in *Oriented* (film), 139, 140; pinkwashing and, 6; Puar on, 57, 59–62, 70, 72; Schulman and, 32, 37, 38, 41, 157n4, 162n61; Spade on, 101, 106
Israeli Gay Youth, 99
Israel/Palestine and the Queer International (Schulman), 31, 51
Israel/Palestine conflict: class promoting critical thinking about, xii–xix, xx; conflation of leftist LGBTQ Israelis with Israeli conservative government on, 7; Davis on intersectionality with Ferguson, Missouri, 82, 85–93; disproportionate campus attention to, 4; incertitude and differences of view, importance of respect for, 2–5; origins and history of, 17–20; Palestinian LGBTQs and, 11–17; pinkwashing and, 2, 6–7 (*see also* pinkwashing); Spade's maps of Palestinian land loss, dishonesty of, 102–5; Third Narrative on, 28–29

Jadaliyya, 57
Jaffa riots (1921), 18
Jerusalem Open House, 17, 96–98
Jewish State, The (Herzl), 119, 184n21
Jewish Voice for Peace (JVP), 43, 101, 161n46, 178n19
Johnson, Alan, 114, 115
Johnson, Dorian, 87
Judt, Tony, 119–20

Kala-Meir, Sara, 95–96
Kaplan, Roberta, 96
Keep Not Silent (film), xix
Khrushchev, Nikita, 79, 171n7

King, Martin Luther, Jr., 86, 90–91, 94
Kirchick, James, 12, 44, 161n51
Kramer, Martin, 22

Larson, Jonathan, 43, 161n45
Lawfare, 4
League of Nations, 103
Lebanese Civil War, 32, 157n4
Lebanon, 9, 19, 117, 127, 179n32
Leibovitz, Liel, 162n61
Levi, Primo, 122, 129–31
Levinas, Emmanuel, 122, 126–29
Lewis, Bernard, 157n9
LGBTQ community: anti-Israeli animus in, xix–xx; assemblages theory of Puar, 64–65; BDS annexing, 1–5, 29–30; Butler, as lesbian Jewish American queer theorist, 113, 114; conflation of leftist LGBTQ Israelis with Israeli conservative government, 7; Creating Change conference, Spade disrupting, 95–99; Davis and, 78, 79, 81, 173n20; in Egypt, 48, 161n51; homonationalism, Puar on, 7, 46, 54, 62–68, 73, 74, 147n22, 162n55, 168n34; Islam/Muslims and homophobia, 40, 43–47, 141, 160n32, 161n51; Israeli campaigns aimed at, 2, 6 (*see also* pinkwashing); Massad on, 44, 48–49; Palestinian LGBTQs, 11–17, 49, 101–2, 114, 135–36, 150n49, 150n51, 150–51n55, 178n22, 182–83n9; postmodernism and queer BDS academic activists, 133–35; Pride parades, xix, 10–11, 38, 98, 141, 149n40, 177n9; racialized Jewish Israeli gay and lesbian parenting, Puar on, 54, 68–70; same-sex relations in Middle East, 7–11; Schulman addressing Tel Aviv University LGBTQ conference, 39–42; sexuality rights, globalization, and modernization, 2–3, 145n6, 148n27.

See also intersectionality of anti-Zionism, antisemitism, and homophobia; Spade, Dean
Lucas, Michael, 49, 50–51

maiming allegations of Puar, 54, 60–62
maps of Palestinian land loss, by Spade, 102–5
Marks, Jonathan, 163–64n2
Marquardt-Bigman, Petra, 164n4
marriage: consanguineous marriage, Palestinian practice of, 59, 166nn19–20; DOMA (Defense of Marriage Act) in U.S., 96; Israel, marriage equality in, 68–69
martyrdom, 47, 61–62, 167–68nn27–28
Massad, Joseph, 44, 48–49
Meir, Golda, xvii
Men of Israel (film), 49
Merrill, Charles, 10
micro-boycotts, 5, 146n13
Milgram, Stanley, xv
Mizrachi Jews, xi, 10, 20, 32, 34–37, 57, 68, 116, 118, 124, 131
Moore v. Hughes Helicopter, 83
Mor, Shany, 102, 104
Morsi, Mohamed, 48
Moses, as binational, 123, 124
Moses and Monotheism (Freud), 123
Movement for Black Lives, 173n24
Moynihan, Daniel Patrick, 172n14
Mozer, Yariv, 16, 101
Murray, Ed, 106
Muslim Alliance for Sexual and Gender Diversity, 95
Muslims. *See specific entries at* Islam and Muslims
Muslims for Progressive Values, 8
Muzzlewatch, 43

Nakba, 179n34. *See also* Arab-Israeli War
National Council of Jewish Women, 100

nationalism and the nation-state: binationalism, 112, 117, 119–20, 124, 126; Butler on, 113, 116–18; homonationalism, Puar on, 7, 46, 54, 62–68, 73, 74, 147n22, 162n55, 168n34
National Jewish Fund, 103
National LGBTQ Task Force, 95, 96–99
National Women's Studies Association (NWSA), BDS resolution of, xiii, 143n2
Nazis, 18, 20, 32, 33, 35, 80, 104, 131, 156n93, 158n16, 178n28, 180n1. *See also* Holocaust
Nelson, Cary, xx, 5, 6, 55, 56–57, 115, 146n13
Netanyahu, Benjamin, 6, 40, 42, 130, 156n92
New Haven Register, viii, ix
New Israel Fund, 100
New York City, Schulman on, 39
New York Lesbian, Gay, Bisexual, & Transgender Community Center, 49
New York Times, 31
9/11, 7, 91
Normal Life (Spade), 99, 109
Nusseibeh, Sari, 27–28

Obama, Barack, 87, 109–10
Omar, Ilhan, 17
one-state solution, 18, 25, 119–20
Operation Cast Lead (2008), 37, 72
Operation Hot Winter (2008), vii, 40–41
organ harvesting: Hamas engaged in, 94, 134; Puar's allegations against Israel, 54, 56–58, 74, 165n13, 165n16, 165–66n17
Oriented (documentary), 135–42
Orthodox and ultra-Orthodox Judaism, x, xix, xxi, 1, 6, 10–12, 32, 38–39, 57, 68–69
Oslo Accords and Oslo II, 25, 65, 81, 105

Ottoman empire, 35, 102–3, 158n16, 178–79n28
Oz, Amos, 134–35

Palestinian Authority (PA): authoritarianism of, 14; corruption in, xxi, 46; LGBTQ Palestinians, treatment of, 15, 16, 17, 114, 150–51n55, 182–83n9; stunting allegation of Puar and, 58; West Bank controlled by, 105
Palestinian Campaign for the Academic and Cultural Boycott of Israel (PACBI), 25, 45
Palestinian Economic Policy Research Institute (MAS), 58
Palestinian Liberation Organization (PLO), 104, 157n4
Palestinians: collaborating with Israel, 114, 181–82n5; consanguineous marriage, practice of, 59, 166nn19–20; as historical identity, 104; as LGBTQs, 11–17, 49, 101–2, 114, 135–36, 150n49, 150n51, 150–51n55, 178n22, 182–83n9; Puar's allegations regarding Israeli treatment of (*see* Puar, Jasbir); Schulman engaging with, 43–47, 49; Spade's maps of land loss by, 102–5. *See also* Israel/Palestine conflict
Parting Ways: Jewishness and the Critique of Zionism (Butler), 25, 115, 117–19, 121, 125, 126, 132
Payne v. Travenol, 83
Peel Commission, 18
People in Trouble (Schulman), 43, 161n45
performative use of Jewish identity by Butler, 121–22, 123
PFLAG, 99, 100
Phalangists, 157n4
Philo of Alexandria, 147n23
pinkwashing, 1–17; BDS advocacy and, 1–5, 8, 11–14; "Brand Israel" campaign, 2, 101; concept of, 1–5; conflation of leftist LGBTQ Israelis with Israeli conservative government, 7, 149n43; defined, 1–3; historical background, 5–7, 144n2; postmodernism of queer BDS academic activists and, 134, 142; Puar on, 2, 7, 8, 11, 13, 14, 54, 62, 68–70; same-sex relations in Middle East and, 7–11; Schulman on, 1–2, 6–8, 11–13, 51; Spade on, 2, 16, 96, 97, 99–107, 109–10
Pinkwashing Exposed (Spade documentary), 16, 99–105
Pleitgen, Fred, 175n46
police in Israel and America compared by Davis, 91
postmodernism: of *Oriented* (documentary), 135–42; queer BDS academic activists and, 133–35, 141–42
Powell, Colin, 154n86
Pride parades, xix, 10–11, 38, 98, 141, 149n40, 177n9
Protocols of the Elders of Zion, 24
Puar, Jasbir, 53–75; on academic freedom, 53–54, 164n4; on assemblages, 54–55, 59, 61, 62–68, 70, 73, 133, 168n34; BDS advocacy and, 53, 54, 56, 60, 61, 68–70, 72, 73; blood libel of, 53, 163–64n2, 165n16; on cis-gendered Israeli masculinity, 67–68; conspiracy theories of, 53–56, 73–75; Davis and, 55, 81, 89; on exposure of Palestinian children to violence, 54, 71–73; on homonationalism, 7, 46, 54, 62–68, 73, 74, 147n22, 162n55, 168n34; on maiming strategy of Israel against Palestinians, 54, 60–62; on organ harvesting from Palestinians by Israel, 54, 56–58, 74, 165n13, 165n16, 165–66n17; on pinkwashing, 2, 7, 8, 11, 13, 14, 54, 62, 68–70;

postmodernism and, 133–35; on racialized Jewish Israeli gay and lesbian parenting, 54, 68–70; Schulman and, 46, 55; Spade and, 55, 109; storytelling and political discourse, use of, 55; on stunting of growth of Palestinian children by Israel, 54, 58–60
Putin, Vladimir, 71, 171n11

Qambuta, 135
Queen Boat incident (2001), 161n51
Queers Undermining Israeli Terrorism (QUIT), 144n2

race/racism: Black Lives Matter, 82, 86, 89, 93, 173n24; Civil Rights movement, 86, 89, 93; Ferguson, Missouri, and Israel/Palestine, Davis on intersectionality of, 82, 85–93; Hamas, human trafficking of Africans in Sinai by, 94, 175n46; nonwhiteness of almost half of Israelis, 31, 90; UN Resolution 3379 on Zionism as racism, 81, 154n87, 172n14. *See also* Davis, Angela
Rashaida, 175n46
Raz-Krakotzkin, Amos, 124
Reform Judaism, 125
Rent (musical), 43, 161n45
reverse pinkwashing, 11
Right to Maim, The (Puar), 54, 61, 62, 63
Robbins, Bruce, 121
Rodinson, Maxime, 89
Rojanski, Rachael, 157n2
Russia. *See* Soviet Union / Russia

Sabra and Shatila massacres, 32, 127, 157n4
Sachar, Harold, 171n13
Sadat, Anwar, 104, 179n29
Said, Edward, 119, 122–24
Sanchez, Illich Ramirez ("Carlo"), 170n1

Sandinistas, 170n1
Sarsur, Ibrahim, 10
Save the Children, 71
Schlissel, Yishai, 11, 177n9
Schulman, Sarah, 31–51; on American military and Jewish state power, 34–39, 41, 42, 159n21; antisemitism and, 31, 34–37, 47, 50; BDS advocacy of, 31–34, 39–42, 46, 48, 50; black-and-white views of, 40–41, 47, 51; Butler and, 40, 41, 47, 50; Davis and, 81, 89; emergence of anti-Israel stance, 31–34; end of state of Israel, suggesting, 39, 50; family background of, 31–33; intersectionality, failure to deal with, 33, 40, 45; Jewish identity, disavowal of, 42–43; Larson accused of plagiarism by, 43, 161n45; Lucas and, 49, 50–51; Palestinians, engaging with, 43–47, 49; on pinkwashing, 1–2, 6–8, 11–13, 51; postmodernism and, 133–35; Puar and, 46, 55; on return to America, 47–50; Spade and, 109; Tel Aviv, journey to, 39–42
Second Intifada, 6, 25, 56, 57, 58, 101, 181–82n5
security barrier / apartheid wall, 25, 46, 90, 155n88
Sephardic Jews, 36
settler colonialism: BDS advocacy and, 25, 26, 155–56n92; Butler on, 113, 114, 116, 118, 123, 125, 126, 131, 134; Davis's intersectionality theory and, 89, 90; intersectional hate crimes and, xv, xvii; Puar on, 55, 56, 65; Schulman on, 50; Spade on, 97, 101, 106, 108
Sharansky, Natan, 183–84n21
Shatila and Sabra massacres, 32, 127, 157n4
Shenhav, Yehouda, 124
Shoah. *See* Holocaust
Siege Busters, 49

Simpson, Hannah Elyse, 96
Singer, Isaac Bashevis, 32, 33
el-Sisi, Abdel Fattah, 48
Six-Day War (1967), 81, 90, 104, 126
Slepian, Arthur, 100
Solzhenitsyn, Aleksandr, 79–80
Some of My Best Friends Are Zionists (documentary), 121
Song of Myself (Whitman), 126
Soviet Union / Russia: antisemitism in, 80, 171n11; anti-Zionism of, 78–82, 171n13; Davis's engagement with, 77–81, 83, 91, 94, 173n20; human rights violations by, 13, 41, 81; Jews emigrating to Israel from, 34
Spade, Dean, 95–110; BDS advocacy of, 96, 97, 99, 102, 105, 106, 109–10; black-and-white views of, 101, 107–8; as conspiracy theorist, 106, 108, 109–10; Creating Change LGBTQ conference, disruption of, 95–99; Davis and, 81, 89, 109; maps of Palestinian land loss, dishonesty of, 102–5; op-ed on right-wing leveraging of trans issues, 99, 105–7; on pinkwashing, 2, 16, 96, 97, 99–107, 109–10; postmodernism and, 133–35; Puar and, 55, 109; Schulman and, 109; Seattle panel of Israeli LGBTQ organizations and, 99–101, 105
Stagestruck: Theater, AIDS, and the Marketing of Gay America (Schulman), 161n45
StandWithUs, 100, 106, 107
Stark, Debra Pogrund, 108
Stern, Kenneth, xiv, xvi, 3
Stillwell, Cinnamon, 164n5
Students for Justice in Palestine (SJP), 24
stunting allegation of Puar, 54, 58–60
suicide bombings, 25, 68, 101, 167–68nn27–28, 179n32
Survival in Auschwitz (Levi), 130

Taliban, 71
Tehila, 99
Terrorist Assemblages (Puar), 11, 63, 66, 162n55
Third Narrative, 28–29
Thoreau, Henry David, 91
Thousand Plateaus Capitalism and Schizophrenia, A (Deleuze and Guattari), 54
Ties That Bind (Schulman), 32, 40, 45, 51
tikkun olam, 116, 119, 183n15
Tlaib, Rashida, 17
Toameh, Khaled Abu, 160n32
Trevor Project, 100
Trump, Donald, 107
Truth, Sojourner, 82
two-state solution, xvi, 18, 19, 25, 28, 93, 117, 121, 126, 134, 155n92

uncertainty-identity theory, xv
United Kingdom. *See* Britain
United Nations, viii, 6, 19, 42, 67, 103, 150n51, 172n14; partition plan, 35, 89, 103–4; Relief and Works Agency for Palestine Refugees in the Near East (UNWRA), 19; Resolution 3379 on Zionism as racism, 81, 154n87, 172n14; World Conference Against Racism (Durban Conference), 24–25, 154nn86–87; World Happiness Report, 45, 161–62n53
United States v. Windsor, 96
university policies on academic freedom and free speech, 23–24, 180–81n1

Valdary, Chloe, 86, 93–94
Vietnam War, 78

Waller, James, xiv
Waltzer, Ken, 163n2

War of Independence (1948). *See* Arab-Israeli War
War on Terror, 7, 156n92
Warsaw Ghetto Uprising, 40–41
Weber, Max, 115, 183n12
West Bank settlements. *See* settler colonialism
Weymouth, Lally, 170n1
When I See Them I See Us (documentary, 2015), 81, 82, 88, 91, 172n16
Whitman, Walt, 126
Wieseltier, Leon, 119–20
Wilson, Darren, 87
Windsor, Edith, 96
Witzenfeld, Jake, 135
Women, Race and Class (Davis), 84

Yemen, 9, 35, 42, 71–72, 117
Yiannopoulos, Milo, 107
Yiddish, 31–32, 157n2, 181n3
Yudof, Mark G., 163n2

Zertal, Idith, 130
Zionism: Davis's anti-Zionism and intersectionality theory, 81–85; of Herzl, 119, 184n21; historical development of, 17–20; Schulman on, 33–34; Soviet opposition to, 78, 79, 81–82, 171n13; UN resolution on, 81, 154n87, 172n14. *See also* Butler, Judith; intersectionality of anti-Zionism, antisemitism, and homophobia